Baker College of Clin~~ton~~~~Township~~~~Library~~

PROPERTY OF
BAKER COLLEGE LIBRARY
PORT HURON MI

Mass Trauma and Emotional Healing around the World

MASS TRAUMA AND EMOTIONAL HEALING AROUND THE WORLD

Rituals and Practices for Resilience and Meaning-Making

VOLUME 1: NATURAL DISASTERS

Ani Kalayjian and
Dominique Eugene,
EDITORS

PRAEGER
An Imprint of ABC-CLIO, LLC

A B C ⬤ C L I O

Santa Barbara, California • Denver, Colorado • Oxford, England

Copyright 2010 by Ani Kalayjian and Dominique Eugene

All rights reserved. No part of this publication may be reproduced, stored in a retrieval system, or transmitted, in any form or by any means, electronic, mechanical, photocopying, recording, or otherwise, except for the inclusion of brief quotations in a review, without prior permission in writing from the publisher.

Library of Congress Cataloging-in-Publication Data

Mass trauma and emotional healing around the world : rituals and practices for resilience and meaning-making / Ani Kalayjian, Dominique Eugene, editors
      p. cm.
  Includes bibliographical references and index.
    ISBN 978-0-313-37540-8 (set hbk. : alk. paper) — ISBN 978-0-313-37541-5 (set ebook) — ISBN 978-0-313-37542-2 (v. 1 hbk. : alk. paper) — ISBN 978-0-313-37543-9 (v. 1 ebook) — ISBN 978-0-313-37544-6 (v. 2 hbk. : alk. paper) — ISBN 978-0-313-37545-3 (v. 2 ebook)
  1. Disasters—Psychological aspects—Cross-cultural studies. 2. Psychic trauma—Cross-cultural studies. 3. Post-traumatic stress disorder—Cross-cultural studies. I. Kalayjian, Ani. II. Eugene, Dominique.
  BF789.D5M38   2010
   155.9'35—dc22   2009031607

14 13 12 11 10   1 2 3 4 5

This book is also available on the World Wide Web as an eBook.
Visit www.abc-clio.com for details.

Praeger
An Imprint of ABC-CLIO, LLC

ABC-CLIO, LLC
130 Cremona Drive, P.O. Box 1911
Santa Barbara, California 93116-1911

This book is printed on acid-free paper ∞

Manufactured in the United States of America

CONTENTS

Volume 2

HUMAN-MADE DISASTERS

ACKNOWLEDGMENTS

We would like to thank those who have whole-heartedly helped us bring this project to light. Those that diligently gave of their time and patience with all the editing and re-editing that were necessary. We thank you for jumping on board and understanding how vital this book is. With the many disasters that occur, we are grateful for the number of humanitarians that understand the need to provide assistance to people in a meaningful, mindful, and culturally respectful manner, bearing in mind the innate resiliency of those affected by various travesties. This project was long overdue.

Our thanks go out to all of our authors. In addition we thank Gil Reyes, Debora Carvalko, and Tiffany Seisser for pushing this along for us and putting up with all the details.

These two volumes are a celebration of our wonderful Meaningfulworld Research Intern Team (www.meaningfulwrold.com) spearheaded by Elissa Jacobs (Graduate Coordinator of Interns); Miryam Nadkarni (Germany), Bindia Patel (New Jersey), Christina Di Liberto (New Jersey), Eleanor Donovan (Massachusetts), and Yuki Shigemoto (Japan). We thank Miryam for jumping in the mix and doing so well. Special thanks to the Association for Trauma Outreach & Prevention Board, especially our Vice President Georgina Galanis for her wisdom and valuable insights, and for Nicole Moore for her consistent input in addition to her participation in a few of the humanitarian missions.

Thank you to our significant others and family members—Murat Koroglu, Mama Kalayjian, and siblings; Der Hyre Vertanes, Zarmine, Kevork, and Vasken and their spouses (Ani); Davidicus Schacher and Germaine

Castre (Dominique)—who supported us and put up with us and who tolerate our passions, giving us the space to accomplish our goals, and for giving us unconditional love, encouragement, and moral and spiritual support. Thanks also go out to Clifford Robinson for encouraging private practice and my Angel Heart Mental Health Consulting partners Dr. Lori Williams Dobbs and Myisha Driver (Dominique).

A very special gratitude to all the survivors that we worked with to gather the important data necessary to share with you (our readers), to their families and communities, we express our immense gratitude to you all around the world. This is also an outcome of a true partnership developed from all of ATOP/Meaningfulworld's Humanitarian Outreach Missions around the world.

We express utmost gratitude to the Universe, the Almighty, and Spiritual Guides and Angels for putting us on this path, guiding us to fruition one step at a time, and helping us to disseminate this invaluable collective work.

INTRODUCTION

More than one billion people have been directly affected by violence and disaster throughout the world. The rest of us are living with its generational impact. Kalayjian has speculated that as more disasters occur, those disasters will impact a larger number of people and places, costing a large sum of capital to recover (1995). As interest in and literature about psychological aspects of resilience, coping, and survival related to trauma and disasters accelerate dramatically over the years, our mission is to maximize scientific, cultural, spiritual, and other practices to reduce suffering, minimize disability, and increase resiliency, meaning-making, and healing worldwide. Ultimately, our goal is to prevent all human-made disasters and minimize the impact of natural disasters by preparedness and mindfulness. This handbook will serve the dual function of documenting these developments in the field and, equally or even more importantly, setting the agenda for future development of research and theory in all areas of the discipline of disasters and mass trauma.

In addition, a deliberate effort was made to see that the handbook leaves a mark on the mainstream discipline of psychology of mass disasters mitigation, coping, resilience, and prevention. This handbook focuses on the use of cultural practices, religious and spiritual rituals, and indigenous practices in coping, resilience, and meaning-making after disasters. According to Frankl (1959, 116), "we must never forget that we may also find meaning in life even when confronted with a hopeless situation, when facing a fate that cannot be changed. For what then matters is to bear witness to the uniquely human potential at its best, which is to transform a personal tragedy into a triumph, to turn one's predicament into a human achievement."

A remarkable team of expert authors provide firsthand accounts from survivors of disasters around the globe in the past decade so that the reader can understand the impact of trauma. Group experiences are shared, focusing on self and community empowerment. Group members are empowered not only because they learn by doing but also because they are changed by doing (Hedrick et al. 1992). The authors span the globe with their remarkable experiences and passion for providing culturally sensitive assistance during traumatic times—be it natural or human made disasters. The authors represent various universities such as Columbia University, Fordham University, George Mason's Institute for Conflict Analysis and Resolution on the Institute's International Criminal Court Project, Humboldt State University in Arcata, California, Texas Woman's University, American Universities, Muhlenberg College, the Norwegian University of Science and Technology (NTNU) in Trondheim, Maison des Sciences de l'Homme in Paris, International Christian University in Japan, Université du Québec à Chicoutimi in Canada, Hackensack University Medical Center in New Jersey, Yeshiva University, the University of Applied Sciences in Muenster, Germany, to name a few.

A main thrust of each chapter focuses on emotional healing, rituals, and practices for resilience after mass trauma. The impact of disasters in terms of casualties varies enormously depending on the level of development in the country concerned. This handbook covers the marginalized people around the world, including developing countries. From 1994 to 2003, deaths per reported disaster were on average seven times higher in countries of low development than in highly developed countries (http://www.irinnews.org/webspecials/DR/default.asp). These figures reinforce the value of this handbook since each chapter addresses the impact of disasters on these survivors, and the challenge of recovery when their community support is already compromised.

Chapter 1

EARTHQUAKE IN SOVIET ARMENIA

Coping, Integration, and Meaning-Making

Ani Kalayjian,
Yuki Shigemoto, and
Bindia Patel

Through humor, you can soften some of the worst blows that life delivers. And once you find laughter, no matter how painful your situation might be, you can survive it.

—Bill Cosby

INTRODUCTION

On December 7, 1988, at 11:41 A.M. (Viviano 2004), an earthquake disrupted the industrial cities of northern Armenia. The earthquake measured 6.9 on the Richter scale and, according to Soviet estimates, killed at least 25,000 people. According to European sources, however, as many as 100,000 people died and 530,000 were left homeless (Goenjian et al. 1994). Unfortunately, this was not the only source of devastation. During this time, tension was also growing between ethnic Armenians in Nagorno-Karabakh and military forces of Soviet Azerbaijian. As a result, 200,000 refugees fled to Armenia, settling in the earthquake zone (Viviano 2004). The country was in shambles and in the midst of a serious conflict. Many survivors were affected and as a result developed emotional reactions including post-traumatic stress disorder (PTSD) and depression.

This chapter will focus on the survivors' responses and reactions immediately after the quake, six months later, and one year after the earthquake. Coping, meaning-making, and resilience are also discussed.

LITERATURE REVIEW

Many disasters have occurred and created devastation all around the world. The 1989 Newcastle earthquake in Australia caused approximately 550 survivors to develop symptoms of PTSD (Neria, Nadi, and Galea 2008). Two months after the 1999 earthquake in Turkey over 75 percent of the survivors had PTSD (Kowalski and Kalayjian 1999). Additional research on the same earthquake found that out of 530 Turkish survivors assessed near the epicenter of the earthquake, 23 percent developed PTSD symptoms when evaluated 14 months after the earthquake. After three years, the prevalence of PTSD symptoms was still high, with 11.7 percent of survivors being affected (Basoglu et al. 2004). In Florida, survivors exposed to Hurricane Andrew experienced an increase in PTSD symptoms from 26 percent to 29 percent between 6 and 30 months after the disaster (Norris et al. 1999). The same was witnessed in the 1998 Zhangbei-Shangyi earthquake in China, with an increased prevalence rate of PTSD between three months and nine months after the disaster (Wang et al. 2000). Natural disasters have shown that survivors closer to the epicenter of the disaster develop more severe symptoms of PTSD. However, natural disasters overall affect more survivors than other disasters. It can lead to loss of resources, relocation of the people, and high death tolls (Neria et al. 2008).

In 1999, two separate earthquakes devastated the Marmara region of Turkey (Bal and Jensen 2007). The earthquakes measured 7.4 and 7.2 on the Richter scale, leading this particular earthquake to be classified as one of the 20th century's worst earthquakes. The devastation of this particular trauma lead to approximately 19,000 deaths and 54,000 injuries among the survivors of Turkey (Bal and Jensen 2007). The country sustained massive losses of money and land, leaving the people with the broken pieces of what was once their country.

A study by Basoglu, Kiliç, Salcioglu, and Livanou (2004) assessed the levels of PTSD in survivors from two locations. The first site assessed 530 survivors from the epicenter of the earthquake and the second assessed 420 people from a nearby suburb in Istanbul. Survivors were given a Survivor Information form asking for information on their demographics and history. It also contained the Traumatic Stress Symptom Checklist (TSSC) and Severity of Disability Scale. These scales were used to determine the level of PTSD and depression an individual experienced. The results showed that at Site I, 22 percent of survivors experienced symptoms of PTSD and 15 percent of survivors experienced both PTSD and depression. At Site II, 11 percent of survivors experienced symptoms of PTSD and 6 percent experienced both PTSD and depression (Basoglu et al. 2004).

The closer to the epicenter survivors were, the higher the rates of PTSD and depression. Other research findings show that there are significant correlations between PTSD symptoms and gender, past psychiatric illness, damage to home, participation in rescue work, past trauma, and loss of close ones. However, the greatest factor predicting PTSD was the presence of fear during the earthquake. The authors of the study suggest using behavioral treatments targeted at reducing the fear to treat symptoms of PTSD for this particular natural disaster (Basoglu et al. 2004).

A follow-up study by these authors examined whether a self-help guide given to different survivors by a therapist could alleviate the exposure to fear cues. Eight survivors were assessed at week 10, and at 1, 3, and 6 month intervals for symptoms of PTSD. The findings show that one out of two survivors benefited from the self-help guide, which led to an improvement of PTSD symptoms. A self-help manual is an inexpensive and effective way of educating oneself about the symptoms of PTSD (Basoglu, Salcioglu, and Livanou 2009). Another study conducted on the survivors affected by the 1999 earthquake in Turkey examined the risk factors before the trauma for survivors who developed PTSD (Tural et al. 2004). Out of a sample of 910 survivors, 25 percent were diagnosed with PTSD using the Post-traumatic Stress Disorder Self Test (PTSD-S).

More than half of the survivors during the earthquake in Turkey were children and adolescents (Bal and Jensen 2007). Along with their adult counterparts, they faced hardships that led to the development of symptoms of PTSD. Two hundred and ninety-three (293) children and adolescents living near the epicenter of the earthquake participated in this study. They were given the Post-traumatic Stress Disorder Reaction Index for Children (CPTSD-RI) to assess levels of PTSD. The results discovered that almost 60 percent of Turkish children surviving the earthquake suffered from moderate to very severe levels of PTSD symptoms even 3 years after the 1999 earthquake (Bal and Jensen 2007).

The 1999 Chi-chi earthquake in Taiwan was one of the biggest earthquakes to affect the area in over a hundred years. Approximately 50 percent of the population was left homeless after the earthquake, which measured 7.6 on the Richter scale (Kuo et al. 2007). A group of researchers set out to assess the rates of PTSD in the region. Using the Davidson Trauma Scale, Chinese version (DTS-C) and the Chinese Health Questionnaire (CHQ), the authors of the study found that 16.5 percent of 272 earthquake victims exhibited signs of PTSD. PTSD was more prevalent among women, with 22.2 percent showing symptoms of PTSD while only 9.2 percent of the men exhibited these symptoms (Kuo et al. 2007). The authors concluded that it is vital for survivors to receive psychological counseling after a traumatic event such as an earthquake.

Across studies, the average prevalence rates for depression and general anxiety are 26 percent and 40 percent (Rubonis and Bickman 1991). In this study, survivors who sought outpatient psychiatric help were assessed for symptoms of PTSD. The participants were 156 patients with a mean age of 41. The study found that 76 percent of the participants had symptoms of PTSD. It also evaluated which coping mechanisms the participants used to combat PTSD. The positive coping methods included visiting others, exercising, watching television, attending church and praying; negative coping methods included smoking cigarettes and drinking alcohol. Survivors who watched less television and prayed reported lower levels of PTSD (McLeish and Del Ben 2008).

After the earthquake in Armenia the Mental Health Outreach Project (MHOP) was established to assess levels of PTSD in the surviving community, and establish a rehabilitation program. MHOP consisted of eight stages: pre-assessment, assessment, analysis, community diagnosis, planning, implementation, evaluation, and remodification (Kalayjian 1995).

There are different forms of treatment available to survivors of natural disasters. Smith, Perrin, and Yule (1999) studied cognitive behavior therapy (CBT) as treatment for PTSD in children exposed to trauma. The results show that CBT is an effective treatment and helps improve the symptoms of PTSD over time. Another study conducted by March, Amaya-Jackson, Murray, and Schulte (1998) found that some children with PTSD due to a single incident stressor were able to overcome PTSD symptoms altogether. After a trial of 18 sessions of cognitive behavioral group treatment for 14 children, 8 children were free of PTSD and a further 4 children were free of PTSD at a 6-month follow-up.

Group and individual therapies have also been used to help children who developed symptoms of PTSD from Hurricane Katrina. The study measured disaster-related exposure, post-traumatic stress symptoms, depression, traumatic grief, and distress at preintervention, postintervention, and three weeks postintervention. Both treatment modalities were seen as effective for addressing trauma and grief post disaster (Salloum and Overstreet 2008).

A year-and-a-half after the earthquake in Armenia, the Psychiatric Outreach Program of the Armenian Relief Society of the Western United States evaluated 179 elderly and younger survivors. Using the PTSD Reaction Index, the survivors were assessed for severity of PTSD and the correlation with exposure, age, gender, and death of a family member. Again, the results showed that those closer to the epicenter of the earthquake survivors had higher levels of PTSD. Elderly survivors scored higher on arousal symptoms and lower on intrusive symptoms compared to young adults.

This study indicates the need for mental health therapy after a traumatic natural disaster (Goenjian et al. 1994).

Another group that has been affected by the earthquake in Armenia includes adolescents and children. The survivors were given the Child Posttraumatic Stress Reaction Index and the Depression Self-Rating Scales. The researchers studied the course of PTSD symptoms and administered brief psychotherapy. The survivors were assessed 1.5 years and 5 years after the earthquake. The untreated survivors were at risk for chronic PTSD and depressive symptoms, whereas the treated ones found that they had better chances at relieving the symptoms of PTSD (Goenjian et al. 2009).

MHOP organized and managed by the first author included assessment in these four areas: (1) assessment of survivor characteristics, (2) assessment of event characteristics, (3) issues during disaster relief, and (4) pre- and postdisaster sociopolitical and economic climate.

SURVIVOR CHARACTERISTICS IN ARMENIA

Who were the survivors of the 1988 earthquake in Armenia? They were intelligent, hard-working, peaceful, religious, family-oriented, and hospitable people (Jordan 1978). The Republic of Armenia is geographically the smallest of the former Soviet Republics, with a population of approximately four million, but it is the most entrepreneurial and economically the fastest-growing republic (Walker 1991). The historical record shows an Armenian presence in the general region of Asia Minor and the Caucasus dating back over three millennia (Ishkhanian 1989). Its history throughout the centuries is one of enduring oppression, war, relocation, and survival. From the end of the 14th century until 1991, Armenia had only two years of independence (1918–1920), yet its people, culture, and language have survived. On September 23, 1991, Armenia once again declared independence. For the first time in 71 years, the Armenian people freely elected a president and representatives to the Republic's Parliament, the Supreme Soviet, from a slate of candidates representing a variety of political movements and organizations.

In discussing their history, Armenians mention three things. First, they mention their religion. This is a point of great pride, since Armenia became the first nation to adopt Christianity in 301 A.D. as its national religion. Second, they mention their language. The Armenian language is a distinct branch of the Indo-European family of languages, with a unique 38-character alphabet. Last, they mention their survival of the Ottoman-Turkish genocide. From 1894 to 1923, the Armenian nation was brought to the brink of annihilation as almost two million Armenians, more than half the Armenian population, were massacred by the Ottoman Turkish rulers. To this day, the genocide is denied by the Turkish government. This denial causes tremendous feelings of anger and resentment, with no reparation or resolution (Kalayjian 1991a). During World War II, and for over 70 years under communism, Armenians experienced yet more pain and suffering. This was a system that relied on oppression of individual needs for the sake of the party, and any rebellious gesture could lead to one's disappearance. Pain and suffering continued in the postindependence era (after 1991), because of territorial conflict within Azerbaijan over Nagorno-Karabagh. Adding to the suffering has been the Azeri blockade of Armenia which began in 1988 and as of today (2009) is yet to be lifted.

The literacy rate is comparatively high in Armenia, as virtually all Armenian children attend school for 8 to 10 years from age 6 to 16.

People are industrious yet poor, as the economy has been decimated by decades of Soviet rule, further exacerbated by the Azeri and Turkish blockade.

As in many developing countries, an insurance industry is nonexistent in Armenia. Soviet-designed health care was free in Armenia, but the quality and availability vary greatly.

EVENT CHARACTERISTICS IN ARMENIA

On Wednesday, December 7, 1988, at 11:41 A.M., a devastating earthquake shook the Republic of Armenia (Soviet Armenia) for 40 seconds. This catastrophic destruction occurred in a zone where several plates of the earth's surface converge, which occasionally results in disastrous consequences when movement occurs. Although the quake did not come as a total surprise to American and Soviet experts in the field, according to Purkaru of the geological institute in Frankfurt (Sullivan 1988), the community experienced the quake as a total nightmare due to gross unpreparedness and lack of emergency and evacuation plans.

In 893 A.D., a quake in the same general area of Armenia had caused 20,000 deaths. In 1667, another earthquake in that general region claimed 80,000 lives, and in the late 1800s yet another devastating quake had taken place there. "I have Chernobyl behind me, but I have never seen anything like this," Yevgeny I. Chazov, the Soviet Health Minister, told the government newspaper *Izvestia* after visiting the scene with fellow physicians in 1988 (Fein 1988).

Measuring 6.9 on the Richter scale, the quake occurred in an area highly vulnerable to seismic activity. It destroyed two-thirds of Leninakan, Armenia's second-largest city (now Gumru, population about 300,000), half of Kirovakan (now Vanatzor, population 150,000), obliterated Spitak—the epicenter (a town of about 30,000), and heavily damaged some 56 of 150 villages and towns in the northwest corner of Armenia, near the Turkish border. Initial reports of casualties spoke of thousands, which soon became tens of thousands, and went on to climb day by day to 130,000, even though the official death toll was announced as 25,000. In the end, there were about 500,000 people handicapped, approximately 500,000 children orphaned, and over half a million, one sixth of Armenia's population, left homeless. The exact number of human losses was very difficult to determine for several reasons: the uncertain number of refugees from the February 1988 massacres in the Azerbaijani cities of Baku and Sumgait, the poor record-keeping procedures, and, finally, the Soviet government's covert style of operations. Therefore, the above estimates, or any estimates from this incident, are only provisional. Proportional losses in the United States would have amounted to six million dead and 40 million homeless. The physical damage was estimated at $20 billion (U.S.).

Unlike other earthquakes, where there is often a prediction of occurrence, this event was largely unanticipated by the community. It impacted a very large segment of the local population and caused tremendous property damage. All hospitals, schools, churches, and community centers were severely damaged or destroyed, unlike the Mexican quake of 1986, the San Francisco quake of 1989, and the Los Angeles quake of 1994. Survivors were forced to head for the capital, Yerevan, to receive emergency medical care. This meant traveling four to six hours, instead of the usual two hours, in extremely crowded conditions and on roads that were partially destroyed by the quake. Therefore, the delay caused additional casualties. "My only brother, ten years old, died in my arms in the car going to Yerevan," stated Nayiri, a 16-year-old female Armenian survivor from Spitak (Kalayjian 1995). In the earthquake region, survivors had no areas left intact in their community through which to seek support. In turn, this made relocation a necessity and created additional stress and trauma. Further trauma was caused by the Soviet government when it decided to relocate women and children to Yerevan and other Soviet Republics, while keeping the men in the earthquake zone to help clean up. According to Terr (1989), families cope better if they remain together after a trauma. Therefore, these relocations and separations further aggravated the trauma by shattering and displacing family units.

Assistance from all over the world poured into Armenia. Within the first 10 days, $50,000,000 worth of goods, food and supplies were delivered to Yerevan's airport from around the world, overwhelming the damaged distribution system. This airlift marked the first time since World War II that the Soviet government had accepted disaster assistance from the United States. In all, the American government spent about four million U.S. dollars, and U.S. Air Force and National Guard planes were used to fly in the relief supplies. Private contributions from Americans in the first four weeks following the earthquake reached about 34 million dollars. The grand total given by all countries outside the Soviet Union reached 106 million dollars (Simon 1989). According to U.S. Senator Simon, in view of the fact that the United States represents 20 percent of the world's economy, what the United States did as a nation was not that impressive. However, aid sent by the U.S. government to the Soviet Union, and its acceptance, was unprecedented. When the Marshall Plan was announced in 1948, the Soviets would accept no American aid whatsoever. Therefore, the fact that aid was given and received was a healthy sign (Simon 1989).

ISSUES DURING DISASTER RELIEF

The disaster response was somewhat different in Armenia from that seen in Florida and California. The earthquake received overwhelming international attention because of the interruption of President Gorbachev's visit to the United States. Unfortunately, this did not result in an organized rescue effort. Efforts were extremely disorganized, began too late and resulted in chaos. The warning system was outdated, old-fashioned, or just dysfunctional, and the rescue equipment was either broken or insufficient.

Though assistance poured in from all around the world, Armenia's airport was not equipped to deal with that volume and therefore many planes could not land. The planes that were able to land just unloaded their goods on the runway. Much of the other assistance that went through Moscow did not make it to Armenia in its entirety. This lasted until Armenian voluntary organizations took over the distribution and management of the funds, as well as the goods.

PRE- AND POSTDISASTER SOCIOPOLITICAL AND ECONOMIC CLIMATE

During the 10 months preceding the quake, Armenia was experiencing sociopolitical tension and was economically drained. This was caused by the conflict with neighboring Azerbaijan over Nagorno-Karabagh, a 4,000 square kilometer enclave mostly populated by Armenians and locally ruled by Armenians until 1923, when Josef Stalin gave it to Soviet Azerbaijan. In early 1988, Armenia challenged Gorbachev and put glasnost and perestroika to their first true test, but failed. As a result, over 200,000 Armenian refugees from Azerbaijan came to already overcrowded Armenia. In February 1988, there was yet another massacre in Sumgait, Azerbaijan, where dozens of Armenians were killed, houses were burned, and women were raped and set on fire, according to Vasken Manoukian—the then prime minister of Armenia (personal communication, 1991). Noteworthy is that seismologists described the quake area as a "structural knot," engendered by the interaction of several rigid plates (Sullivan 1988). Ironically, this paralleled the sociopolitical and emotional situation: political agitation, tension, anger, resentment, disappointment, and mistrust, due, at least partly, to rigid attitudes.

ANALYSIS

Psychological and behavioral symptoms were first assessed systematically six to eight weeks after the earthquake due to difficulties obtaining access visas. Over 200 adults and 200 adolescents and children constituted the assessment sample. The site of the assessments varied. Several different layers of the community were observed in their natural environments, that is, school age children and adolescents in their classrooms during recess, in hospitals, shelters, or in their homes; adults at their work places (if they were still employed), in hospitals, at government shelters, or at the homes of their relatives. Geographically, emphasis was placed on the quake zone in Armenia: Leninakan, Kirovakan, Spitak and a few of the villages that were en route to the larger cities. Data from the assessment were used for this analysis.

SHORT-TERM IMPACT OF EARTHQUAKE MANIFESTED IN CHILDREN AND ADOLESCENTS IN ARMENIA: ASSESSMENT OF CHILDREN

Eighty-six percent of the children interviewed or observed (N = 122, F = 60%) displayed at least 4 of the following 10 symptoms: separation anxiety intensified during the night; refusing to go to school; refusing to sleep or to be left alone; conduct disorders; sleep disturbances manifested by bad dreams, frequent awakenings, difficulty falling asleep; regressive behavior manifested by thumb sucking, enuresis and clinging behaviors; hyperactivity; withdrawal; inability to concentrate; and somatic complaints. According to the Reaction Index Scale (Frederick 1986), 82.8 percent of the adolescents interviewed (N = 62, F = 55%) scored over 50, indicating severe levels of post-traumatic stress disorder (PTSD). The most common psychological and behavioral symptoms observed in adolescents were as follows: withdrawal, lack of concentration, aggressive tendencies, nightmares, unusually poor grades in courses in which they had excelled prior to the earthquake, irritability, and increased reports of episodic daydreaming.

ASSESSMENT OF ADOLESCENTS

Responses of adolescents differ somewhat from those exhibited by children and adults. Although a few research findings indicate the short-lived nature of responses by adolescents to disaster, very few studies focus on the frequency and the intensity of those responses. Milgram and colleagues (1988) studied seventh graders nine months after a school bus disaster and found they had very few psychological symptoms. Nadar et al. (1990) assessed children and adolescents after a sniper attack at their school and similarly found their post-traumatic stress symptoms decreased within 14 months after the trauma.

Adolescent disaster stress response differs from those of adults and children. Developmentally, adolescents are in a unique and inherently stressful stage, with distinct emotional and psychological needs (Rutter, Izard, and Read 1986). In addition, adolescents do not have the advantage of increased age and multiple life experiences to rely on, as do adults. In the one-to-one interviews with the adult survivors of Hurricane Andrew, there was a repeated theme of benefiting from previous experiences. Gleser, Green, and Winget (1981) studied children and adolescents one-and-a-half to two years after the Buffalo Creek disaster and found that disaster stress increased from childhood to adolescence. They also found that 20 percent of adolescents (N = 82) 12 to 15 years of age reported anxiety; 30 percent reported depression. Prior healthy coping experiences, a viable family support system, and low level of life event stress are considered to be prerequisites to a healthy adolescent response to a disaster (Andrews et al. 1978). According to Andrews et al., those meeting the above-mentioned prerequisites had a 13 percent risk for psychiatric difficulties, while those not meeting the prerequisites exhibited a 43 percent rate of psychiatric complications.

According to Hardin et al. (1994), who studied 1482 South Carolina high school students a year after Hurricane Hugo, as exposure to the hurricane increased so did symptoms of psychological distress. However, the study by Hardin et al. was limited, as are almost all the studies on natural disasters, by its inability to compare the baseline psychological distress scores of adolescents before and after the disaster. As a whole, the study revealed that social support and self-efficacy are inversely related to psychological distress, which reinforced studies of Baum, Fleming, and Davidson

(1983), Fleming et al. (1982) and Murphy (1987). Social support was an even better protector against psychological distress than self-efficacy, reinforcing studies by Fleming et al., Berndt and Ladd (1989), and others, who found peer support to be essential for teens in distress.

ASSESSMENT OF ADULTS

Two hundred twelve adults (62% female) were interviewed or assessed in Armenia. The Reaction Index Scale was utilized. Over 80 percent scored in excess of 50 on the Reaction Index Scale, indicating severe levels of post-traumatic stress disorder (PTSD). Over 80 percent of those interviewed admitted to having at least five of the psychological symptoms listed.

DIAGNOSES

Community diagnosis is a statement describing a community's response to a disaster. Diagnoses are utilized as classifications to express conclusions based on the data gathered in the preassessment, assessment, and the analysis phases.

Diagnoses generally are abstract and broad labels, or definitions of phenomena that health professionals use to help clients, as well as communities, to change and improve. These labels, or inferences, are utilized to assist professionals in their planning and implementations of care (Kalayjian 1995).

A thorough analysis of the assessment of the impact of the earthquake in Armenia and individual interview conducted by the first author revealed several diagnoses.

Community findings in Armenia Post 1988 Earthquake:

1. 86 percent of the children interviewed had severe PTSD
2. 83 percent of the adolescents interviewed had severe PTSD
3. 81 percent of the adults interviewed had severe PTSD
4. 80 percent of the teachers interviewed in Leninakan (now Gumru) were survivors themselves
5. Over 79 percent of the leaders and government officials interviewed from the quake zone were survivors themselves
6. 80 percent of the mental health professionals interviewed from the quake zone exhibited signs of burnout
7. 98 percent of the survivors in the earthquake zone did not have a mental health professional available to provide care

8. There was only one community mental health outpatient clinic in Leninakan (Gumru), established by the first author

9. Spitak and some 56 affected villages had no mental health providers or centers

10. There were 39.2 physicians for every 10,000 people in Armenia

MENTAL HEALTH OUTREACH PROJECT: SHORT-TERM PLANNING

Coordinating the dispatch to Armenia of teams of Armenian-speaking mental health professionals from the United States, Canada, and Europe was necessary to provide direct patient care. Fluency in the Armenian language, some knowledge of the culture, and emotional stability were key criteria in the selection of the volunteers. Based on the first author's experience, those without knowledge of the language and culture arrived at erroneous conclusions in their assessments of the survivors' mental health and further drained the limited resources of the community by requiring translators. Though the surviving community was fluent in Armenian and Russian, only about 20 percent of the university graduates had a working knowledge of the English language.

Each interdisciplinary team included a psychiatrist, a psychologist, and a psychiatric nurse or psychiatric social worker. Interdisciplinary groups were helpful in many ways. First and foremost, they were to be role models for the professionals in Armenia, where not only did the psychiatrists and psychologists not work collaboratively, but they were also supervised by different governmental ministries. Psychiatry was supervised by the Ministry of Health and psychology supervised by the Ministry of Education. Psychologists were not permitted to care for patients and there were no psychiatric nurses or social workers in Armenia. There were a handful of psychotherapists in Yerevan who were psychiatrists with a year of postpsychiatry training, which frequently took place in Moscow or Leningrad. Each mental health outreach team remained in Armenia for 15–22 days and provided services at the major disaster sites.

Each team was also joined by a psychiatrist and a psychologist from Armenia for the purposes of training, education and role modeling. This was a successful attempt at involving and empowering the survivor community. This integration also enhanced the sharing of a variety of theoretical perspectives and clinical interventions. The first author encouraged the involvement of Soviet mental health professionals from other republics as well. As a result, scholars from Moscow and Georgia joined in the collaborative research effort.

Orientation sessions and workshops in the United States were organized for the volunteer professionals who agreed to serve in Armenia. These sessions were designed to inform, educate and empower the volunteers. This was done through a step-by-step plan using the seven-step Biopsychosocial and Eco Spiritual Model (Meaningfulworld.com).

IMPLEMENTATION

Implementation means putting the plan into effect. This phase directly follows planning, and is followed by the evaluation phase. Implementation is based on specific, unique needs of survivors and their community.

It is absolutely essential to have highly trained and expert mental health professionals conducting the interventions and implementing the plan of care. This phase may take from one month to one year based on the needs of the surviving community, their level of motivation and resources, and the number of mental health professionals available to them. Ideally, the sooner the therapeutic implementation begins, the sooner the community will return not only to its predisaster state of equilibrium, but hopefully to a healthier and more mindful state of being.

The planning phase, emphasizing the short-term goals, began in February 1989 and was reevaluated and modified six months later, in August 1989. During this planning phase, six mental health teams were sent to Armenia to help the survivors of the earthquake, a total of 40 volunteers. They helped over 3,500 earthquake survivors in Yerevan, Leninakan, Kirovakan, Spitak, and in five other villages. The first author, in collaboration with the president of the Committee for Cultural Relations with Armenians Abroad, Garen Dallakian, placed the volunteers in available shelters, hospitals, schools, clinics, and governmental agencies to provide their professional services to a variety of people. Routine cruising, driving, or walking around was also used to detect those who, for many reasons, including fear and suspicion, did not volunteer to seek assistance. Developing a trusting relationship with the survivors was essential. The voluntary nature of the services was stressed and the benefits of the program were listed.

The Mental Health Outreach volunteers possessed expertise in a variety of theoretical methods, and thus clinical approaches also varied. Therapeutic techniques utilized included art therapy, biofeedback, the coloring storybook, drawings (structured and unstructured), family therapy, group therapy, instruction booklets, logotherapy, meditation, play therapy, pharmacotherapy, and short-term psychotherapy. No single clinical intervention alone would have been successful to treat all postquake symptomatology.

SIX MONTH FOLLOW-UP

A six month follow-up evaluation conducted by the first author in Armenia revealed that those survivors (n = 180) who received care from the MHOP's professional teams were:

1. Coping more effectively (78%), based on one-to-one interviews and the survivors' own anecdotal reports
2. Less depressed (50%), based on the interview process and the survivors' own observations
3. Scored lower on the PTSD Reaction Index Scale (80%) (Kalayjian 1994)

In comparison, those survivors who did not receive care from the MHOP's professional teams expressed feelings of hopelessness, helplessness, anger, despair, and apathy. These same survivors, immediately after the quake, were working together cohesively, struggling to survive, helping one another, and hoping that, with the coming of spring, they would spring back to a more stable life. Instead, they had nothing but tanks, tents, and makeshift sheds for basic shelter, air polluted with dust due to the rubble, no running water in many places for 15 hours a day and no electricity for several hours a day. Only about 50 percent of the survivors had homes, 30 percent were in shelters and the remaining 20 percent had relocated to other parts of what was then the Soviet Union or to the United States.

Those who did not benefit from the MHOP or did not receive any psychological support continued exhibiting signs of moderate to severe levels of PTSD. The incidence of suicide, homicide, aggressive outbursts, substance abuse, and spousal and child abuse had increased. Less than 15 percent of the projected construction had been completed in the quake zone. Almost all aid from around the world subsided, and the Azeri blockade continued.

The following are some of the contributing factors as to why some survivors did not participate in the Mental Health Outreach Program:

1. The geographic distance of survivors from the outreach centers
2. The survivor/mental health professional ratio
3. The new modality, that of a talking cure, a concept foreign to the survivors
4. The priority for those survivors was obtaining food, shelter, and clean air to breathe
5. Resistance to treatment and toward authority figures
6. Resistance to foreigners

The first author then recommended the following interventions:

1. Collaborate with and motivate American philanthropic organizations which have enormous resources at their disposal to expedite the reconstruction process. The author began a campaign to inform the public by submitting articles to newspapers and appearing on local radio and television shows to raise the motivation of Americans and Armenian Americans to continue their financial support of Armenia.

2. Continue on-site clinical interventions using the MHOP professional teams for longer stays. The longer time would allow for follow-up and long-term treatments.

3. Engage in on-site education and training of teachers, psychologists, psychiatrists, and other health professionals, as well as invite them to the United States. The purpose of this emphasis is to reach a larger number of survivors and to empower Armenia's professionals by providing them with the necessary instruments, knowledge and expertise in PTSD to help themselves and their communities.

4. Develop community mental health clinics in the affected cities of Leninakan, Kirovakan, and Spitak in order to provide easy access to care for the community.

5. Collaborate with the mental health professionals in Armenia and Moscow to conduct joint research studies.

6. Provide training and orientation for those professionals providing field relief work in Armenia; upon their return provide them with support groups and debriefing sessions.

ONE YEAR FOLLOW-UP

The first author returned to Armenia in April 1991 to evaluate the MHOP and gather more data for the ongoing research. The outpatient clinics in Leninakan (managed by Earthquake Relief Fund for Armenia (ERFA)) and Kirovakan (managed by SOS Armenia) were in place and both clinical care and training were taking place. Two MHOP team members were staying in Armenia for one year each, to supervise, train, and conduct clinical work. About 40 percent of the survivors who visited the clinic had severe PTSD and 15 percent suffered from major depressive disorders. According to Vasken Manoukian, (Kalayjian 1995) the then prime minister of Armenia, only 19 percent of the housing had been completed, leaving thousands of Armenian refugees in need of homes. About 90 percent of the refugees interviewed by the author had severe levels of PTSD. They had escaped beating, rapes, and torture by the Azerbaijanis.

MEANING-MAKING AND RITUALS POST EARTHQUAKE

According to another research study, conducted by the first author six weeks after the earthquake in Armenia, where survivors were asked an open-ended question eliciting the meaning they had attributed to the earthquake, 20 percent (20%) attributed a positive value and meaning to the disaster (Kalayjian 1991b). This is congruent with Quarantelli's notion (1985) that disaster survivors are primarily attempting to cope with the meaning of the trauma and with Frankl's assertion (1978) that meaning is available under any condition, even the worst conceivable one. This is somewhat contrary to Figley's belief (1985) that one of the fundamental questions a victim needs to answer in order to become a survivor is "Why did it happen?" The first author's research findings indicated that a question of that type forced the survivor to remain in the past, in the role of a victim, without a rational or satisfactory answer. It also left the survivor filled with feelings of self-induced guilt and therefore, trapped in a cycle of destructive behavior. Viktor Frankl, the author of *Man's Search for Meaning*, in a personal communication, labeled this type of "why" question as the "wrong question." Any question that begins with a "why" has a built-in presumption that there is someone responsible for it and that there is a clear reason behind it. In this case, it was a natural disaster. Those survivors from Armenia who were preoccupied with the question of "Why did this happen?" were dissatisfied with the scientific answer that the plates moved, pressure was built up and finally the tension was released. Interestingly, these were the survivors who remained helpless, more depressed, and showed higher scores on the PTSD Reaction Index Scale.

In Armenia, those survivors who were preoccupied with the "why" were uninterested in the scientific explanation. They countered with the questions, "Why us? What have we done to deserve this?" This question, "Why was my child, my parents or my school affected?," implied that trauma and disaster happen to bad, sinful or unworthy people, attributing a negative meaning to the disaster. They expressed a lot of guilt and self pity. These survivors connected the earthquake to the genocide, globalized all their historic unresolved traumas in one, and felt even more overwhelmed by their memories.

Survivors who attributed a positive meaning focused instead on the present moment and the meaningful experiences they had gained by helping or receiving help from one another and from the world. One survivor from Armenia stated: "Look at how the world has come to help us (the Armenians), the closed Soviet system has opened its doors, there is more communication, caring and sharing" (Kalayjian 1995).

According to the first author's research findings (1991b), 20 percent of the survivors in Armenia were convinced that they were indomitable, echoing the words of Nietzsche (1872), who said, "That which does not kill me makes me stronger."

In addition, during the intervention, the first author saw survivors praying and showing awe to their country by bending their knees and kissing the soil. Their spiritual rituals were seen in many scenes, and 7- and 40-day commemorations were also conducted for the victims of the earthquake. However, when they were required to move to another geographic location, the majority of the people strongly resisted. Some survivors expressed anger and mentioned that they were not leaving the land where their ancestors had lived for three centuries.

Black humor was used generously to distance survivors from the enormity of the trauma and from the crippling pain of multiple losses and to help them transform their suffering. The following is an example: "Ara, a survivor, is half buried under a massive boulder. His brother is standing on top of the boulder, engaging him in conversation to keep him alive until rescue forces arrive. After a couple of hours Ara moans "I am cold, I am cold!" His brother replies jokingly: "Shall I throw another boulder onto you?"

DISCUSSION

The results that many survivors, including adults and children, showed PTSD symptoms were consistent with past research (Azarian et al. 1994; Azarian, Miller, and Skriptchenko-Gregorian 1996; Pynoos et al. 1993). Pynoos et al. also conducted their research near the epicenter of the earthquake, Spitak and Gumri (Leninakan), and found that more than 70 percent of the children reported severe PTSD symptoms. One of the reasons of this unusually high number of children reporting PTSD may be explained by the number of people killed in the earthquake, with many children left as survivors (Pynoos).

In addition, it is in line with some studies that the majority of children still reported PTSD symptoms even after one year (Pynoos et al. 1993). This could be due to several reasons, for example that the majority of children had been separated from their families, that the housing and food were not enough for the survivors, and that the political conflict still existed.

RECOMMENDATIONS FOR THE FUTURE

According to the first author's observations and evaluations, there is the need for at least a 20 year continued on-site clinical intervention program with three groups:

1. The earthquake survivors
2. The refugees from Azerbaijan
3. The former government's Communist Party leaders who expressed feelings of shame, doubt, defeat, resentment, and uncertainty due to the collapse of the Soviet Union

In Armenia, when addressing the educational arena, it is recommended that a 20-year plan be established for schools in clinical psychology, social work and nursing, as well as training programs in interpersonal and behavioral modalities. For example, the Armenian General Benevolent Union and the University of California have founded the American University of Armenia. It opened its doors in the fall of 1991, offering MA degrees in business, industrial engineering, and earthquake engineering. Future programs could be in the fields of clinical psychology with specialty programs in social work, counseling, and psychiatric nursing.

REFERENCES

Andrews, G., Tennant, C., Hewson, D. M., and Valliant, G. E. 1978. "Life Event Stress, Social Support, Coping Style and Risk of Psychological Impairment." *Journal of Nervous Mental Disorders* 66: 307–16.

Azarian, A., Miller, T. W., and Skriptchenko-Gregorian, V. 1996. "Baseline Assessment of Children Traumatized by the Armenian Earthquake." *Child Psychiatry and Human Development* 27 (1): 29–41.

Azarian, A., Skriptchenko-Gregorian, V., Miller, T. W., and Kraus, B. F. 1994. "Childhood Trauma in Victims of the Armenian Earthquake." *Journal of Contemporary Psychotherapy* 24 (2): 77–85.

Bal, A., and Jensen, B. 2007. "Post-traumatic Stress Disorder Symptom Clusters in Turkish Child and Adolescent Trauma Survivors." *European Child and Adolescent Psychiatry* 16 (7): 449–57.

Basoglu, M., Kilic, C., Salcioglu, E., and Livanou, M. 2004. "Prevalence of Posttraumatic Stress Disorder and Comorbid Depression in Earthquake Survivors in Turkey: An Epidemiological Study." *Journal of Traumatic Stress* 17: 133–41.

Basoglu, M., Salcioglu, E., and Livanou, M. 2009. "Single-Case Experimental Studies of a Self-Help Manual for Traumatic Stress in Earthquake Survivors." *Journal of Behavior Therapy and Experimental Psychiatry* 40: 50–58.

Baum, A., Fleming, R., and Davidson, L. M. 1983. "Emotional, Behavioral, and Physiological Effects of Chronic Stress at Three Mile Island." *Journal of Counseling and Clinical Psychology* 51: 565–72.

Berndt, T. J., and Ladd, G. W. 1989. *Peer Relationships in Child Development.* New York: Wiley and Sons.

Fein, E. 1988. "Toll Put in Tens of Thousands from Quake in Soviet Armenia." *New York Times,* December 9.

Figley, C. R. 1985. *Trauma and Its Wake.* New York: Brunner-Mazel.

Fleming, R., Baum, A., Gisriel, M., and Gatchel, R. R. 1982. "Mediating Influences of Social Support on Stress at Three Mile Island." *Journal of Human Stress* 8: 14–22.

Frankl, V. E. 1978. *The Unheard Cry of Meaning.* New York: Simon and Schuster.

Frederick, C. J. 1986. "Children Traumatized by Catastrophic Situation." In *Posttraumatic Stress Disorder in Children,* ed. S. Eth and R. Pynoos, 73–99. Washington, DC: American Psychiatric Press.

Gleser, G. C., Green, B. L., and Winget, C. 1981. *Prolonged Psychosocial Effect of Disaster: A Study of Buffalo Creek.* New York: Academic Press.

Goenjian, A., Walling, D., Steinberg, A., Roussos, A., Goenjian, H., and Pynoos, R. 2009. "Depression and PTSD Symptoms among Bereaved Adolescents 6 1/2 years after the 1988 Spitak Earthquake." *Journal of Affective Disorders* 112 (1): 81–4.

Goenjian, A. K., Najarian, L. M., Pynoos, R. S., Steinberg, A. M., Manoukian, G., Tavosian, A., and Fairbanks, L. A. 1994. "Post-traumatic Stress Disorder in Elderly and Younger Adults after the 1988 Earthquake in Armenia." *American Journal of Psychiatry* 151 (6): 895.

Hardin, S. B., Weinrich, M., Weinrich, S., Hardin, T. L., and Garrison, C. 1994. "Psychological Distress of Adolescents Exposed to Hurricane Hugo." *Journal of Traumatic Stress* 7 (3): 427–40.

Ishkhanian, R. 1989. *Badgerazart Aadmountioun Hayotz.* [A pictorial history of Armenians.] Armenian SSR: Arevig Press.

Jordan, R. P. 1978. "The Proud Armenians." *National Geographic* 153: 846–73.

Kalayjian, A. S. October, 1991(a). "Genocide, Earthquake, and Ethnic Turmoil: Multiple Traumas of a Nation." Paper presented at the 7th Annual Convention of the International Society of Traumatic Stress Studies, Washington, DC.

Kalayjian, A. S. 1991(b). "Meaning in Trauma: Impact of the Earthquake in Soviet Armenia." Paper presented at the VIII World Congress of Logotherapy, San Jose, CA.

Kalayjian, A. S. 1994. "Mental Health Outreach Program Following the Earthquake in Armenia: Utilizing the Nursing Process in Developing and Managing the Post-Natural Disaster Plan." *Issues in Mental Health Nursing* 15 (6): 533–50.

Kalayjian, A. S. 2005. "Eight Stages of Healing from Mass Trauma." Presentation at United Nations, New York September 7–9.

Kowalski, K. M., and Kalayjian, A. S. 2001. "Responding to Mass Emotional Trauma: A Mental Health Outreach Program for Turkey Earthquake Victims." *Safety Science*: 29: 71–81.

Kuo, H. W., Wu, S. J., Ma, T. C., Chiu, M. C., and Chou, S. Y. 2007. "Post-traumatic Symptoms Were Worst among Quake Victims with Injuries Following the Chi-chi Quake in Taiwan." *Journal of Psychosomatic Research* 62: 495–500.

March, J. S., Amaya-Jackson, L., Murray, M. C., and Schulte, A. 1998. "Cognitive Behavioral Psychotherapy for Children and Adolescents with Post-traumatic

Stress Disorder after a Single Incident Stressor." *Journal of the American Academy of Child and Adolescent Psychiatry* 137: 585–93.

McLeish, A.C., and Del Ben, K.S. 2008. "Symptoms of Depression and Post-traumatic Stress Disorder in an Outpatient Population Before and After Hurricane Katrina." *Depression and Anxiety* 25: 416–21.

Meaningfulworld.com. *Stage III: Cultivating a Meaningfulworld View and Seeds of Forgiveness.* Available at: http://meaningfulworld.com/index.php?option=com_content&task=view&id=233&Itemid=24.

Milgram, N., Toubiana, Y., Klingman, A., Raviv, A., and Goldstein, I. 1988. "Situational Exposure and Personal Loss in Children's Acute and Chronic Stress Reactions to a School Bus Disaster." *Journal of Traumatic Stress* 1 (3): 339–52.

Murphy, S.A. 1987. "Self-Efficacy and Social Support: Mediators of Stress on Mental Health Following a Natural Disaster." *Western Journal of Nursing Research* 9 (1): 58–86.

Nadar, K., Pynoos, R., Fairbanks, L., and Frederick, C. 1990. "Children's Post-traumatic Stress Disorder Reactions One Year after a Sniper Attack at Their School." *American Journal of Psychiatry* 147 (11): 1526–1530.

Neria, Y., Nadi, A., and Galea, S. 2008. "Post-traumatic Stress Disorder Following Disasters: A Systematic Review." *Psychological Medicine* 38: 467–80.

Nietzsche, F. [1872, 1887] 1956. *The Birth Of Tragedy* and *Of the Genealogy of Morality.* New York: Doubleday.

Norris, F.H., Perilla, J.L., Riad, J.K., Kaniasty, K., and Lavizzo, E.A. 1999. "Stability and Change in Stress, Resources, and Psychological Distress Following Natural Disaster: Findings from Hurricane Andrew." *Anxiety Stress Coping* 12: 363–96.

Pynoos, R.S., Goenjian, A., Tashjian, M., Karakashian, M., Manjikian, R., Manoukian, G., et al. 1993. "Post-traumatic Stress Reaction in Children after the 1988 Armenian Earthquake." *British Journal of Psychiatry* 163: 239–47.

Quarantelli, E.L. 1985. "An Assessment of Conflicting Views on Mental Health: The Consequences of Traumatic Events." In *Trauma and its Wake,* ed. C.R. Figley, 173–215. New York: Brunner-Mazel.

Rubonis, A.V., and Bickman, L. 1991. "Psychological Impairment in the Wake of Disaster: The Disaster-Psychopathology Relationship." *Psychological Bulletin* 109: 384–99.

Rutter, M., Izard, C.E., and Read, P.B. 1986. *Depression in Young People: Developmental and Clinical Perspectives.* New York: Guilford Publishing.

Salloum, A., and Overstreet, S. 2008. "Evaluation of Individual and Group Grief and Trauma Interventions for Children Post Disaster." *Journal of Clinical Child and Adolescent Psychology* 37 (3): 495–507.

Simon, P. 1989. "U.S. Government Should Do More to Help Armenian Rebuild." *Journal of Armenian Assembly of America* 16: 3–4.

Smith, P., Perrin, S., and Yule, W. 1999. "Cognitive Behavior Therapy for Post-Traumatic Stress Disorder." *Child Psychology and Psychiatry Review* 4 (4): 177–82.

Sullivan, G. 1988. "Pressing Rock Masses Mark Center Quake." *The New York Times,* December 9.

Terr, L. C. 1989. "Family Anxiety after Traumatic Events." *Journal of Clinical Psychiatry* 50 (11): 15–19.

Tural, U., Coskun, B., Onder, E., Corapcioglu, A., Yildiz, M., Kesepara, C., Kara-kaya, I., Aydin, M., Erol, A., Torun, F., and Aybar, G. 2004. "Psychological Consequences of the 1999 Earthquake in Turkey." *Journal of Traumatic Stress* 17 (6): 451–59.

Viviano, F. 2004. "The Rebirth of Armenia." *National Geographic* 205 (3): 28–49. http://ngm.nationalgeographic.com/feautures/world/asia/Armenia/Armenia-text.

Walker, B. 1991. *Armenia at Crossroads* [Television broadcast]. Los Angeles: CBS News.

Wang, X., Gao, L., Shinfuku, N., Zhang, H., Zhao, C., and Shen, Y. 2000. "Longitudinal Study of Earthquake-Related PTSD in a Randomly Selected Community Sample in North China." *American Journal of Psychiatry* 157: 1260–1266.

Chapter 2

NORTHRIDGE EARTHQUAKE IN SOUTHERN CALIFORNIA

Lessons Learned and Meanings Discovered

Ani Kalayjian and
Christina Di Liberto

A man is called selfish not for pursuing his own good, but for neglecting his neighbor's.

—Richard Whately

INTRODUCTION

Many Californians have feared the major release of seismic tension, and on Monday, January 17, 1994, their forebodings came to devastating fruition. At the bracing hour of 4:31 A.M., the Northridge community experienced a surge of vibrations that measured 6.7 on the Richter scale. Given the hour and the fact that it was Martin Luther King Day, a national holiday, the level of casualties was significantly lower it might have been. In a population of roughly 10 million, the earthquake's estimated death toll was 61 people and the number of injuries was measured around 7,300 people (Kalayjian 1995).

The high velocity of the concussive tectonic motion placed the structural integrity of buildings under tremendous stress. Consequently, during the subsequent periods of aftershocks, buildings whose architecture was compromised by the initial shock were vulnerable to further damage and potential collapse. As previously mentioned, the Northridge earthquake measured 6.7 on the Richter scale, resulting in the demolishment of six major freeway ramps, the displacement of hundreds of thousands of survivors, and the temporary closing of 23 hospitals due to incurred structural damage.

The situation of the survivors postquake was dire, and the Federal Emergency Management Agency (FEMA) responded to the Northridge community's needs without hesitation. FEMA, in coordination with other governmental aid programs and local community organizations, supplied many of the survivors with the appropriate provisions, financial assistance, and shelter that their particular situation required.

Although the response to the Northridge earthquake was immediate and expeditious, it was not entirely comprehensive. Due to socioeconomic and immigration status, there were many individuals in need that did not receive proper aid. The progression of events following the earthquake made clear the need for protocol reformation. The earthquake also revealed architectural reinforcement measures that needed to be taken in order to prevent the compromise of infrastructure and better insure the safety of community members in the event of future earthquakes.

The impact an earthquake can impose on a community is often apparent in physical casualties, injuries, and structural damage. However, the experience of a disastrous event such as an earthquake can have potentially traumatic and lasting psychological effects. Months after the initial event, researchers found that 67 percent of the adults interviewed had severe posttraumatic stress disorder (PTSD), 88 percent of the children interviewed demonstrated severe PTSD, and 50 percent of mental health workers showed signs of developing PTSD (Kalayjian 1995). Consequently it has been theorized that, depending on the circumstances, one's psychological state has either a positive or negative influence on one's overall state of physical health. Regarding the Northridge earthquake, researchers found that the psychological stress experienced by certain survivors as a result of the earthquake led to the impairment of their autonomic nervous systems and their immune systems (Segerstrom et al. 1998).

In this chapter the authors are interested in exploring the multifarious impact of the Northridge earthquake on the community regarding the infrastructure, local residences, medical facilities, the psychological well-being of the survivors, and rituals and practices used for meaning-making and resilience.

LITERATURE REVIEW

Event Characteristics

An aspect that is rather intriguing about this particular earthquake is the fact that it was consistently described as being erratic. For example, certain buildings were damaged by the quake while adjacent ones were left fully intact. Similarly, buildings that were in close proximity to the epicenter were left unharmed, whereas others were thoroughly demolished. An estimated 200 buildings suffered major damage as a result of the earthquake, most predominantly ones six stories and under (Kalayjian 1995).

Unsurprisingly, the earthquake had a significant impact on the area's infrastructure as well. As a result of the quake, six major freeways were compromised, including collapse of the elevated ramps from the Antelope Valley freeway to the Golden State Freeway. Three ramps connecting southbound Route 14 to southbound I-5 collapsed as well as one connecting southbound Route 14 to northbound I-5. The impairment of such freeways hindered the availability and accessibility of emergency relief. The reparation costs were estimated to cost $100 million, the highest amount the Federal Highway Association (FHA) can issue in order to aid emergency relief. The FHA initiated the restoration process the day following the earthquake (Kalayjian 1995).

Another major post-quake concern was the loss of medical facilities and the consequential impact on inpatients. In Canoga Park, 2 of the 28 Cigna Healthcare outpatient stations were forced to close. An estimated 34 hospitals suffered damages as a result of the earthquake (Kalayjian 1995).

Although the earthquake's primary impact was on infrastructure, there were negative ecological consequences as well. In the San Fernando and Santa Clarita Valleys, ARCO's line 1 running from San Jaoquim Valley to a refinery near Long Beach, had four ruptures in the piping system. The most significant rupture spilled an estimated 3,000 gallons into the Santa Clara River for a stretch of 12 miles (Kalayjian 1995).

Summary of Event Characteristics

1. No prediction or warning
2. Severe infrastructure damage
3. Oil leak
4. Erratic behavior of quake
5. Unusual pounding due to unusually large vertical accelerations
6. Especially devastating to buildings with less than six stories
7. 1.1 million lost electrical power and gas service
8. 3,500 aftershocks
9. 34 hospital buildings and medical offices were damaged
10. 61 people were killed
11. 7,300 people were injured
12. Californians thought it was the Big One (Kalayjian 1995)

Survivor Characteristics

The Northridge population, as of 1990, was reported to be 69 percent white, 7.4 percent African American, 0.8 percent Native American, 9.6 percent Asian, 25.8 percent Hispanic, and 13.2 percent other ethnicities. California was ranked first in terms of gross state product, totaling $744.73 billion in economic output. As of 1993, with 5,285,000 students, California was also ranked first in public education enrollment. California was ranked 35th in the nation with $4,584 per student; 79.7 percent of the student population attain four years of high school, and 25 percent four years of college or more (Kalayjian 1995).

Members of the Southern California community have historically experienced a range of natural disasters such as earthquakes, mudslides, fires, and floods. Given the precarious nature of the region, many of the surviving residents were insured for earthquakes (Kalayjian 1995).

Summary of Survivor Characteristics

1. Education: Public education enrollment taking first in the nation
2. Economy: As of 1990, $744.73 billion gross state product
3. Religion: Mostly Christian, but mixed
4. Survivors: Largely white American, long-term residents of the area
5. Small number of Mexican and African Americans
6. Largely established communities who have experienced earthquakes
7. Area with most damage was Northridge, where there was a large student population from all around the United States
8. Survivors were from all socioeconomic levels
9. Insurance: Most were insured (Kalayjian 1995)

Issues during Disaster Relief

One major issue of the Northridge earthquake was the fact that it was without warning. Despite this, the evacuation protocol was executed expeditiously, and the response of the Federal Emergency Management Agency (FEMA) was timely. The programs that were implemented through FEMA were intended to provide temporary assistance to community members, such as home rehabilitation and emergency financial relief. In response to the earthquake, FEMA set up relief clinics throughout the hardest hit areas, including the services of professional nurses and mental health practitioners. Although the assistive relief centers were set up promptly, after about a month many of them had been closed down (Kalayjian 1995).

One aspect of these programs that should be noted is the fact that they are not designed to improve the previous living situation of any community member, and are only expected to assist them in returning to the state of their situation prior to whatever disaster might have occurred. Correspondingly, if victims of a disaster are properly insured, they are required to go through their respective insurance companies as the primary source of assistance (Bolin and Stanford 1998).

Another confounding issue was the obstruction of traffic flow to the southern Californian community. Since residents were heavily reliant on personal transportation, the destruction of traffic routes led to an influx in public transportation usage. Metrolink, a light-rail system, experienced a 300 percent increase in morning commuters, maintaining about 70 percent of new ridership after normal traffic conditions had been restored (Kalayjian 1995).

The outreach to those who were impacted by the disaster but were residing in the United States illegally, in particular immigrant Mexican farmers, was also another major issue in terms of disaster relief. As many of the crisis counseling and emergency relief programs were governmentally organized, those with questionable immigration status were apprehensive about using their services, and therefore did not necessarily receive the amount of aid they needed after the disaster. In order to access this community, the project COPE (Counseling Ordinary People in Emergencies) coordinated with the Catholic Charities and Clinicas del Camino Real, local organizations in whom the community felt a level of confidence. These local organizations historically have provided the necessary services regardless of immigration status, thus affording those who were concerned with their residency status an opportunity for accessible postquake assistance (Bolin and Stanford 1998).

The legality of their immigration status was not the only obstacle at hand for the immigrant farming community. Another barrier that had to be faced was language. Many of the farmers were monolingual Mexican immigrants who have difficulty communicating with monolingual Americans. The inability to speak the language impaired their ability to express their particular needs and access the proper emergency relief. In an effort to better reach the victims, project COPE, the Catholic Charities, and Clinicas del Camino Real organized crisis counseling services that were Spanish-speaking and culturally sensitive. This was extremely pertinent to the provision of crisis counseling services. The process of counseling necessitates the expression and exposition of one's personal reaction and emotional state, requiring an effective level of communication between the survivor and the crisis counselor (Bolin and Stanford 1998).

Socioeconomic Environment

On March 3, 1991, Rodney King was the victim of police brutality committed by the Los Angeles Police Department. The accused officers were later charged in the attack, but were then acquitted on all accounts. The court's decision, in conjunction with the brooding racially charged tension, led to the 1992 Los Angeles riots, where many households and commercial establishments were looted and then set on fire. The events preceding and following the Rodney King trial exemplify the underlying social inequalities facing the Los Angeles community.

Short-Term Planning

In response to the 1994 earthquake, the American Red Cross (ARC) provided the Northridge community with assistance and relief. From New York State, ARC dispatched 15,000 trained relief workers in an effort to attend to the postquake needs of the survivors. The operation was able to harbor over 22,000 refugees in 47 shelters as well as provide around 1.7million meals (Kalayjian 1995).

The Clinton administration was very effective in authorizing and issuing the necessary funding and assistance in an expeditious manner. Within a week they announced an initial $7.5 billion aid package, which included $3.9 billion for FEMA and $1.35 billion package for the Federal Highway Association. As the disaster occurred within the United States, there was no waiting period required in order to access the impacted community (Kalayjian 1995).

Governmental agencies not only tended to the physical needs of the surviving community, but to those of an emotional nature as well. Within two weeks of the earthquake, FEMA implemented a $35 million crisis counseling and outreach services package designed to assist the survivors with their emotional reaction to the disaster. In 18 Red Cross Service shelters, volunteers trained by ARC collaborated with local mental health professionals offering to meet with the survivors individually and to discuss their particular needs (Kalayjian 1995).

Community Diagnoses

1. Quake referred to as the Big One
2. 34 percent of survivors interviewed planned to relocate
3. 67 percent of the adults interviewed had severe PTSD
4. 88 percent of the children interviewed demonstrated severe PTSD
5. 50 percent of mental health workers were showing signs of PTSD

6. 30 percent of teachers and educators in the affected area had severe PTSD

7. Based on interviews taken, survivors seemed content with relief efforts

8. 98 percent of the survivors complained about the influx of traffic jams (Kalayjian, 1995)

Post-Earthquake Housing Issues

What is interesting about the Northridge earthquake is the fact that it is considered to be one of the first disasters after which information regarding the community damage was systematically catalogued. The information gathered postquake now allows researchers to conduct a comparison analysis between issues faced by tenants and single-family homeowners (Comerio 1997).

The violation of the structural integrity of many apartments left numerous tenants displaced and without housing. In response to their situation, FEMA coordinated with both Housing and Urban Development (HUD) and the California Governor's Office of Emergency Services (OES) to ensure short-term rental assistance to community members in need. Within two months of the disaster, they were able to find housing accommodation for 130,000 middle-class and low-income families. FEMA issued housing assistance checks for two to three months to all but 12,000 of those who received temporary housing assistance. Recipients of these checks could request an extension to up to 18 months, but most did not take advantage of that option. As with the receipt of crisis counseling, many of those with questionable legal status abstained from requesting housing assistance out of fear of deportation. Fortunately, many sought the aid of local organizations and charities for assistance with their housing rehabilitation (Comerio 1997).

Although the renting community faced many hardships, those experienced by the single-family homeowners were far more complicated and costly. Within three to six months after the earthquake, the initial data from insurance companies estimated a total of 1.5 billion dollars worth of damage for the city and 2.5 billion dollars worth of damage for insurance reimbursements. The data also show that 288,000 homeowners received an average of $3,000 from FEMA's Minimal Home Repair program, 265,000 homeowners received an average of $30,000 in indemnification, and 74,000 homeowners received an average $31,000 in low-interest loans from the Small Business Administration. In total, governmental agencies and private insurance companies provided the Northridge community with an estimated $25.7 billion in financial assistance, of which 50 percent was designated for housing reparation, 25 percent for transportation, and 20 percent for the repair of local commercial establishments (Comerio 1997).

Remodification

The occurrence of any major natural disaster, through its devastating impact, will illuminate what aspects of the area's infrastructure are designed to withstand the shock and differentiate them from those that require remodification in order to be better suited for future disasters. The 1994 Northridge earthquake made clear that the architecture of certain buildings needed to be restructured, the most pressing being the hospitals.

As a consequence of the earthquake, some 23 hospitals were forced to suspend some if not all of their services and incurred an estimated $3 billion in damages. Exacerbating the situation is the nature and purpose of a hospital. Many of the infirm are either bedridden or have significantly limited mobility. That in conjunction with the inadequacy of the hospital's structure allows for a high level of patient vulnerability. The impact of the 1994 earthquake demonstrated that certain measures needed to be taken in order to better insure the safety of the hospital staff and residents. As a result, the California legislature ratified SB 1953, the Hospital Facilities Seismic Safety Act. The act was an amendment to the already existing HFSSA, the 1973 Hospital Facilities Seismic Safety Act following the 1972 Sylmar earthquake (SB 1953).

The SB 1953 Hospitals Facilities Seismic Safety Act mandated that all 2,700 general and acute inpatient facilities upgrade their nonstructural emergency systems such as backup generators and exit lighting by the year 2002, and if they were at risk of collapsing, they were to be rebuilt by the year 2008. It also stipulated that all buildings should be constructed to be fully operational following an earthquake by the year 2030. Although the act undoubtedly will improve the condition of California hospitals and significantly lower the potential for injuries, it also will result in the condemning of those facilities, particularly those located in the inner-cities, that do not have the financial means to meet the structural remodification requirements of SB 1953. Though they may be architecturally unfit, their removal may result in the limitation of proper health care accessibility for those living in the inner-city areas. That being said, it is equally important to have facilities that are structurally designed to cope with any potential seismic vibrations. If the facilities are unable to procure enough funding to ensure their proper reconstruction, perhaps governmental financial assistance should be pursued (SB 1953).

Issues Faced by Nursing and Health Facilities as a Result of the Earthquake

Although there has been a significant amount of attention placed on the impact of the Northridge earthquake on general and acute care facilities, the issues faced by the nursing facilities has been overlooked. In an effort to gain further information regarding how nursing facilities were affected by disasters, Saliba, Buchanan, and Kington (2004) investigated how nursing facilities responded to the Northridge earthquake.

Through the California Office of Emergency Services, Department of Health Services, Office of Statewide Health Planning and Development, and the Los Angeles Building Inspector's Office they were able to diagnose nursing facilities that were damaged as a result of the earthquake. In order to do so, they utilized the maps of California Health Facility Planning areas and determined 7 areas, totaling 144 facilities, which were significantly affected by the earthquake. Another interesting, and unfortunate, finding was that in all the public data they collected through the *Los Angeles Times*, there was not a single piece covering the impact the earthquake had on nursing facilities or even considering them health facilities (Saliba, Buchanan, and Kington 2004).

Surveys were mailed to each facility investigating such topics as their 5 phases of disaster planning: anticipation and prevention, alert and warning, immediate postevent assistance and relief, and rehabilitation, as well as their incurred damages, postdisaster assistance, and any changes in admittance patterns postquake. Of the 113 facilities that submitted responses, 23 (20%) reported the existence of extensive structural damage, and 5 of them had to close as a result. With regard to changes in admissions after the earthquake, 31 percent of the facilities noted that they received a higher number of requests relating to the disaster than standard admissions (Saliba, Buchanan, and Kington 2004).

One major issue that was reported by 74 percent of the respondents was the inadequacy of the central communication system. This resulted in nursing facilities being unable to communicate their needs and space availability during the crucial postdisaster period. Of the damaged facilities, five reported the absence of their medical director, and six reported the absence of a physician during the first 24-hour period after the disaster. This exemplifies how some facilities were devoid of the necessary trained medical professionals during a period of great urgency and importance. As with SB 1953, Hospital Facility Seismic Safety Act, regulations should be set in place that would require nursing facilities located in areas vulnerable to potential earthquakes to implement structural reinforcement and effective disaster planning (Saliba, Buchanan, and Kington 2004).

Concordance between Worry and Immune System Dysfunction as a Result of the Earthquake

The devastation a natural disaster inflicts upon a community is undoubtedly not solely experienced in casualties and demolishment of buildings, but psychologically as well. The impact a disaster can have on a survivor's psyche and emotional wellbeing can be debilitating and has the potential to be quite lasting if left untreated by mental health professionals. It should also be noted that there is a close synergy between the emotional state of individuals and their overall physical health. Therefore, if a survivor is experiencing psychological trauma, emotional problems may translate into infringements upon their physical health (Segerstrom et al. 1998).

For example it has been argued that anxiety is associated with malfunctioning of the autonomic nervous system (ANS), which is a portion of the peripheral nervous system primarily responsible for the maintenance of homeostasis in the human body. A constituent of the human immune system significantly related to the ANS is the natural killer cell system (NK), which is comprised of nonspecific cytotoxic cells responsible for killing virally infected cells and preventing the metastasis of particular tumors. It has been found that exposure to acute stressors activates the ANS, resulting in an increase of NK cells. However, it has also been conjectured that with the exposure to chronic stressors the converse will occur, and the number of NK cells will actually decrease. The interaction between chronic stressors, ANS, and NK functioning may prove to be demonstrative of the connection between anxiety and the immune system (Segerstrom et al. 1998).

In an effort to explore further the interaction between the experience of a traumatic event and physical health, Segerstrom, Solomon, Kemey, and Fahey conducted a longitudinal study investigating the relationship between anxiety and immune system dysfunction as a result of the Northridge earthquake. The participants of the study were asked to complete questionnaires and had their blood taken 2, 8, and 15 weeks after the earthquake. The researchers utilized an analysis of covariance (ANCOVA) in order to make a better comparison between the three time points and the level of anxiety (high anxiety being above the median and low anxiety below the median) (Segerstrom et al. 1998).

A significant main effect of anxiety on the NK counts is such that high worriers had a lower count of NK cells than low worriers at all three time points. After controlling for the trait anxiety, a significant negative linear relationship was also found between high levels of anxiety and the number of NK cells at all three time points. The results indicate an association between high levels of anxiety and the disruption in appropriate NK counts after the earthquake. Individuals who suffered from higher levels of anxiety were prone to having lower NK cells, compromising their immune system and leaving them vulnerable for potential ailments (Segerstrom et al. 1998).

METHOD

Participants

The author interviewed individuals experiencing primary and secondary trauma as a result of the earthquake. Based on previous experience, the first author has found that children, adolescents, and the elderly tend to be the populations most vulnerable to the impact of a traumatic event. Participants of this study also included members of the mental health, educational, and governmental communities.

Procedure

The environment after the Northridge earthquake was quite tumultuous and agitated, necessitating an expeditious assessment. The author selected the Reaction Index Scale as the most appropriate diagnostic instrument for effective implementation, based on its perspicuity and succinctness. The scale consisted of 28 items (20 for children), where each item was scored on a range between zero and 4 for a total of 80 possible points. The Reaction Index Scale was utilized for adults as well as children.

The author also used structured and unstructured drawings in order to assess the level of trauma experienced by children under the age of 10. For the structured drawings, children were given specific instructions as to what to include in their drawing, such as their house at the time of the quake, and another drawing depicting a safe place, while incorporating themselves, their family members, and anything else they considered to be significant. In the event that the children were resistant to the structured drawing assignment, they were asked to compose an unstructured drawing depicting anything they wished to include.

With children who were resistant to both structured and unstructured drawing, the author utilized play therapy as an assessment instrument. For the purposes of this study, houses, trees, animals, cars, and significant figures were incorporated in order to allow them to communicate the emotional experiences they could not express verbally or graphically.

RESULTS

After careful analysis, the results indicated that of those who participated, 67 percent of the adults, 88 percent of the children, and 50 percent of the educators in the affected area were suffering from severe PTSD. Of the mental health professionals in the affected area 50 percent suffered from PTSD, indicating secondary traumatization.

BAKER COLLEGE of CLINTON TWP LIBRARY

Meaning-Making

The experience of any traumatic event has the potential to shift an individual's perspective and promote the reevaluation of priorities. In the event that the lives of loved ones are placed in jeopardy, an individual may learn to better appreciate elements of his or her life that are matters of the heart, and place less of an emphasis on those that are materialistic.

Southern California is home to notoriously materialistic areas such as Hollywood, LA, and Beverly Hills. These areas are infamous for placing a high value on image, materials, and consumption. However, after experiencing the earthquake, many were given the opportunity to place their life approaches into perspective. In interviewing the participants, it was noted that 40 percent established a positive meaning in their experiences of the earthquake because it allowed them to realize the transience of material items, as they learned to appreciate others more than material goods. Many of the participants gave assessments such as "I went through many quakes in my life, always replaced all the china and the broken crystal. This time is different, this time I learned something about life's meaning. This time I'm not going to replace the unnecessary crystal. I now value my friends and family, and will put all my energy to be with them," "Materials are here today and gone tomorrow, from now on I am going to invest in people," and "This (quake) was a good lesson to me of life, not material. I did not lose my life and the lives of the loved ones, thank God, and that is what counts."

CONCLUSION

With the destruction of six major freeways, the suspension of 23 hospitals, the displacement of hundreds of thousands of residents, $25.7 billion in financial assistance, and the estimated casualty toll, the impact of the Northridge earthquake was indubitably calamitous and extensive. In addition to the physical damage, lives of the resident community were seismically shifted and dramatically altered, requiring the financial and supportive aid of both governmental agencies and local community outreach programs. The horrific impact of the earthquake led to the illumination of certain aspects of disaster relief protocol that were in need of remodification.

For example, because many of the aid programs were implemented by governmental agencies, there was a portion of the affected community that did not receive appropriate aid out of fear of deportation. The aid programs have to be residency-blind to extend adequate outreach assistance to this community. One possibility is to grant immunity to those with questionable immigration status for the duration of the assistance process, with the understanding that they would then apply for the appropriate residency documentation afterwards.

The implementation of SB 1953 Hospitals Facilities Seismic Safety Act is another example of how the impact of the earthquake harvested necessary remodification strategies. With the suspension of 23 hospitals it became apparent that health care service facilities located in seismically precarious areas were in need of renovation that would reinforce the architectural structure and lessen their vulnerability.

On January 17, 1994, the Northridge residents experienced a series of seismic convulsions of devastating proportions. The event had an extensive and devastating impact on their homes and community, as well as on their overall state of psychological and physical health. While the earthquake was comprehensively destructive and traumatic, it led to an awareness of problematic emergency relief protocol and vulnerable structural composition. Insight gained from the earthquake illuminated what reformative measures had to be taken both systemically and architecturally in order to better prepare the community and to insure the safety of its members in the event of future earthquakes.

A given experience will provide an individual with new information and allow for varying shifts in perspective. These particular shifts function as a catalyst for marked personal growth, and therefore can lead to an overall appreciation for the experience. For many of the survivors, the experience of the earthquake, however subjectively traumatic, led to the reorganization of their priorities in life and the attainment of insight regarding what is personally meaningful.

REFERENCES

Bolin, R., and Stanford, L. 1998(a). "The Northridge Earthquake: Community-based Approaches to Unmet Recovery Needs." *Disasters* 22 (1): 21–38.

Bolin, R., and Stanford, L. 1998(b). *The Northridge Earthquake: Vulnerability and Disaster.* Abingdon, UK: Routledge.

Comerio, M.C. 1997. "Housing Issues after Disasters." *Journal of Contingencies and Crisis Management* 5 (3): 166–78.

Kalayjian, A.S. 1995. *Disasters and Mass Trauma: Global Perspectives on Post Disaster Health Management.* Long Branch, NJ: Vista Publishing.

Saliba, D., Buchanan, J., and Kington, R.S. 2004. "Function and Response of Nursing Homes during Community Disaster." *American Journal of Public Health* 94 (8): 1436–1441.

SB1953. 1997. The Hospital Facilities Seismic Safety Act.

Segerstrom, S.C., Solomon, G.F., Kemeny, M.E., and Fahey, J.L. 1998. "Relationship of Worry to Immune Sequelae of the Northridge Earthquake." *Journal of Behavioral Medicine*, 21 (5): 433–50.

Chapter 3

USING PLAY TO SUPPORT CHILDREN TRAUMATIZED BY NATURAL DISASTERS

Chuetsu Earthquake Series in Japan

Akiko J. Ohnogi

Play is itself a therapy.

—D. W. Winnicott

INTRODUCTION

Despite centuries of trauma, the effects of trauma on children have only recently been recognized (Saylor and DeRoma 2002). Research on the effects, as well as the emotional and psychological support for children, is still in its infancy. However both areas are slowly being developed (La Greca et al. 2002).

The purpose of this chapter is to provide basic information on children's responses to trauma, and briefly outline play-based interventions that have been helpful in providing emotional and psychological support to traumatized children. The age range of children covered in this chapter will be limited to preschool and school-aged children (Schaefer et al. 2008). As psychological work with traumatized children can be effectively and appropriately conducted with children regardless of their culture (Schaefer et al. 2005), specific work with the Niigata Prefectural Psychiatric Medical Center staff will be discussed in line with the summarized information. The hope of this author is for readers to increase their understanding of children's reactions to crisis and the importance of developmentally appropriate and timely psychological and emotional interventions. Japanese cultural rituals used to help children who have experienced natural disasters and specific rituals conducted by Niigata earthquake survivors will be integrated as part of meaning-making.

MISCONCEPTIONS OF ADULTS CONCERNING TREATMENT OF TRAUMATIZED CHILDREN

Before we start analyzing the misconceptions adults have concerning child trauma treatment, we need an answer to the following question: What is trauma?

According to Eth and Pynoos (1985), psychic or psychological trauma is the effect on a person who has experienced an extremely stressful situation (one that is outside the range of normal human experience). Individuals who are exposed to a traumatic event may become temporarily helpless. Often, experiences that are out of an individual's control and/or are unpredictable, such as natural or man-made disasters, life threatening diseases, or injury, war, abuse, and murder or suicide of a loved one, are sources of psychological trauma for adults as well as for children.

> Although typically, research on children and trauma is focused on their resiliency as compared to adults, there is another side to trauma in children. The assumption that all children are resilient is a common but inaccurate notion. In reality, many children can benefit greatly from emotional and psychological support following a disaster (Shelby 1997).

Many children who are exposed to a crisis exhibit reactions that impair their daily functioning. In addition, the crisis may also impair or delay the child's development and growth (Silverman and La Greca 2002). Often, the parents or caregivers have been victims of the same trauma that the child has experienced. As a result, they are simultaneously trying to process their own trauma and therefore are not always able to provide assistance to their child/children. Thus, it is not surprising that many children's emotional and psychological needs are neglected, leading to further complications that could be prevented with appropriate and timely intervention (La Greca and Prinstein 2002).

While it is essential for children to be provided with the opportunity to talk about and play out their trauma experiences, many adults mistakenly attempt to protect their child from having to remember and deal with traumatic events. Often, adults believe that children will become more distressed or traumatized if they are reminded of the trauma, and if left alone will forget the incident. However, research has demonstrated that despite these well-meant attempts, children who are left alone and unsupported will develop inappropriate defenses that could ultimately affect the child's wellbeing and personality (Schaefer 1994).

In order to reduce the risk of long-term negative effects of trauma, it is crucial for adults to help children confront, integrate, and master their trauma reactions. Also, timely intervention is necessary so that children do not continue exhibiting symptoms for years (Galante and Foa 1986). Although most adults think of school-aged children when they think of children, infants and younger children are also significantly affected by trauma. Emotional reactions to traumatic experiences are greatly influenced by the child's age at the time of the trauma (Gurwitch et al. 2005), thus necessitating developmentally appropriate trauma interventions.

When adults attempt to manage their emotional reactions to a traumatic event, they often speak in detail of the stressful experience. Abreaction is a human being's instinctual motivation to recreate the experience through the articulation of it. Like adults, children have the same need to work through their trauma reactions by retelling their story of survival in detail (Schaefer 1994). However children, unlike adults, use play to communicate and express themselves (Landreth 2002). Therefore, when working through a traumatic experience, children need to use play and not words to master their experience (Axline 1960; Landreth 2002; Moustakas 1959; Schaefer 1993; Winnicott 1971).

For those children affected by the 2004 Chuetsu earthquake series, it was important to give them information about what they experienced in an appropriate way, as not all the children knew what an earthquake was. For many, this could have been accomplished through play. This way, children can express their feelings about the traumatic experience, diffuse fear of the trauma, and recognize and integrate their emotions (Gil 1991).

The play interventions that were taught to support personnel in Niigata were selected based on research regarding effective ways to treat children and adolescents for trauma. The goals of these activities were to help decrease trauma reactions, increase appropriate coping skills, correct misattributions, encourage social support, and create a sense of hope for the future.

NATURAL DISASTER AND PSYCHOLOGICAL TRAUMA IN CHILDREN

Natural disasters occur all over the world and no one is immune to them. All persons, regardless of where they live or their socioeconomic status, are affected by natural disasters. The psychological effect that natural disasters have on individuals can be quite severe, as most natural disasters are unpredictable, and result in mass destruction and fatalities (Young, Ford and Watson 2005). Many children who are victims of natural disasters experience significant emotional distress for an extended period of time posttrauma (Vogel and Vernberg 1993).

How trauma symptoms are exhibited and affect a child depends on the level of exposure to a trauma, disruption of daily activities, access to support, and coping skills (Vogel and Vernberg 1993). If the trauma experience is severe, the possibility of long-term post-traumatic stress responses is great. A child's subjective experience of the trauma also plays a large role in determining the acuteness and duration of the post-traumatic stress reactions.

As children often cannot recognize danger until after it has occurred, they primarily rely on adults to protect them from frightening events, and do not fully comprehend their physical and emotional reactions to trauma. Children will become especially upset if adults that they rely on are distressed (NCTS 2005a). Many parents view their children after a trauma as having grown up too fast, while the children themselves feel that they missed out on being a kid (NCTS 2005a).

The greater the change in lifestyle as a result of a trauma, the longer and more difficult recovery will be. Therefore, recovery will require more intervention for a child who is struggling with both post-traumatic stress reactions and grief (FEMA 2005). Other factors that influence recovery include how often a child faces trauma and loss reminders as well as the child's temperament, fears, strengths and coping skills.

A child's total number of psychological and/or behavioral difficulties (e.g., anxiety, behavior problems, and inattention) appears to increase following a disaster. Traumatic experiences remain on the minds of children, adolescents, and adults for a long time following the trauma. Children's school performance can also be seriously affected as a result of intrusive thoughts and reactions to reminders, as well as fears that inhibit them from venturing far from their parents, and so on. Various strong negative emotions and physical reactions, in addition to viewing the world differently, may decrease with time. However, there will be objects, people, places, and events that may trigger these emotional, physical, and cognitive reactions. Similarly, although most children's symptoms disappear after a while, some continue to experience significant trauma-related symptoms for an extended period of time, up to several years after the trauma (Vernberg 2002).

Typical symptoms exhibited by children who experienced a trauma include various posttrauma reactions such as constant images and thoughts about the disaster; fear, and belief that another traumatic event will occur; feelings of losing control over their own safety and life in general; concern that someone will be injured or killed; hyperalertness and oversensitivity; avoidance of situations and places that remind them of the trauma; regression to an earlier developmental level; dread that they will be separated from family members; apprehension of leaving their parent(s); anxiety or panic, especially when separated from caregivers; distress that they will be abandoned or neglected; intense emotions such as denial, anger, sadness, irritability, and fear; conduct problems; physical ailments, such as headaches and stomachaches which are often difficult to distinguish from medical conditions; wanting to talk about the disaster repeatedly; isolating self from others; and sleep difficulties including nightmares and/or enuresis (Eth and Pynoos 1985; FEMA 2005; Frederick 1985; Galante and Foa 1986; Gurwitch et al. 2005; Schaefer 1994). Traumatized children do not only feel more vulnerable and helpless, but they also view their futures as unpredictable and feel powerless to prevent future disasters. Although the list above includes some examples of typical symptoms exhibited by children, responses differ depending on the developmental level of the child, as well as other factors (Frederick 1985; Ohnogi 2006).

Perry (2001) found that traumatized children who have experienced fear, threat, unpredictability, frustration, helplessness, hunger, and pain have altered cardiovascular regulation, affective lability, behavioral impulsivity, increased anxiety and startle response, and sleep abnormalities. The brains of these children are at risk for developing into unregulated brain systems that would respond poorly to future psychosocial stressors.

EARTHQUAKES

Earthquakes are caused by underground boulders that suddenly shift, resulting in massive and often destructive movement of the ground. The initial impact of earthquakes last only a few minutes, but the aftershocks can last from hours to even months. However, aftershocks generally occur within two hours of the quake. Although milder than the original earthquake, aftershocks can be quite damaging both physically to the landscape and emotionally to survivors. In terms of psychological effects, as earthquakes are unpredictable, it is difficult to warn people ahead of time, and therefore the suddenness, unpreparedness, and loss of control increases negative emotions and stressors (La Greca and Prinstein 2002).

The unpredictability of earthquakes makes evacuation to safe locations very difficult. Therefore, compared to other natural disasters, earthquakes can result in more casualties and injuries, creating more emotional and psychological trauma to victims (La Greca and Prinstein 2002). Separation from family members and spending hours not knowing their whereabouts, as well as seeing severely injured people and dead bodies, is very traumatic.

Of the children who experienced the earthquake, those who were closer to the earthquake's epicenter and those whose homes were located near the epicenter experienced more severe and prolonged post-traumatic stress disorder (PTSD) symptoms (La Greca and Prinstein 2002). Children felt more threatened and had a greater sense of loss when they were closer to the disaster and/or experienced a greater amount of personal loss.

Trauma reminders evoke various posttrauma stress reactions in victims. Perceived motion of the ground (e.g., a truck rumbling), movement of objects (e.g., the wind causing a lamp to sway), and loud noises are reminders of the earthquake and can trigger trauma reactions. Whether victims were inside or outside when the earthquake occurred affects the individual's perception of how safe certain places are. Similarly, distress associated with prior traumatic experiences or losses can be renewed by the experience of an earthquake.

PLAY, CHILDREN, AND TRAUMA INTERVENTIONS

For all children, regardless of their culture, play is something that is natural (Axline 1960). Play facilitates physical, cognitive, verbal, and social development. In addition, it helps release extra energy, rejuvenates expended energy, provides opportunities to practice various skills, relieves stress, promotes creativity, and provides an optimal level of arousal. For children, play is something that they need to do, and they can become so engrossed in it that they lose awareness of time and their surroundings. Various thoughts and emotions, both positive and negative, can be safely expressed through play. Play is a necessary developmental activity that all children must engage in, in order to develop psychologically, physically, socially, culturally, and cognitively (Landreth 2002). Play also enhances creativity, problem solving skills, and abstract thinking.

Play can help facilitate normal child development as well as alleviate abnormal behavior (Gil 1991). Children use play as a natural and self-therapeutic process to deal with trauma (Erikson 1963). Play helps to enhance adjustment, decrease misbehavior, decrease symptoms of trauma, and increase social support experience. A child's unconscious preoccupations and anxiety are often expressed through play and drawings. Both are safe ways for children to positively and effectively work on multiple issues (Ohnogi 2007). In addition, play helps children satisfy their egos by working through a past event, assimilating and gaining control over this event by gradually and repeatedly digesting and gaining mastery over the trauma (Piaget 1962). In order to understand, assimilate, and master a traumatic experience, children reenact and recreate their experience through play (Erikson 1963).

Although play is a self-healing process for children, depending on how the play progresses, it can lead either to mastery of the trauma or to a retraumatizing experience (Schaefer 1994). Children can heal through self-initiated play reenactments if they have mild stress reactions, as play helps them gain control and assimilate the trauma. However, if the child is reacting moderately or severely to the trauma, play can create further symptoms if appropriate support is not provided. These children may frantically exhibit the same play themes over and over again, retraumatizing themselves through the repetitive and compulsive play. Resolutions will not be found, anxiety will increase, and feelings of helplessness and fear will be reactivated. Unless a professional intervenes, this cycle of retraumatizing play will not end (Terr 1981).

Once children are able to reenact a traumatic experience in play, they are more open to dealing with their various emotions, cognitions, and behaviors about the real trauma experience. Terr (1991) states that "untreated, all but the mildest of childhood traumas last for years." Interpretation of the play and experienced trauma helps children more readily express their reactions to the trauma and accept reality and their reactions (Shelby 2000).

Many play therapists who work with traumatized children combine several therapeutic strategies (Schaefer 1994). Abreaction, cognitive reappraisal, a supportive relationship, and crisis intervention are some of the main principles applied in play therapy treatment. Usually, interventions immediately following a natural disaster are short-term, apply to all victims of the trauma, and rely heavily on including the community in treatment. However, interventions that are made several months post disaster are focused more on those individuals who are having the most difficulty.

In order to avoid overwhelming a child, traumatic play must be organized so that the child plays out parts of the trauma a little at a time (Schaefer 1994). A child must be given the opportunity to take time to work through the traumatic experience through play repetition. This slow and gradual process ensures that the tragic memory is integrated into the self, making defense mechanisms less necessary. As a result, symptoms decrease (Schaefer 1994).

PLAY INTERVENTION FOR NIIGATA EARTHQUAKE CHILD VICTIMS

Japan is an island in Asia, with a population of approximately 128 million people (over 10% of the population lives in the capital, Tokyo). The entire island is located on top of four fault lines: the Eurasia plate, the Pacific Ocean plate, the Sea of Philippines plate, and the North American plate. Due to the geological placement, there are M1–2 tremors daily in Japan. Therefore, small earthquakes are an integral part of life.

The Chuetsu earthquake series that hit the North Eastern part of Japan on October 23, 2004, was a M6.8. Aftershocks came on October 23, 2004,

October 24, 2004, and October 25, 2004, totaling over 1,000 tremors. Financial losses amounted to 300,000,000 yen (US$2,500,000), and there were 67 deaths (4 children) as well as 4,805 injuries. In addition, 100,000 buildings were damaged and 103,000 people were forced to relocate or were displaced. To further complicate matters, a snowstorm hit the area soon after the quake. Many people either died or became seriously ill as a result of living in their cars, because they were afraid to live inside buildings or temporary housing (Kimura et al. 2006). Despite the severity of the earthquake, relatively few people and buildings were affected, as the earthquake hit a part of Japan that was not densely populated.

The author of this chapter had the honor, after the earthquake, of being invited to the Niigata Prefectural Mental Health and Medical Center, the largest and most well-equipped hospital in the Chuetsu area that provides services to children and adolescents, to help train the staff in psychological interventions. The importance and significance of play for children, along with the importance of utilizing various new activities and games to continue helping children deal with their trauma responses, were taught to all staff, including psychiatrists, psychotherapists, nurses, teachers, and social workers. The activities were a combination of common interventions used in the treatment of children plus those cognitive behavioral techniques designed by Janine Shelby (2004) and the UCLA trauma team. Each activity had several goals, such as to: (a) normalize reactions; (b) assess current coping mechanisms and reinforce healthy ones; (c) assess and modify misattributions and cognitive distortions; (d) decrease hyperarousal and panic symptoms; (e) increase self-soothing; (f) identify and change intrusive re-experiencing; (g) decrease isolation and withdrawal and reinforce the ability to seek helpful social support; (h) decrease regressive behaviors by focusing on strengths and resources; (i) identify loss reminders and trauma triggers; and (j) leave the child with a sense of hope (Shelby et al. 2004). The support personnel were trained in the play techniques to enable long-term emotional support of the children who were affected by the earthquake.

A few of the activities that were taught to support personnel included:

- Conducting puppet shows to address the children's fears and correct misattributions
- Writing and reading a story about the earthquake, typical responses, and helpful coping strategies, while acting out the story
- Practicing yoga and breathing exercises to decrease anxiety
- Making coping bracelets/necklaces as a visual reminder of their support systems and self-strengths, as well as serving as a lucky charm
- Building a new village together to instill hope and a sense of community as well as a sense of control over their environment

- Creating magazine collages to assess current coping mechanisms and reinforce healthy ones
- Changing the words to well known songs in order to develop new songs about hope and safety
- Blowing bubbles to symbolize the blowing away of bad feelings
- Having a transitional object like a worry stone to touch and rub when feeling anxious or scared
- Blowing up different sized balloons symbolizing different amounts of pent up emotion and being able to control the release of emotion to obtain relief
- Assigning different colors to different feelings in order to identify and distinguish a range of emotional responses to trauma
- Identifying within a group same versus different feelings and thoughts on various topics, to create a feeling of community as well as a sense of individuality
- Tinman versus ragdoll activity to experience the physical difference between feeling tense and relaxed and learning how to control muscle tension
- Engaging in group activities to decrease isolation and reinforce the importance of seeking social support

CULTURAL, RELIGIOUS, AND OTHER RITUALS USED FOR COPING, RESILIENCE AND MEANING-MAKING

When individuals experience a natural disaster such as an earthquake, various rituals are used for coping, resilience, and meaning-making. Many of these rituals in Japan are based on Shinto and Buddhist beliefs of protecting the community, providing a sense of security and saving souls, although they are blended with nonreligious traditional beliefs. Unlike in many other cultures, Shinto and Buddhist based rituals are conducted more because they are considered part of the Japanese culture than because an individual believes in the Shinto or Buddhist faith. Therefore, many Japanese people, even if they are of a different religion or do not subscribe to any religious beliefs, engage in many of the following rituals because they have been passed down as the Japanese means of obtaining emotional and psychological relief. Many people who engage in these rituals are not even aware that these rituals originated from Shintoism and/ or Buddhism.

All of the following Japanese cultural rituals for coping, resilience, and meaning-making are used with children, regardless of age, gender, or socioeconomic status, and are exhibited in their play after experiencing a trauma. Therefore, having various toys and objects, which can either literally or symbolically represent the trauma experiences, to use in play is necessary both in nonprofessional and professional intervention.

The following are examples of some of the more popular rituals for coping, resilience, and meaning-making in Japan. They are organized into several categories; (a) rituals that are conducted on an individual basis when the need arises; (b) rituals that are conducted on an individual basis depending on when the trauma occurred or during which season; (c) rituals that are conducted as a community when the need arises; (d) rituals that are conducted as a community depending on when a trauma occurred or during which season; (e) rituals that are conducted individually either when the need arises or dependent on when a trauma occurred or during which season; (f) rituals that can be conducted either individually or as a community when a trauma occurred or during which season.

Rituals That Are Conducted on an Individual Basis When the Need Arises:

- Incense (*okou*): Special incense is used to create a sacred space and is lit at various locations (e.g., family altars or grave) for both the deceased and survivors to enjoy. Some people take comfort in believing that Buddha appears in the smoke from the incense. Different kinds of incense are used during different prayers, for different purposes, and in different locations
- Paper charm (*ofuda*): Placing a blessed paper charm at various places (e.g., front door of house) in the home to protect the house from future negative events
- Flowers (*hana wo ikeru*): Placing flowers at the site where a trauma occurred, or on the desk of a child who passed away
- Ancestors (*gozennzosama*): Speak to ancestor spirits and ask them to protect those who survived a trauma
- Charms (*omamori*): Carry around a blessed charm for a specific purpose, for example, being able to return home after being evacuated due to an earthquake
- Purification ceremony (*oharai*): Having a Shinto or Buddhist priest recite prayers to bless/protect a person, object or place
- Folk tales (*minkansetsuwa*): Telling traditional stories based on stories of Gods (*shinwa*)
- Recite sutras (*okyou*): Having a Buddhist priest sing prayers for specific purposes based on various Buddhist scriptures for comfort and purification of evil and trauma

- Stake (*kui wo tateru*): Placing a blessed stake in the ground where a trauma has occurred in order to bless the place and protect it from future traumas

Rituals That Are Conducted on an Individual Basis Depending on When a Trauma Occurred or During Which Season:

- Doll's festival (*hinamatsuri*): An annual ceremony conducted on March 3rd, when parents pray that a specific doll take the place of their female child and carry away all her traumas. Elaborate doll arrangements (*hina-dan*) along with offerings of sake and special candy (*hina arare*) are displayed in the main room of every household that has a female child between mid February until March 3rd. Care must be taken to remove the doll on the morning of March 4th; otherwise the doll will not take the place of the child and trauma will befall the child

- Boy's festival (*tango no sekku*): An annual ceremony conducted every May 5th, when parents pray that their male child will grow up safely without any traumatic experiences. Specific warrior figures (*kabuto, yoroi, katana, bushi ningyou, kintarou*) and large fish, such as streamers (*koi nobori*) fitted to poles, are set up and special rice cakes are eaten (*kashiwamoch, chimaki*)

- 753 Festival (*shichi go san*): A ceremony conducted for three-year-old girls and boys, five-year-old boys, and seven-year-old girls to grow up safely. The numbers 3, 5 and 7 are chosen because they are considered lucky numbers. The family, including the child, dresses in their best kimonos and visits a shrine on November 15th to have a Shinto priest bless the child. Special candy (*chitose ame*) made and sold only on this occasion is placed in a special bag and given to the blessed child. Professional pictures are often taken so that the child can appreciate the purification ceremony when he/she is older. Also, this is a time for children to remember his/her deceased parents or for parents to remember a deceased child

- Bon Festival (*obon*): An annual Buddhist festival when ancestors and deceased relatives come to visit the homes of their descendents in mid-July in Tokyo and mid-August throughout the rest of Japan. Family graves are visited and a fire is lit (*mukaebi*) to welcome the ancestors. The family places their deceased relatives' favorite foods and drinks on the family altar three times a day, along with flowers, candles and incense. The home that the ancestors and deceased relatives visit during this festival is usually that of the first born son. Relatives gather at the house where the spirits are visiting to remember the dead who have come back to visit

- Death Anniversary (*ishuuki*): Recognizing the one year death/trauma anniversary by gathering together as a family, group, or community, and remembering the trauma and those who passed away. Additional ceremonies are conducted on the 3rd year (*sanschiiki*), 7th year (*nanashuuki*), 13th year (*jyuusanshuuki*), 17th year (jyuunanashuuki), 23rd year (*nijyuusann-shuuki*), 27th year (*nijyuunnanashuuki*), 33rd year (*sanjyuusanshuuki*), and 50th year (*gojyuushuuki*)

Rituals That Are Conducted as a Community When the Need Arises:

- Candle lighting (*rousoku wo tomosu*): Candles are lit to provide a sense of relief to both the survivors and deceased spirits as well as recognize the victims' passing. This occurs at the place where the trauma occurred or at the school victims attended

- Children's songs (*warabeuta*): Songs accompanied by dance and games designed to both remind children of the trauma and its effects as well as those who passed away (e.g. *kagome*)

- 1,000 Cranes (*sennbazuru*): The community folds 1,000 paper cranes out of origami paper in hopes for happiness, longevity, and recovery from trauma

- Build shrines (*jinjya wo tateru*): Building a new shrine to bless the trauma-affected land and protect it from future disasters

Rituals That Are Conducted as a Community Depending on When a Trauma Occurred or During a Particular Season:

- Mountain fires (*gozan no okuribi*): Large fires on five mountains in Kyoto are lit (*okuribi*) on August 16th in the symbols of: large (*dai*), small (*myou*), dharma (*hou*), shrine gate (*torii*) and boat (*fune*)" to send beloved deceased spirits back after having welcomed them home for a time.

- Water lanterns (*mizu tourou*): Water lanterns are placed in the river near the location of a trauma to signify the cleansing or washing away of evil and trauma. Those sending off the water lanterns write prayers and poems of hope on all four sides of the paper lantern

- Doll floating (*nagashi bina*): Special dolls which are supposed to take away all the bad luck from a child are floated down rivers

- Lights (*tentou*): Modern electrical lights are lit in various commercial buildings in cities near trauma sites throughout Japan in lieu of water candles

- Moment of silence (*mokuto*): Observing a moment of silence as a community on the anniversary of a trauma

- Annual ceremonies (*maitoshi no gishiki*): Ceremonies that include activities of mourning, remembering the trauma, and celebrating recovery, survival, and the community's bond

- Festivals (*omatsuri*): Festivals with choreographed dances, drums and music, as well as various food and activity stations. To celebrate those who have survived disasters and encourage them to continue living positively, while remembering and appreciating those who were victims of the disasters

Rituals That Are Conducted Individually Either When the Need Arises or Depending When a Trauma Occurred or During a Particular Season:

- Visit grave (*hakamairi*): Visiting the family grave to light incense and candles, place flowers, food and drinks for the ancestors and thank them for protecting the surviving family members. Often, Buddhist priests bless and say prayers for the surviving family members
- Family altar (*butsudan* for Buddhists or *kamidana* for Shintoists): Praying at one's family altar and performing candle lighting and other such rituals
- Shrine and temple (*jinjya* and *otera*): Visiting a Shinto shrine or Buddhist temple to thank the Gods for protecting the survivors and ask the Gods for various favors

Rituals That Can Be Conducted Either Individually or with the Community, Either When the Need Arises or When the Trauma Occurred or During a Particular Season:

- Priest prayer (*oharai*): Having a Shinto or Buddhist priest bless a person, place or object. Families usually ask for continued protection, no more trauma, spiritual support in reconstruction and recovery of the trauma site, and the opportunity to return to their home town. It is thought to be helpful for people, especially children and adolescents, to focus and think seriously about something important, ridding themselves of evil or negative thoughts and/or confusion, and/or helping them feel hopeful and positive when something negative befalls them
- Dance and song (*odori to uta*): Dancing and singing usually conducted by Shinto priests (*kannushi*), or assistant priestesses (*miko*) in shrines, or Buddhist priests (*obousan*) or nuns (*ama*) in temples while surviving victims of a trauma look on. Songs and dances are specifically tailored to the needs of the individual or community

OTHER CULTURAL RITUALS THAT HAVE BEEN CONDUCTED SPECIFICALLY FOR THE CHUETSU EARTHQUAKE

The following activities are/were conducted on the date and time of the earthquake or the anniversary date and time of the death of a person who perished in the earthquake (Mainichi Shinbum Chihouban 2008; Niigata Nippo 2007; personal communication with Chikae Takahashi at Niigata Prefectural Mental Health and Medical Center, 2004, 2005, 2006, 2007, 2008):

- Annual memorial services in various parts of Japan at community squares, school gyms and civic halls, attended by community members and relatives of those who passed away due to the earthquake
- Observance of a moment of silence by all residents in the Chuetsu area
- Mayors and major governmental figures throughout Japan deliver speeches to raise hope and awareness
- Smoke/fire signal/beacon relay at various mountain castle ruins and mountain tops throughout the Chuetsu area
- Display photographs of the effects of the earthquake and temporary living spaces provided for victims are placed in various locations throughout Chuetsu
- Make public diaries of surviving victims and village memorial records
- Ceremony for community members who have chosen to return to their villages
- Elementary and junior high students sing "thank you" in appreciation for Japan-wide support
- Ceremony to plant cherry blossom trees at earthquake sites
- Place flowers at sites of death due to the earthquake

IMPLICATIONS

Natural disasters are frightening and difficult for children to comprehend and deal with. This is especially true as natural disasters are unpredictable and unexpected, and the adults that children often rely on become temporarily unable to provide them with reassurance, guidance, and support. Daily routines, homes, and neighborhoods are often forever changed, which can cause children to become fearful, confused, or anxious. Those children who are cared for by adults who are overly alarmed by the trauma will feel that there are real and present dangers. Similarly, those children who are cared for by adults overwhelmed with a sense of loss will feel their own losses more intensely. While research has demonstrated that almost all children who have experienced a trauma have emotional issues and exhibit posttrauma reactions, such as anxiety, regression, dependency, depression, academic difficulties, and interpersonal conflicts, it is important that these children be allowed the opportunity to work through their trauma. Often, adults ignore or minimize the psychological and emotional effects of the disaster experience on children, and mistakenly believe that they should be shielded from painful memories.

Despite these well-meant but potentially dangerous reactions of adults, children will naturally play out their posttrauma reactions in an effort to work through their various emotions. Repetitive engagement and replaying of the stressful and traumatic events is very natural, and if a child has been mildly traumatized, this posttrauma play can actually decrease symptoms. However, for moderate to severe cases of trauma, and for those without appropriate family support, professional intervention is necessary for the child to work through their psychological and emotional pain.

In order to heal after a disaster and begin to cope with a new reality, children need to play. As children are still in the midst of developing their verbal skills, they require toys, drawings, games, puppets, music, and books to facilitate their expression of emotions. Through play-based interventions, children are able to make sense of their world, explore their fears, problems, and frustrations, and work through them. Unfortunately, psychological interventions with children are a relatively new practice. The unpredictability of natural disasters coupled with difficulties associated with research has limited empirical research. Only though integration and combination of various empirically validated therapeutic factors can treatment of traumatized children become powerful enough for these interventions to be successful. The hope of this author is for continued refinement of various play-based interventions to assist these traumatized children worldwide.

REFERENCES

American Academy of Child and Adolescent Psychiatry (AACAP). 2004. *Helping Children after a Disaster.* Available at: http://www.aacap.org/cs/root/facts_for_families/helping_children_after_a_disaster.

Axline, V. M. 1960. *Play Therapy.* New York: Ballantine Books.

Erikson, E. H. 1963. *Childhood and Society.* 2nd ed. New York: W. W. Norton & Co.

Eth, S., and Pynoos, R. S. 1985. "Interaction of Trauma and Grief in Childhood." In *Post-traumatic Stress Disorder in Children*, ed. Eth, S., and Pynoos, R. S. 171–86. Washington, DC: American Psychiatric Press.

Federal Emergency Management Agency (FEMA). 2005. *Helping Children Cope with Disaster.* Available at: http://www.fema.gov/rebuild/recover/cope_child.shtm.

Frederick, C. J. 1985. "Children Traumatized by Catastrophic Situation." In *Post-traumatic Stress Disorder in Children*, eds. Eth, S., & Pynoos, R. S. 73–99. Washington, DC: American Psychiatric Press.

Galante, R., and Foa, D. 1986. "An Epidemiological Study of Psychic Trauma and Treatment Effectiveness for Children after a Natural Disaster." *Journal of Child and Adolescent Psychiatry* 25: 3357–3363.

Gil, E. 1991. *The Healing Power of Play: Working with Abused Children.* New York: The Guilford Press.

Gurwitch, R.H., Silovsky, J.F., Schultz, S., Kees, M., and Burlingame, S. 2005. *Reactions and Guidelines for Children Following Trauma/Disaster.* Available at: http://www.apa.org/practice/ptguidelines.html.

Kimura, R., Hayashi, H., Tatsuki, S., and Tamura, K. 2006. *Behavioral and Psychological Reconstruction Process of Victims in the 2004 mid-Niigata Prefecture Earthquake.* Proceedings of the 8th U.S. National Conference on Earthquake Engineering. Available at: http://www.seis.nagoya-u.ac.jp/reo/06NCEE_Reo.pdf.

La Greca, A.M., and Prinstein, M.J. 2002. "Hurricanes and Earthquakes." In *Helping Children Cope with Disasters and Terrorism*, eds. La Greca, A.M. et al. Washington, DC: American Psychiatric Association.

La Greca, A.M., Silverman, W.K., Vernberg, E.M., and Roberts, M.C. 2002. "Children and Disasters: Future Directions for Research and Public Policy." In *Helping Children Cope with Disasters and Terrorism,* eds. La Greca, A.M. et al. Washington, DC: American Psychiatric Association.

Landreth, G.L. 2002. *Play Therapy: The Art of the Relationship.* 2nd ed. New York: Brunner-Routledge.

Mainichi Shinbun Chihouban. 2008. *Niigata Chuuetsu Jishin.* Available at: http://mainichi.jp/area/niigata/jishin/index.html.

Moustakas, C.E. 1959. *Psychotherapy with Children: The Living Relationship.* New York: Harper & Row.

National Child Traumatic Stress Network (NCTS). 2005(a). *Age-Related Reactions to a Traumatic Event.* Available at: http://www.nctsnet.org/nccts/nav.do?pid=ctr_aud_prnt_what.

National Child Traumatic Stress Network (NCTS). 2005(b). *Child Trauma Intervention Model: Three Tiers of Mental Health Intervention.* Available at: http://www.nctsnet.org/nctsn_assets/ppt/powerpoints/intervention_model.ppt.

Niigata Nippo 2007. *Chuuetsu Jishin 3 Nen, Kakuchi de Tsuitou Shiki.* Available at: http://www.niigata-nippo.com/tyuetsujishin/.

Ohnogi, A. 2006. "Play Based Psychological Interventions with Traumatized Children: Work with Tsunami Orphaned Sri Lankan Children." *International Journal of Counseling and Psychotherapy* 4: 17–36.

Ohnogi, A. 2007. "Creating Safe Space for Children in Play Therapy." *International Journal of Counseling and Psychotherapy* 5: 55–71.

Perry, B.D. 2001. *Violence and Childhood: How Persisting Fear Can Alter the Developing Child's Brain.* Available at: http://www.childtrauma.org/cta materials/Vio_child.asp.

Perry, B.D., Pollard, R.A., Blakley, T.L., Baker, W.L., and Vigilante, D. 1995. *Childhood Trauma, the Neurobiology of Adaptation and Use-Dependent Development of the Brain: How States Become Traits.* Available at: http://www.trauma-pages.com/a/perry96.php.

Piaget, J. 1962. *Play, Dreams, and Imitation in Childhood.* New York: Norton, W.W.

Saylor, C., and DeRoma, V. 2002. "Assessment of Children and Adolescents Exposed to Disaster." In *Helping Children Cope with Disasters and Terrorism,* ed. La Greca, A. M., Silverman, W. K., Vernberg, E. M., & Roberts, M. C. 35–54. Washington, DC: American Psychological Association.

Schaefer, C. E. 1993. "What Is Play and Why Is It Therapeutic?" In *The Therapeutic Powers of Play,* ed. Schaefer, C. E. 1–16. Northvale, NJ: Jason Aronson.

Schaefer, C. E. 1994. "Play Therapy for Psychic Trauma in Children." In *Handbook of Play Therapy. Vol. 2: Advances and Innovations.* ed. O'Connor, K. J., and Schaefer, C. E. 308–19. New York: John Wiley & Sons.

Schaefer, C. E., Kelly-Zion, S., McCormick, J., and Ohnogi, A., eds. 2008. *Play Therapy for Very Young Children.* New York: Jason Aronson.

Schaefer C. E., McCormick, J., and Ohnogi, A., eds. 2005. *International Handbook of Play Therapy.* New York: Jason Aronson.

Schwarz, E. D., and Perry, B. D. *The Post-Traumatic Response in Children and Adolescents.* Available at: http://www.childtrauma.org/ctamaterials/ptsd ChildAdoles.asp.

Shelby, J. S. 1997. "Rubble, Disruption, and Tears: Helping Young Survivors of Natural Disaster." In *The Playing Cure: Individualized Play Therapy for Specific Childhood Problems,* ed. Kaduson, H. G., Cangelosi, D., and Schaefer, C. E. 143–70. Northvale, NJ: Jason Aronson.

Shelby, J. S. 2000. "Brief Therapy with Traumatized Children: A Developmental Perspective. In *Short-Term Play Therapy for Children,* ed. Kaduson, H. G., and Schaefer, C. E. 69–104. New York: The Guilford Press.

Shelby, J., Bond, D., Hall, and Hsu. 2004. "Enhancing Coping among Young Earthquake Survivors." Unpublished work, currently being refined.

Silverman, E., Vernberg, M., and Roberts, M. C., eds. "Helping Children Cope." In *Helping Children Cope with Disasters and Terrorism,* eds. La Greca, A. M., Silverman, W. K., Vernberg, E. M., & Roberts, M. C. 107–38. Washington, DC: American Psychological Association.

Silverman, W. K., and La Greca, A. M. 2002. "Children Experiencing Disasters: Definitions, Reactions, and Predictors of Outcomes." In *Helping Children Cope with Disasters and Terrorism,* eds. La Greca, A. M., Silverman, W. K., Vernberg, E. M., & Roberts, M. C. 11–34. Washington, DC: American Psychological Association.

Terr, L. C. 1981. "Forbidden Games: Post-Traumatic Child's Play." *Journal of the American Academy of Child Psychiatry* 20: 741–59.

Terr, L. C. 1983. "Play Therapy and Psychic Trauma: A Preliminary Report." In *Handbook of Play Therapy,* eds. Schaefer, C. E., and O'Connor, K. J. 308–19. New York: John Wiley and Sons.

Terr, L. C. 1991. "Childhood Traumas: An Outline and Overview." *American Journal of Psychiatry* 148: 10–20.

Vernberg, E. M. 2002. "Intervention Approaches Following Disasters." In *Helping Children Cope with Disasters and Terrorism,* eds. La Greca, A. M., Silverman, W. K., Vernberg, E. M., & Roberts, M. C. 55–72. Washington, DC: American Psychological Association.

Vernberg, M., and Roberts, M. C., eds. 2002. "Helping Children Cope." In *Helping Children Cope with Disasters and Terrorism,* eds. La Greca, A. M., Silverman, W. K., Vernberg, E. M., & Roberts, M. C. 405–24. Washington, DC: American Psychological Association.

Vogel, J., and Vernberg, E. M. 1993. "Children's Psychological Responses to Disaster." *Journal of Clinical Child Psychology* 22: 464–84.

Winnicott, D. W. 1971. *Playing and Reality.* London: Tavistock Publications.

Young, B. H., Ford, J. D., and Watson, P. J. 2005. *Helping Survivors in the Wake of Disaster.* Available at: http://mentalhealth.samhsa.gov/dtac/Federal Resource/Response/17-Helping_Survivors_in_Disaster.pdf.

Chapter 4

COPING WITH THE EARTHQUAKE IN PAKISTAN

A Religio-Culturally Informed Treatment

Ani Kalayjian,
Nicole Moore, and
Kate Richmond

Religions do not restrict; men do! How can we loosen up if our "traditional" clothes are so restrictive?

—Ani Kalayjian

On the morning of October 8, 2005, at 8:50 A.M., an earthquake registering 7.6 on the Richter scale hit northern Pakistan (Brennan and Waldman 2006). The powerful earthquake caused widespread destruction in northern Pakistan as well as damage in Afghanistan and northern India. In Pakistan, approximately 73,276 to 82,000 people, out of a population of 165,803, were killed by collapsing buildings, landslides and rockslides (World Health Organization 2005). In addition, approximately 106,000 people were injured. Since Saturday is a normal school day in Pakistan, many students were buried under collapsed school buildings. Moreover, because it was the month of Ramadan, most people were taking a nap after their predawn meal and thus did not have time to escape from their homes during the earthquake. An additional 30 million people lost their homes because most buildings in the ravaged areas were constructed of stone, brick, concrete blocks, or unreinforced masonry, which could not withstand the earthquake (World Health Organization 2005).

The experience of a natural disaster is the ultimate challenge to meaning-making (Brown 2008). The chaos and disorganization following a disaster challenges prior systems of beliefs. At the most basic level, a disaster demonstrates the ineffectiveness of faith, spirituality, prayer, spells, and charm. This is especially true for disasters that occur on or around religious holidays or holy days, as was the case in Pakistan (Brown 2008). Pakistan consists of more than 136 million Muslim people, and Islamic traditions not only shape legislative processes, but also health-related practices (Ash 1997; Farooqi 2006). Thus, it was crucial for mental health providers to incorporate religio-cultural rituals in the treatments of survivors following the earthquake.

In this chapter, we discuss how religio-cultural beliefs were incorporated into the treatment of mental health concerns following the earthquake in Pakistan. We begin by situating the experience of Pakistani survivors in the context of the larger literature on psychological effects following a natural disaster. Following this, we report on the unique psychosocial and spiritual influences of the earthquake on survivors living in Pakistan. We then describe important steps in developing a culturally sensitive outreach program and offer lessons learned from a Biopsychosocial and Spiritual Model that can be applied to other disasters that specifically educate and assist female survivors in Pakistan.

TRAUMA FOLLOWING A NATURAL DISASTER

Asia is the most disaster-prone area of the world, partly because of its geographic location in relation to earthquakes (Kokai et al. 2004). While natural disasters can cause a wide range of psychological distress, studies of psychological outcome in this region are limited, partly due to the fact that psychiatry and psychology are not well recognized in these countries (Kokai et al. 2004). Thus, following the earthquake in Pakistan, clinicians referred to more global studies of survivors' mental health to shed light on the psychological health of survivors in Pakistan. Such studies suggest that survivors suffer a wide range of psychological difficulties as a consequence of the extreme stress associated with natural disasters, including depressive symptoms (e.g., major depressive disorder and dysthymia), a range of anxiety disorders, and other adjustment disorders (Doherty 1999; Elhai, North, and Frueh 2005; Norris et al. 2005; Stevens and Slone 2005).

Within the literature, Acute Stress Disorder and Post-traumatic Stress Disorder have received particular attention in relation to natural disasters, and multiple studies have examined clinical and subclinical Post-traumatic Stress Disorders (PTSD) among survivors (Lantz and Buchalter 2005). Such studies report that survivors experience many of the symptoms necessary to meet criteria for PTSD, including intense fear, helplessness, hyperarousal, emotional numbing, reexperiencing the trauma through images and flashbacks, and avoidance of people, places, and things that recall the traumatic experience (Rosen et al. 2001). These symptoms may become chronic and interfere with the ability to function and interact in society productively (Lantz and Buchalter 2005).

Clearly, PTSD seems like an obvious diagnostic fit for symptoms usually seen among survivors following a natural disaster. Nevertheless, significant issues remain unresolved regarding the appropriateness of using the PTSD diagnosis with regard to postdisaster clinical assessments and interventions. The literature regarding whether survivors meet full criteria for PTSD is mixed, and there is debate as to whether post-traumatic psychopathology is transient or long-lasting. A review of the literature of various cross-sectional studies of selected subgroups following disasters showed the prevalence of post-traumatic stress disorder (PTSD) has been estimated to vary between 4 and 80 percent (Acierno et al. 1999; Carr et al. 1995; Karanci and Rustemeli 1995; Kato et al. 1996; Madakasira and O'Brien 1987; McFarlane and Potts 1999; Paradatos et al. 1990; Saigh 1992; Schlenger et al. 1999).

Some researchers speculate that these variations may reflect cross-cultural differences (Ruzek et al. 2007). For example, survivors of Mexican descent are likely to report attacks of nervousness, which include depression, pain, physical illness, weakness, and weight loss. These experiences do not entirely fit into the PTSD mold, but are nevertheless important in assessing the subjective experience of traumatic stress. Additionally, because postdisaster assessments tend to prioritize the DSM symptoms of PTSD as the gold standard for post-traumatic assessment, some argue that other presenting symptoms may be overlooked. Ehrenreich (2003) proposes that because most studies use the DSM criteria of PTSD as an outcome measure, clinicians and researchers may be ignoring other pressing symptoms not accounted for by PTSD—namely spiritual doubts, loss of inner sense of connection to others, or loss of a belief in a just world.

THE VALUE OF MEANING-MAKING IN PAKISTAN

The idea that experiences of trauma cause disruption in meaning-making has been well established in the literature (Carver 1999; Solomon 2003). In the 1950s, Viktor Frankl created logotherapy, which specifically focused on developing the "will of meaning," as an antidote to symptoms associated with trauma. The tenets of logotherapy (freedom of will, will to meaning, and meaning of life) stem from existentialism and aim to promote spiritual renewal and freedom in the face of psychological stressors. Meaning-making is an ongoing process of introspection, learning, and action in order to exercise the will to live again. Frankl (1962) proposed that meaning-making promotes empowerment and self-determination, while reducing anxiety and depression.

The Islamic concept of self and metaphysical theory is a core concept of humanistic and existential theories (Farooqi 2006). This concept suggests that although humans are created on *ahsan-ul-taqvim* (the best of designs), they also have the capacity to choose to do evil and, thus, descend into a lower state (Farooqi 2006). In order to achieve ideal mental health, a person must actively differentiate between good and evil and choose to live in accordance with the teachings of the Quran and Hadith. Conceptually, mental disturbances stem from doubt and conflict related to living in agreement with Allah's will.

Because Pakistan is a developing Muslim country, the majority of its citizens follow the traditions of the Holy Book of Quran and Hadith in their daily lives (Farooqi 2006; Raja 2004). Islamic spiritual healing focuses on identifying a purposeful way of "being in the world" and on upholding a strong devotion to Allah's will (Farooqi 2006). To achieve this, there are many prescribed rituals, traditions, and folk beliefs that are derived from the Quran and Hadith. Health related practices incorporate beliefs in spirits, premonitions, demons, jinns, fairies, and dreams. Treatments may include the use of certain items (*taweez*) for protection and luck, miracle healings, exorcisms, ancestor worship, and voodoo or charms, or the supernatural power of some traditional healers (Farooqi 2006). In Pakistan, mental health services are costly, and there is a considerable shortage of trained, licensed mental health providers (So-kum Tang 2007). Thus, many Pakistani people seek treatment from more affordable, traditional healers, including Pirs, Aamils, Hakims, Muslim Saints, magicians, palm readers, and/or folk healers (Farooqi 2006).

A traditional healing practice, the Islamic Faith/Spiritual Healing, is a popular approach in dealing with mental health concerns (Farooqi 2006). By first developing a strong and trusting relationship, Muslim Saints/Sufis aim to facilitate meaningfulness and devotion by promoting empathetic understanding, catharsis, and insight. Muslim Saints/Sufis use verses from the Quran and then bless an inanimate object (e.g., cloth, paper) by breathing on it. The person is asked to keep it, as well as follow detailed instructions about chores and prayers (Farooqi 2006).

CULTURAL CONSIDERATIONS

The Pakistan earthquake was not gender neutral (Brennan and Waldman 2006). Therefore, during the morning of the Ramadan holiday, while the men were out, most women were at home. Women were particularly affected by the disaster and accounted for more than 75 percent of displaced people (World Health Organization 2005). Pakistan operates under a patriarchal system, where roles and status are defined (Farooqi 2006). Since women are known as the primary caretakers, they were responsible for those affected by the disasters, including all the injured as well as the elderly, men, and children. These added tasks increased the women's fragile emotional and physical well-being, leaving them more fragile.

In disaster situations, gender based violence seems to increase (World Health Organization 2005). An increase in stress and lack of employment for men may lead to emotional, physical, and sexual abuse for women. Since women do not have as many outlets for coping, they resort to adopting more negative strategies. Women's vulnerability in the aftermath of the earthquake was elevated by their inequality in addition to limited access to resources and decision making power. Cultural norms and childcare responsibilities inhibited women from accessing relief centers. In one case, a woman whose leg was crushed and turning gangrenous was denied treatment by her husband.

In certain settings, women are forbidden to interact with male members, which limited women's ability to access treatment from male relief workers (Brennan and Waldman 2007). Women were also systematically marginalized because they were not registered as household heads and thus were not able to receive distributions of food. In the camps, there was limited freedom for women, and their social networks and support systems became narrower. There was an increase in unwanted pregnancies due to lack of activities, and the sex industry became part of the interaction between refugee and displaced populations. The loss of ability to take care of the family, financial aid stigma, lower levels of literacy, and low ownership of land placed women on the verge of destitution (World Health Organization 2005). Opportunities were not clearly available for women, specifically because education and health care was limited.

MENTAL HEALTH ASSESSMENT FOLLOWING THE EARTHQUAKE

The Mental Health Outreach Project (MHOP), a disaster relief organization of Association for Trauma Outreach and Prevention (ATOP), (not for profit, 501 (c)3) has organized teams of professional volunteers to go to areas following natural disasters. As a first response team, MHOP volunteers provide initial psychological assessments to surviving community members of natural disasters and therefore are in a unique position to make recommendations about interventions and treatment. MHOP provided such services during the aftermath of the 2005 earthquake in Pakistan.

When MHOP arrived in Pakistan, three months after the earthquake, the availability of psychological services in Pakistan was limited. There were reportedly 37 mental health/psychosocial support teams with 150 personnel, who met with 13,000 people in a country of 165,803 (Mental Health,

2006). Prior to providing mental health support, data were collected by MHOP in order to assess the mental health needs.

METHOD

Participants

One hundred and five survivors of the Pakistan Earthquake were recruited to participate in the initial assessment. Participants consisted of students, professors and workers of the university. Of the 105 respondents, 12 were men and 93 were women. Education levels varied, but more than half of the participants were in graduate school. The majority of the respondents were between 20 to 29 years old (82%). Demographic information can be found in Table 4.1.

Measures

The Post-Traumatic Stress Reaction Index Scale (RIS) developed by Frederick (1977) and revised by Kalayjian (2002) was used to gather assessment data. This instrument was chosen for its clarity and conciseness. The Reaction Index Scale is a two-part questionnaire that consists of 39 items. The first section includes items that are consistent with the DSM criteria for PTSD. The items are scored on a scale of 0 (indicating none of the time) to 4 (indicating much of the time) with sum scores inverted. The second section of the questionnaire consists largely of questions indicating level of exposure, purpose in life, and lessons learned.

Following the scoring of the RIS/R, the percentages of mild, moderate and severe PTSD were calculated. Scores from 12 to 24 were defined as mild PTSD, scores of 25 to 39 were termed moderate, scores of 41 to 59 were categorized as severe, and scores of 60 and higher were deemed as very severe. All assessment measures were translated using accepted procedures, and back translated, prior to arrival.

Procedure

MHOP arrived three months following the disaster. The first part of the assessment and study was conducted in Islamabad, Pakistan, 100 kilometers from the epicenter of the earthquake. Fatima Jinnah Women's University invited the MHOP team to an international conference on the Pakistan earthquake that involved social, human and gender issues. One of the goals was to work with the students, community, and leaders who were exposed to the earthquake.

Table 4.1
Demographic Characteristics of Total Participants (N = 109)

Characteristic	N	%
Education		
No education	1	.9
Grammar school	3	2.8
High school	14	12.8
Some college	24	22.0
College grad	10	9.2
Graduate school	54	49.5
Marital status		
Single	84	77.1
Married	22	20.2
Divorced	1	.9
Employment status		
No (unemployed)	70	64.2
Yes (employed)	20	18.3
Part time	2	1.8
Student status	12	11
Age		
Under 20	5	3.4
20–29	87	59.6
30–39	10	6.8
40–49	2	1.4

The second part of the assessment and study was done in Muzaffarabad, Pakistan, 19 km from the epicenter. MHOP was invited by a local community leader who worked with the local mosques, and community. Participants voluntarily came seeking help. As the MHOP presence became more visible, more women agreed to participate in the study. When available, local people who were proficient in English were identified to serve as translators. These individuals needed to possess strong communication skills and empathy. Translators included a male administrator from Karachi, and female students.

ASSESSMENT RESULTS

Levels of post-traumatic stress were determined based on the scores of the revised Reaction Index Scale (RIS/R). Twelve percent of respondents' scores indicated below mild levels of PTSD scores. Forty one percent of respondents' scores indicated a level of mild PTSD, 26 percent of respondents' scores indicated a moderate PTSD, 19.6 percent indicated a level of severe PTSD, and the scores of 1.1 percent of respondents indicated a level of very severe PTSD. As predicted, the level of PTSD in the participants was high (i.e., reaching the level considered diagnosable according to the cut-off point for the RIS/R scale). About half of the respondents (47%) scored at least moderate or higher levels of PTSD on the RIS/R scale, and 21 percent of respondents revealed severe or very severe PTSD.

The RIS/R scores showed significant sex differences with regard to PTSD scores, with men reporting higher levels of PTSD ($M = 39.72$; $SD = 19.65$) than women ($M = 25.41$; $SD = 12.50$; $t(86) = -3.28, p<.001$.

Age was not found to be statistically related to PTSD level; however, there was a trend suggesting that older individuals experienced less PTSD than younger individuals and that age might be a significant factor with a larger sample. Table 4.2 displays PTSD scores by specific demographic variables.

A one-way between-groups analysis of variance was conducted in order to examine the influence of education status and PTSD levels. There was a statistically significant difference among the five age groups [$F(4, 90) = 13.5, p<.001$]. The effect size, calculated using eta squared, was .38. Post hoc comparisons using the Tukey HSD test showed that the mean score for Grammar School ($M = 48.50, SD = 4.94$) was significantly different from Some College ($M = 24.95, SD = 12.21$), College Grad ($M = 19.66, SD = 15.30$), and Graduate School ($M = 22.77, SD = 11.13$). Additionally, the mean PTSD score for High School ($M = 45.58, SD = 9.42$) was significantly different from Some College ($M = 24.95, SD = 12.21$), College Grad ($M = 19.66, SD = 15.30$), and Graduate School ($M = 22.77, SD = 11.13$).

There was a relationship between respondents' indication of negative effects on their current relationships and PTSD levels ($r = .324$, p<.01). However, several other variables were not related to PTSD scores. These variables included speaking with a crisis worker ($r = -109$, ns) and having a close friend affected by the earthquake ($r = 198$, ns).

Table 4.3 shows the relationship between PTSD level and ability to find pleasure in tasks of daily living, the discovery of clear-cut goals in life, and the experience of ability to find meaning, purpose or a mission in life. The results show that level of PTSD was correlated with ability to face daily tasks, and with the ability to find meaning, purpose or a mission in

Table 4.2
Means and Standard Deviations for the Age and Education Level on PTSD Level

	M	SD	F	p
Age			1.57	.19
Under 20	40.33	10.21		
20–29	26.07	13.91		
30–39	27.86	13.79		
40–49	26.00	24.04		
50–59	52.00			
Total	26.99	14.18		
Education			10.70	<.001
No education	52.00			
Grammar school	48.50	4.95		
High school	45.58	9.42		
Some college	24.95	12.21		
College grad	19.67	15.31		
Graduate school	22.78	11.13		
Total	26.99	14.19		

life *after* the earthquake (i.e., scores on the RIS/R scale were lower for individuals who rated higher on their ability to face daily tasks and to find meaning in life since the earthquake). This demonstrates the importance of meaning-making in minimizing the development of PTSD.

Finally, three PTSD factors, avoidance/numbing, reexperiencing trauma, and arousal, were found to be related to participants' ratings of their ability to find meaning following the earthquake (see Table 4.4).

DISCUSSION OF ASSESSMENT

Results suggest that there was a range of PTSD symptoms. Because most participants from this assessment had higher levels of education, we suspected that education level would significantly differentiate reports of PTSD symptoms. Consistent with this hypothesis, education level was significantly related to reports of PTSD symptoms. These results appear consistent with the fact that those with higher education had a better cognitive understanding of the nature of the disaster and potential reactions. It is also likely that those with higher education had better resources and opportunities necessary to rebuild their livelihood, compared to those with

Table 4.3
Relationship between PTSD Level and Ability to Find Pleasure in Tasks

PTSD	M	SD	Before				After		
			PTSD	Facing	Discovered	Ability	Facing	Discovered	Ability
Before									
Facing my daily tasks is:	6.07	1.14	-.009		.761**	.593**	.096	.064	-.080
I have discovered:	5.96	1.34	.054			.756**	.045	.072	-.067
Ability to find meaning, purpose, or a mission in life	5.93	1.25	-.82				.035	.131	.018
After									
Facing my daily tasks is:	4.63	2.02	-.273*					.637**	.558**
I have discovered:	5.64	1.67	-.180						.779**
Ability to find meaning, purpose, or a mission in life	5.68	1.68	-.278**						

Pre-post difference	Change	T	D
Facing my daily tasks is:	-2.83	-8.13**	28
I have discovered:	-1.36	-3.12**	27
Ability to find meaning, purpose, or a mission in life	-1.26	-2.80**	27

Note: * $p < .05$, ** $p < .10$. Sample sizes for each analysis in parenthesis. Pre- and post-change scores

Table 4.4
Correlations for PTSD Diagnostic Criteria by PTSD

	Avoidance/Numbing	Re-experiencing	Arousal
Facing my daily task:	−.294**	−.186	−.272**
I have discovered:	−.231	−.181	−.108
I regard my ability to find meaning, purpose, or a mission in life as:	−.353**	−.250*	−.166

Note: * p < .05, **p < .10

less education. Results also confirm that meaning-making is an important component of postdisaster recovery, and aspects of meaning-making predict levels of PTSD.

THE SIX STEP BIO-PSYCHOSOCIAL AND SPIRITUAL MODEL

Following the initial need assessment, the MHOP team implemented the six step bio-psychosocial and spiritual model. Since religio-cultural factors influence the manifestation of psychological distress, this specific intervention was developed by Kalayjian (2002) to be used in MHOP to work with survivors following the earthquake. The steps were not intended to be covered in sequential order. Rather, they were designed to be flexible in order to respond to the organic evolution of issues brought up by survivors. Informed by the Islamic Faith/Spiritual Healing tradition, the six step model consisted of: expression of feelings; empathy; validation; meaning discovery and expression; information dissemination; and breathing and relaxation exercises. The following is a discussion of the six-step model, as it was implemented with groups of survivors three months following the earthquake.

Expression of Feelings: Survivors were first encouraged to express their feelings at present regarding the earthquake. A predominant feeling expressed was fear. Statements like "I am afraid to go back to my home" were frequently expressed. Survivors also expressed great fear of noise and activities inside their homes. Many people did not want to go back to their daily tasks. One woman said, "I can not do laundry again because I see the earthquake." Other feelings expressed by the survivors included anger (towards themselves, family members for dying, forces of nature, and the government for slow response in distributing relief and rebuilding the community), uncertainty as to whether another earthquake would occur because there were dozens of after shocks, sadness over loss of loved ones, and livelihood and anxiety over the future (where to live, what work would be available, schooling). Many of these fears were similar to those expressed by survivors of other disasters, both natural and human-made (Kokai et. al. 2004).

Survivors also reported tremendous guilt and sadness related to images in nightmares and flashbacks. One survivor stated, "My brother was standing outside of his house, when the house fell on him, and the ground buried his body." Survivors especially expressed guilt over not being able to save their children, spouses, relatives or friends.

Empathy and Validation: In order to develop rapport and comfort with mental health providers, the next two steps were developed to offer reassurance that psychological stresses were normal. Feelings of the survivors were validated by using statements such as, "I can understand," or "It makes sense that . . ." Psychoeducation was provided about how survivors from around the world have coped in the wake of natural disasters.

In some cases, verbal validation was limited due to the language and Islamic norms. Women and men did not want to participate in dialogue together. In those cases, female survivors listened attentively to their male neighbors and sometimes used a nonverbal expression of empathy. Therapeutic touch such as holding a female survivor's hand or gentle hugging after a particularly emotional release was also used in a culturally-appropriate manner. The group participants were encouraged to interact with one another both in and outside the group. This was done to encourage mutual support and identification with one another's experience (Bleich, Gelkopf, and Solomon 2003). In all female group sessions, it was observed that women were bonding with each other for the first time since the earthquake. Some female survivors were too afraid to leave their houses or tents due to fear of another earthquake.

In one case, a woman started to doubt her response and the events of the earthquake. As the team spoke with her and worked through her feelings and thoughts, she responded "I thought my mind and heart were playing tricks on me." She further stated, "I did not understand myself." Using Eagan's (1982) concept of "accurate empathy," the MHOP team members expressed awareness of the individual's circumstances. Consistent with the Islamic Faith/Spiritual Healing tradition, the woman was encouraged to actively seek spiritual connection and harmony with Allah's will.

Meaning Discovery and Expression: To help promote a sense of purposefulness and "being in the world," which is connected with the Islamic

Faith/Spiritual Healing tradition, survivors were asked a series of questions: "What lessons, meaning, or positive associations did you discover as a result of this disaster?" These questions were aimed at developing insight, helping promote their meaning-making process, and ultimately gaining a spiritual awareness. Many of the people in the frontier area, who were closer to the epicenter, responded by stating, "Allah is punishing us." One man said, "It was because there were prostitution houses in the mountains." Some women stated that their husbands told them "it was because of women's bad behavior." These comments were acknowledged, but then were challenged by asking survivors to consider what meaning and positive associations were gained that brought them closer to Allah's will.

Survivors began to focus on their strengths in being able to survive and the new meanings about survival and life that arose out of their difficult and traumatic experiences. In one case, a woman said, "everyday I am more thankful for my family and health." Another woman said, "I have no more physical possessions, but I am happier each day for my surviving child." One man said, "My neighbor and I have been feuding, but we came together to rescue and feed the people." These comments were discussed with the context of Islamic teachings related to trusting and listening to the teachings of life (Farooqi 2005).

Feelings of heroism also emerged in the groups. Survivors reported pulling people out of rubble. For example, people came together with broken limbs to move rubble and give assistance to others. Villages worked together to bring food and water up the mountain without having a road to travel with a vehicle. Some participants did not feel heroic, but rather felt guilty for not saving others or not doing enough. In this tragedy, many people were traumatized because they were able to stay on the cell phone with their loved one until he or she passed or the battery died. They may have been caught trapped under rubble and no one could get to them. The survivors felt great guilt, frustration and helplessness, but then they also discussed feelings of being brave and courageous. Again, this was discussed within the context of empowerment, particularly because their positive actions reflected good deeds, in accordance with Allah.

Information Dissemination: During this stage, psycho-education was used to explain how, why, and where an earthquake occurred. By sharing this information, in a nontechnical framework, survivors gained knowledge and practical tips about how to survive and live during the aftermath of the earthquake. Such knowledge was aimed at minimizing fear of the unknown and was used to empower people by giving them an understanding of the natural disaster. By having accurate information, survivors become aware of warning signals and systems, which helped them prepare for future disasters, as well as make better-informed decisions about healing and recovery.

Breathing and Movement Exercises: In the last stage, experiential, therapeutic, and mindful breathing exercises were taught for relaxation and the reduction of anxiety and fear. The underlying premise of this step is that if the startle-response or alarm-reaction adversely affects the respiratory patterns (e.g., gasping, thoracic breathing, breath holding), then normalizing the respiratory patterns with diaphragmatic breathing will lead to an improvement in health and performance, as well as a lessening of the negative effects of the human stress response. This seemed to be challenging for survivors who were not familiar with this form of exercising and body movement. There was an initial sense of shyness and uncomfortableness, which was addressed by encouraging participants to visualize a prayer or passage from the Quran. The participants appeared to respond more positively to the instruction of these simple exercises over subsequent days.

There were both logistical and practical circumstances that limited the extent to which assessments could be carried out in large numbers due to mudslides and pending outbreaks of violence because of the resurgence of feudal battles and terrorists. Limitations common in cross-cultural research were encountered in this project, including language and cultural differences, finding private and quiet space to hold groups, and participants with limited time to devote to groups (since other daily self and family care necessities took precedence).

In some cases, the translators did not want to translate anything negative a woman was saying about her husband, brother, father, mother-in-law or family. In addition, the team's questions to the women were not always translated. In some cases, the female translators were speaking to male members of society and this was not always welcomed. Furthermore, facilitating the six-step model in the rural area was quite challenging because of the education level and lack of translators. Nevertheless, clinical observations of the use of the six-step Bio-Psychosocial and Spiritual Model with these groups of earthquake survivors suggested the effectiveness of this model in this particular context. In particular, by incorporating aspects of the Islamic Faith/Spiritual Healing tradition, the six step model was successful in promoting meaning making among the survivors.

REFERENCES

Acierno, R., Kilpatrick, D. G., and Resnick, H. C. 1999. "Post-traumatic Stress Disorder in Adults Relative to Criminal Victimization: Prevalence, Risk Factors, and Comorbidity." In *Post-traumatic Stress Disorder: A Comprehensive*

Textbook, ed. P.A. Saigh and J.D. Bremner, 44–68. Needham Heights, MA: Allyn & Bacon.

American Psychiatric Association. 1980. *Diagnostic and Statistical Manual Disorders*, 3rd ed. Washington, DC: American Psychiatric Association.

Anderson, N.C. 1980. "Post-traumatic Stress Disorder." In *Comprehensive Textbook of Psychiatry*, ed. H.I. Kaplan, A.M. Freedman, and B.J. Sadlock, 1517–1525. Baltimore, MD: Williams & Wilkins.

Armenian, H.K., Morikawa, M., Melkonian, A.K., Hovanesian, A.P., Harutunian, N., Saigh, P.A., Akiskal, K., and Akiskal, H.S. 2000. "Loss as a Determinant of PTSD in a Cohort of Adult Survivors of the 1988 Earthquake in Armenia: Implications for Policy." *Acta Psychiatrica Scandinavica*. Munksgaard 102: 58–64.

Bleich, A., Gelkopf, M., and Solomon, Z. 2003. "The Psychological Impact of Ongoing Terrorism and Suicide Bombing on Israeli Society: A Study of a National Sample." *Journal of the American Medical Association* 290 (5): 612–20.

Brennan, R.J., and Waldman, R.J. 2006. "The South Asian Earthquake Six Months Later: An Ongoing Crisis." *The New England Journal of Medicine* 354 (17): 1769–1771.

Brier, J. 1997. *Psychological Assessment of Adult Post-traumatic States*. Washington, DC: American Psychological Association.

Brown, L.S. 2008. *Cultural Competence in Trauma Therapy: Beyond the Flashback*. Washington, DC: American Psychological Association.

Cao, H., McFarlane, A.C., and Klimidis, S. 2002. "Prevalence of Psychiatric Disorder Following the 1988 Yan Nan (China) Earthquake: The First 5-Month Period." *Social Psychiatry & Psychiatric Epidemiology* 38: 204–12.

Carr, V.J., Lewin, T.J., Webster, R.A., Hazell, P.L., Kenardy, J.A., and Carter, G.L. 1995. "Psychosocial Sequelae of the 1989 Newcastle Earthquake: Community Disaster Experience and Psychological Morbidity Months Postdisaster." *Psychological Medicine* 25: 539–55.

Carver, C.S. (1999). "Resilience and Thriving: Issues and Models and Linkages." *Journal of Social Issues* 54: 245–66.

Creamer M., and Burgess, P. 2001. "Post-traumatic Stress Disorder: Findings from the Australian National Survey of Mental Health and Well-Being." *Psychological Medicine*.

Doherty, G.W. 1999. "Cross Cultural Counseling in Disaster Settings." *The Australasian Journal of Disaster and Trauma Studies* 20: 1–15.

Egan, G. 1982. *The Skilled Helper*. 2nd ed. Monterey, CA: Brooks/Cole.

Ehler, A., Mayou, R.A., and Bryant, B. 1998. "Psychological Predictors of Chronic Post-traumatic Stress Disorder after Motor Vehicle Accidents." *Journal of Abnormal Psychology* 107: 508–19.

Ehrenreich, J.H. 2003. "Understanding PTSD: Forgetting 'Trauma'." *Journal of Social Issues* 3 (1): 15–28.

Elhai, J.D., North, T.C., and Frueh, B.C. 2005. "Health Service Use Predictors among Trauma Survivors: A Critical Review." *Psychological Services* 2: 3–19.

Farooqi, Y. N. 2006. "Traditional Healing Practices Sought by Muslim Psychiatric Patients in Lahore, Pakistan." *International Journal of Disability, Development and Education* 53 (4): 401–15.

Fletcher, K. E. 1996. "Childhood Post-Traumatic Stress Disorder." In *Child Psychopathology,* ed. E. J. Marsh and R. A. Barkley, 242–76. New York: Guilford Press.

Frederick, C. J. 1977. "Current Thinking about Crises and Psychological Interventions in United States Disasters." *Mass Emergencies* 2: 43–50.

Horwitz, M. J. 1976. S*tress Response Syndromes.* 2nd. ed. New York: Jason Aronson.

Horwitz, M. J., ed. 1999. *Essential Papers on Post-Traumatic Stress Disorder.* New York: New York University Press.

Karanci, A. N., and Rustemeli, A. 1995. "Psychological Consequences of the 1992 Erzincan Earthquake." *Disasters* 19: 8–18.

Kato, H., Asukai, N., Miyake, Y., Minakawa, K., and Nishiyama, A. 1996. "Posttraumatic Symptoms among Younger and Elderly Evacuees in the Early Stages Following the 1995 Hanshin-Awaji Earthquake in Japan." *Acta Psychiatrica Scandinavia* 93: 477–81.

Kessler, R. C. 2000. "Post-traumatic Stress Disorder: The Burden to the Individual and to Society." *Journal of Clinical Psychiatry* 61 (5): 4–12.

Kessler, R. C., Sonnega, A., Bromet, E., Hughes, M., and Nelson, C. B. 1995. "Post-traumatic Stress Disorder in the National Comorbidity Survey." *Achieves of General Psychiatry* 52: 1048–1060.

Kessler, R. C., McGonagle, K. A., Zhao, S. et al. 1994. "Lifetime and 12-month Prevalence of DSM-III-R Psychiatric Disorders in the United States: Results from the National Comorbidity Survey." *Archives of General Psychiatry* 51: 8–19.

Kokai, M., Fujil, S., Shinfuku, N., and Edwards, G. 2004. "Natural Disaster and Mental Health in Asia." *Psychiatric and Clinical Neurosciences* 58: 110–16.

Latz, M. S., and Buchalter, E. N. 2005. "Post-Traumatic Stress Disorder: When Current Events Cause Relapse." *Clinical Geriatrics* 13 (2): 20–23.

Madacasira, S., and O'Brien, K. F. 1987. "Acute Post-traumatic Stress Disorder in Victims of Natural Disaster." *Journal of Nervous and Mental Disease* 175: 266–90.

McFarlane, A.C., and Potts, N.C. 1999. "Post-traumatic Stress Disorder: Prevalence and Risk Factors Relative to Disaster." In *Post-traumatic Stress Disorder: A Comprehensive Textbook,* eds. P. A. Saigh and J. D. Bremner, 92–102. Needham Heights, MA: Allyn & Bacon.

McNally, R. J., Bryant, R. A., and Ehlers, A. 2003. "Does Early Psychological Intervention Promote Recovery from Post-traumatic Stress?" *Psychological Science in the Public Interest* 4 (2): 45–79.

Norris, F H. 2005. *Psychosocial Consequences of Natural Disasters in Developing Countries: What Does Past Research Tell Us about the Potential Effects of the 2004 Tsunami?* Available at: U.S. Department of Veterans Affairs, National Center for PTSD Web site: http://www.ncptsd.va.gov/facts/disasters/fs_earlyint_disaster.html.

Papadatos, Y., Nikou, K., and Potamianos, G. 1990. "Evaluation of Psychiatric Morbidity Following an Earthquake." *International Journal of Social Psychiatry* 36: 131–36.

Perry, S., Difede, J., Musngi, G., Frances, A. J., and Jacobsberg, L. 1992. "Predictors of Post-traumatic Stress Disorder after Burn Injury." *American Journal of Psychiatry* 149: 931–35.

Raja, R. 2004. "The Role of Religion and Spirituality in Health Care." *Journal of College of Physicians and Surgeons Pakistan* 14 (8): 1–3.

Rosen, C. S., Chow, H. H., Murphy, R. T., Drescher, K. D., Ramirez, G., Ruddy, R., and Gusman, F. 2001. "Post-traumatic Stress Disorder Patients' Readiness to Change Alcohol and Anger Problems." *Psychotherapy* 38 (2): 233–44.

Ruzek, J. I., Brymer, M. J., Jacobs, A. K., Layne, C. M., Vernberg, E. M., and Watson, P. J. 2007. "Psychological First Aid." *Journal of Mental Health Counseling* 29: 17–49.

Saigh, P. A. 1992. "History, Current Nosology, and Epidemiology." In *Post-traumatic Stress Disorder: A Comprehensive Textbook,* ed. P. A. Saigh, 1–28. Boston: Allyn & Bacon.

Schlenger, W. E., Fairbank, J. A., Jordan, B. K., and Caddell, J. M. 1999. "Epidemiology of Combat Related Post-traumatic Stress Disorder." In *Post-traumatic Stress Disorder: A Comprehensive Textbook,* ed. P. A. Saigh and J. D. Bremmer, 69–91. Boston: Allyn & Bacon.

Schnyder, U., and Moergeli, H. 2003. "The Course and Development of Early Reactions to Traumatic Events: Baseline Evidence from a Nonintervention Follow-up Study." In *Reconstructing Early Intervention after Trauma: Innovations in the Care of Survivors,* eds. R. Orner and U. Schynder. Oxford, England: Oxford University Press.

Schnyder, U., Moergeli, H., Klaghofer, R., Buddeberg, C. 2001. "Incidence and Prediction of Post-traumatic Stress Disorder Symptoms in Severely Injured Accident Victims." *American Journal of Psychiatry* 158: 594–99.

Scott, W. J. 1990. "PTSD in DSM III: A Case in the Politics of Diagnosis and Disease." *Social Problems* 37: 294–310.

So-krum, Tang, C. 2007. "Post-Traumatic Growth of Southeast Asian Survivors with Physical Injuries: Six Months after the 2004 Southeast Asian Earthquake-Tsunami." *Australasian Journal of Disaster and Trauma Studies* (1): 405–29.

Solomon, Z. 2003. *Coping with War Induced Stress: The Gulf War and the Israel Response.* New York: Plennum.

Stevens, S., and Slone, L. June, 2005. *Tsunami and Mental Health: What Can We Expect?* Available at: U.S. Department of Veterans Affairs, National Center for PTSD Web site: http://www.ncptsd.va.gov/facts/disasters/fs_early int_disaster.html.

World Health Organization. 2005. *South Asian Earthquake*. Available at: http://www.who.int/hac/crises/international/pakistan_earthquake/en/index.html.

Yehuda, R., and McFarlane, A. C. 1995. "Conflict between Current Knowledge about Post-traumatic Stress Disorder and Original Conceptual Basis." *American Journal of Psychiatry* 152: 1705–1713.

Chapter 5

COPING WITH HURRICANE ANDREW

Preparedness, Resilience, and Meaning-Making

*Ani Kalayjian,
Eleanor Donovan, and
Yuki Shigemoto*

Ask not what the world needs, ask what you need to come alive because what the world needs is people like you—who have come alive.

—Howard Thurman

INTRODUCTION

On August 24, 1992, a devastating hurricane with 120–140 mph winds, heavy rain, and a surging tide slammed into the 200-mile belt from Key West to Fort Lauderdale. Officials reported that the storm left over 250,000 people living in Florida homeless. As it ended its journey across the Gulf of Mexico, Hurricane Andrew struck New Orleans. It moved inland over sparsely populated marshlands, making the damage worse in small towns along Interstate 90 from Morgan City to New Iberia. In total, over 750,000 people evacuated and over 250,000 people were displaced. Also, 8,373 single-family homes and 8,974 mobile homes were destroyed, with more than 37,000 homes having major damage and 40,000 with minor damage. 180,000 people were left homeless, and a total of 52 hurricane related deaths were reported in Florida, Louisiana, and the Bahamas. The property damage cost around $30 billion and the estimated insurance loss was $18 billion. This chapter aims at presenting the outcome of the six month and one year follow-up in Florida, while highlighting some of the coping mechanisms and rituals victims used in order to heal from Hurricane Andrew's trauma.

Although the rescue mission left a lot to be desired, Floridians and the Federal Emergency Management Agency (FEMA) have developed a better understanding since Hurricane Andrew, assuring that following a natural disaster, joint damage assessment teams will be on the ground within 10 hours. FEMA has since learned to work closely with state disaster agencies and has found quicker means by which to provide aid to disaster victims. Additionally, victims and residents in the impacted region are now better prepared for a natural disaster. In collaboration with FEMA, a statewide campaign on hurricane preparedness has been launched to educate and prepare residents for a future disaster, and alleviate their fears and uncertainty. All of these measures are done in order to empower residents—for it is when residents become disempowered that they feel helpless and hopeless. It becomes a psychological downward spiral that can be extremely difficult to rise out of, especially when basic material resources such as food and shelter are lacking. Resources such as food, clothing, and shelter must be attainable or reestablished in survivors' lives if they are to begin coping emotionally with and recover from the damage done by a natural disaster.

Survivors cope with trauma in a myriad of ways. Some suffer anxiety, shock, feelings of helplessness and hopelessness, intense anger, post-traumatic stress disorder (PTSD), depression, and psychosomatic illness such as constant headaches and nausea. Many are unable to find appropriate outlets to release their frustration and anger, and subsequently fall into negative behavior patterns of drinking, using drugs, stealing, or acting in a verbally and/or psychically abusive way toward loved ones. Feeling helpless and hopeless, survivors resort to these substances or actions as a way to numb the pain or temporarily feel powerful and in control. Some, however, cope with the disaster by helping others and relying on their faith. Pain and suffering caused by massive losses after natural disasters may cause a fruitful tension, making the community aware of what could be, appreciate what is, and prevent what ought not to be. These tensions may help the community to come together and act responsibly and collectively. Massive traumatic losses not only create a crisis in the community; they create opportunity for survivors to understand their obligation to one another and to the earth, and also help the community *feel* such obligation. Above all, crises carry the potential for opportunity where residents can reach out and help community members care for each other. It may well be a paradox that traumatic disasters that disrupt the way of life of a community may lead to a spiritual evolution as long as the community can learn from and find positive meaning in a communal crisis (Kalayjian 1995).

LITERATURE REVIEW

In the aftermath of a natural disaster, it is natural for survivors to fall into a state of shock, unable to comprehend or appraise what occurred, the extent of the damage, and the scope of their loss. Emotionally, many feel anxious, restless, hopeless, angry, and irritable. They are angry at the lack of control they now have over their lives, and are unable or unwilling to grasp or accept that they are survivors of a natural disaster. Their global meaning, consisting of beliefs, goals, and subjective feelings has been shattered by the trauma (Park and Ai 2006). Yet, according to crisis theory, disasters do not necessarily result in the development of mental illnesses or psychiatric disabilities for the majority. While it is normal for many to go through stages of helplessness, numbness, shock, a sense of loss, and/or denial, generally speaking, these feelings do not have to be permanently debilitating. Rather, it depends on how survivors process the trauma through a negative or positive appraisal of meaning. While it has been shown that a negative appraisal further generates the distress of post-traumatic symptoms, the process to acquire a positive appraisal stimulates an unprecedented growth in survivors (Park and Ai 2006). This personal growth begins with the disruption of one's worldview or global meaning from trauma, and carries on throughout the entire process of meaning-making (Park and Ai 2006).

According to crisis theory, it is believed that social support can greatly influence the way we cope with disasters, and can help us return to our emotional equilibrium state. Social support during times of distress further helps stimulate victims' growth by reestablishing a sense of foundation and community. In the darkness of disaster grows an opportunity to create light—the human spirit endures, and we can cultivate the ability to create a positive out of a negative event.

Dealing with trauma in the wake of disaster, according to psychologists, occurs in two phases: the Impact Phase and the Recoil Phase (Mauro 1992). Phase one, the Impact Phase, often involves feelings of shock, denial, anger, and restlessness. Post-traumatic stress disorder (PTSD), depression, and certain psychosomatic illnesses can arise in this initial phase as survivors are forced to estimate their losses, find new shelter, and adjust to an entirely new and seemingly bleak reality. Many have different ways of coping and struggle even to accept the fact that they are survivors of a natural disaster. For example, according to Erikson (1976a), in the wake of the 1972 Buffalo Creek flood, survivors reported feeling demoralized, disoriented, and a loss of connection with social networks (as quoted in Crabbs and Heffron 1981). Additionally, in the aftermath of Hurricane Hugo, survivors reported feeling anxious, sad, numb, and angry (Shelby and Tredinnick 1995). Amidst these varying levels of PTSD, a common theme amongst survivors is an overwhelming sense of loss: loss of one's material comforts and security, and loss of one's social networks. Emotionally recovering from distress in this stage can take several weeks or months, and depends upon a reinvestment or revival of physical resources in survivors' lives (Hobfoll and Lilly 1993; Mauro 1992). That is, basic needs such as food, clothing, and shelter must be attainable or reestablished in survivors' lives if they are to begin emotionally coping with and recovering from the damage done by a natural disaster. This second stage of coping and adjustment is known as the Recoil Phase and can last for years (Mauro 1992).

While looking at Hurricane Andrew, Crabbs and Heffron (1981) note that survivors claimed having difficulties in establishing and maintaining relationships, as well as feelings of loss of personal confidence as a result of PTSD. The feelings of helplessness after trauma are rampant, and initially, are natural. To recognize a feeling of helplessness is to recognize that there are greater forces (such as a natural disaster) at work, which one may not be able to control. This realization is an essential first step to cope with natural disasters and grow—for when one achieves acceptance of that which one cannot control, more energy is left to focus on what one *can* control. What we can control is ourselves, our responses, and our attitudes. Therefore, in the first stages of coping with PTSD, insight into one's own strengths and resilience is crucial. Shelby and Tredinnick (1995) caution that a therapeutic response must focus on a victim's preexisting strengths and how these strengths might be realized and employed.

Shelby and Tredinnick (1995) further note that coping after trauma can actually be beneficial for a person's self-growth: "These experiences [of a natural disaster] sometimes create an enhanced capacity to learn new coping behaviors and problem-solving skills. Indeed, learning that occurs during a crisis state often tends to last, and coping behaviors adopted during the crisis tend to be utilized during stressful situations in the future" (493). In effect, the experience of a crisis actually generates the opportunity for victims to create "adaptive patterns for the future," which they otherwise may not have possessed (493).

SURVIVOR CHARACTERISTICS

According to the U.S. Census Bureau (2007), the population in Florida has grown from 2.8 million in 1950 to 13 million in 1990 and approximately 16 million in 2000. Florida's top industry is tourism. Other industries include agriculture, manufacturing, and international trade.

Florida's residential population is 83.1 percent white, 13.6 percent African American, 0.3 percent Native American, 1.2 percent Asian, and 1.8 percent other races. Hispanics may belong to any of the above racial groups. A majority of the Hispanic residents (62.5%) live in the southern part of the state. Although survivors were mostly Americans, there were a large number of legal and illegal residents from Cuba, Haiti, Jamaica, and Mexico (Kalayjian 1995).

Miami, located in southern Florida, is the second largest city in the state. Miami experienced one of its most monumental population booms during the 1960s, when about 260,000 Cuban refugees arrived seeking freedom. Furthermore, Florida ranks 4th in the United States in public education enrollment and 29th in expenditures per pupil. Florida's gross state product, as of 1990, was $244.62 billion, placing it 6th in the nation and ahead of most small nations.

Hurricane Andrew struck a wide area and impacted a community of varying socioeconomic levels. Some survivors who had resided in Homestead for over 30 years had experienced another devastating hurricane in 1965. Although there was a lack of coherence and community homogeneity as a whole, there were several pockets of cohesion. These included senior citizens, illegal immigrants, legal immigrants, the armed forces, and recently relocated families from the northern and western parts of the country. Various homeowners' insurance policies were available to residents and many of them purchased insurance, but not all obtained special hurricane or flood insurance (Kalayjian 1995).

EVENT CHARACTERISTICS

On Sunday, August 23, 1992, a ferocious hurricane slammed across the Gulf of Mexico with 120 mph winds, heavy rain, and a surging tide. Four people were reported dead as a result of the storm and over 250,000 Floridians were left homeless. By 1:30 A.M. that morning, high winds in advance of the storm toppled trees and knocked out electrical transformers in the Miami Beach area and sunk boats in Biscayne Bay, moving westward at 18 mph with wind speeds of approximately 140 mph. By 2 A.M., the eye of the storm passed south of Miami between Homestead and Cutler Ridge, which meant that the strongest winds struck the Homestead, Cutler Ridge, and Coconut Grove areas. The strong east-to-west winds pushed the hurricane along a bit faster than might otherwise have been the case, causing it to clear Florida in a relatively brief three hours. The hurricane was a category 4 storm on the Saffir-Simpson scale of hurricane intensity, with category 5 being the strongest. The course of this storm appeared to closely follow that of Hurricane Betsy in 1965, a Category 3 storm that struck both Southern Florida and New Orleans causing $1.5 billion worth of damage and killing 75 people (Kalayjian 1995).

Residents of Dade County, which includes Miami Beach, Key Biscayne, Fort Lauderdale, Homestead, and other low-lying coastal areas, were urged by authorities to evacuate. However, the residents underestimated the damage that such a storm can cause and did not adhere to the official orders. Some said, "We trust Mother Nature," while others explained, "It can't be that bad, we're going to ride it out," and "You've got to die sometime. It can't be that bad." Many people organized hurricane parties and bought cases of beer, chips, and cigarettes to celebrate, some in denial and some to numb the pain of the impact.

It seemed some individuals were lulled by the hope that Hurricane Andrew would turn northward at the last minute toward Georgia and the Carolinas, as Hurricane Hugo did in 1989 and as several other storms have done in recent years. However, a high pressure system extending east from Jacksonville kept that from occurring and pushed the storm westward. The evacuation orders, which began Sunday morning, covered a 200-mile belt from Key West to Fort Lauderdale, east of the main coastal highways, U.S. Route 1 and Interstate 95. The evacuation orders extended to low-lying areas, to mobile home communities further north, and to areas along the southwestern coast. One million people were told to evacuate. In Dade County 70,000 people spent the night in 48 shelters set up in churches and schools. By 7:30 P.M. a Dade County official stated they had exhausted their resources and could no longer provide any special evacuation assistance to those who might have needed it.

On that Sunday evening most of the Southern Florida gas stations, hardware stores, pharmacies, and groceries that had been mobbed with customers since midnight on Saturday were closed. The few stores that did remain open did not have such essentials as water, flashlight batteries, canned goods or bread. In hardware stores, people were waiting in line for hours to buy sheets of plywood to board up their windows. Plywood prices originally quoted at around $22 per sheet had increased to $40. There was the overall absence of basic public services such as water, electricity, gas, and telephones.

On August 24, 1992, several thousand National Guard troops were sent in to join local law enforcement officers who were trying to prevent looting, which was reported throughout the day in the hurricane-devastated area. Miami and Dade County imposed a curfew from late evening to early morning. Main roads, especially U.S. Route 1 and side streets, were filled with debris, parts of roofs, sailboats, other pieces of furniture, and palm trees that had been yanked out of the ground with balls of roots and turf still attached. The roads were further jammed by residents who had evacuated the area the day before and were now returning to their homes. Street signs were blown off their designated poles, creating additional problems for taxi drivers and residents.

At the South Miami Hospital in Homestead, the generator failed and there was no running water or telephones. Staff had to work day and night to help the injured and evacuate patients to a nearby hospital. One man described the situation by saying, "I spent two years in Vietnam and I have not seen anything like this."

ISSUES DURING DISASTER RELIEF

Hurricane Andrew caught the community by surprise. Although some people were prepared, having bought batteries, groceries, bottled water and plywood to board up their windows, most people had not taken seriously the threat of the storm. The majority reacted by saying, "We've been hearing these threats every year; nothing is going to happen; I am sure we'll deal with this," and "Not me, I think this one will blow over us. This area hasn't been hit in a long time." These attitudes, borne of familiarity and disbelief, led to greater shock immediately following the hurricane. Many members of the community intended to ride out the storm no matter what anyone said. Although the authors were not there during the initial disaster relief, they were able to follow the relief process by way of radio and television announcements. Many survivors stated that this had been the closest that they had ever come to death. The community reacted with overwhelming fear and uncertainty.

Red Cross volunteer forces began to intervene immediately with shelters in churches, schools, and other community outreach centers. Other volunteer groups, including church groups, were organized to assist the surviving community. The Red Cross expenditure was estimated at $77 million, with 12,150 workers serving over 4.78 million meals and providing 16,565 medical treatments. The Red Cross also established 230 shelters in Southern Florida, housing 85,154 people. Some additional psychological and spiritual counseling was provided through the Red Cross, Federal Emergency Management Agency (FEMA), the National Organization of Victim Assistance (NOVA), clergy, nurses, and other hospital staff.

Hospitals in the area, especially SMH Homestead Hospital and South Miami Hospital, were treating survivors around the clock. SMH Homestead Hospital displayed a sign over the doorway to its emergency room that read, "We beat Andrew like nobody else could." Professional nurses, psychologists, and other staff donated their time and expertise to help those in need. Although SMH Homestead Hospital itself sustained $2 million in damages and had to close for five days to repair, clean, stock, and restore utilities, most of the employees worked nonstop. Some of the employees did not come back; they chose to relocate. One nursing unit at SMH Homestead Hospital lost over 50 percent of its staff. Fortunately, volunteers and traveling nurses from across the nation arrived to fill in where necessary.

FEMA was also visible some time later. Although initially FEMA received criticism for being late, they were effective in providing travel trailers to qualified applicants—often to families of five or six. According to FEMA, there were a total of 184,893 applications, including 46,982 families who requested assistance. As part of short-term planning, home loans to 17,511 were approved for $389 million and 5,097 small business loans were approved for $226 million. Emergency grants of 66,590 were approved for $187 million, of which 61,616 families received emergency food stamps totaling $25.8 million; 7,236 disaster unemployment claims were submitted totaling over $12.4 million.

On Friday, August 28, 1992, four days after the hurricane, Pentagon officials announced that 5,000 troops were being sent from Fort Bragg in Fayetteville, North Carolina, along with portable kitchens, medicine, supplies, helicopters, and bulldozers. They set up tents for shelters and kitchens to feed 6,000 people three meals a day. Nevertheless, a professional disaster relief specialist characterized this response as "modest and tardy."

On Monday, August 24, 1992, the Medical Examiner's Office, which is equipped to handle an average of 10 deaths a day, had to deal with 66 bodies. Offices of Emergency Management were also overwhelmed. Kate Hale, director of Dade County's Office of Emergency Management, announced on Sunday night before the hurricane that the resources of her office had been completely exhausted and that they would no longer be able to provide special evacuation assistance to those in need. By midnight Sunday, 21,000 people had gone to public shelters in Broward County, north of Miami. Some shelters were packed to twice their capacity, prompting county officials to ask for emergency donations of food.

On August 27, 1992, Dade County officials directed the County Attorney to file a Federal lawsuit in an effort to postpone a statewide primary election scheduled for Tuesday on the grounds that extensive hurricane damage would not allow Dade County voters access the polls.

Other calamities occurred during the relief. Two people were killed and another was injured as a small plane carrying aid to the victims of the hurricane crashed onto the roof of a house in Miramar, near Miami. Channels of communication were disrupted; there were no telephones, electricity, or mail. Community members tried to deal with this chaotic state by staying with friends, neighbors, or at places of work (Kalayjian 1995).

PRE- AND POSTDISASTER SOCIOPOLITICAL AND ECONOMIC CLIMATE

Before Hurricane Andrew, both politically and economically, the community was in a state of equilibrium. After the hurricane, though, there was a tremendous problem caused by the migrant construction workers who traveled from South Carolina, Georgia, Alabama, even as far away as Michigan and New Jersey, to make a quick buck. They lived in roadside camps with their shotguns and 9-mm pistols, drugs, and drinks. In one incident, a roofer was stabbed 100 times; in another, soldiers who patrolled the area reported seeing a roofer bite off another man's ear and then spit it out. Local police officers referred to them as "roofers from hell" (Booth 1993). The wife of a roofer from Indiana said, "The price of one's life is less than a 12-pack of beer." According to Cathy Booth, a survivor in Key Largo (1993), one carpenter from Pennsylvania was living in his aging scout van at "Camp Mad Max" because he couldn't afford a hotel. Thieves had taken his car battery, radio, tools, and even his Penn State floor mats. His body was covered with infected mosquito bites, and on his back, antibiotic cream covered a patch of ringworm. He was planning to cure it himself by sanding down the skin and then washing it with Clorox.

The first author, who traveled to South Florida, met several survivors who complained about the roofers and the construction people. One survivor said that she had gone through eight different construction companies in less than two months with no success. Mary, a registered nurse from the SMH Homestead, said that the first contractor took the deposit and never returned, the second contractor came and promised to return the next day and never did, and the third one came to give the estimate and began drinking an alcoholic beverage. Mary then fired the third contractor, but the damage had already been done: She had already taken three days off from work with no compensation, and now while still living in a trailer, was without a reliable contractor.

METHOD

Implementation began immediately after Hurricane Andrew in Southern Florida. No waiting period was essential to access since the hurricane occurred in the United States. The Reaction Index Scale was the instrument utilized once again for its brevity and clarity to measure the level of PTSD, and additional questions were asked in order to elicit what changes in survivors' personal and social lives had occurred. The study sample consisted of 127 individuals who had survived Hurricane Andrew. Respondents were selected randomly from several shelters in Southern Florida, as well as South Miami Hospital at Homestead.

A six-month follow-up study in Florida revealed that many communities were still in chaos. People were still walking wounded, suffering emotionally from posthurricane trauma. The authors conducted research to indicate the level of PTSD. According to DSM-IV (American Psychiatric Association 1994), PTSD is categorized as an anxiety disorder with the following symptoms experienced for over one month of duration following exposure to a traumatic event: persistent reexperiencing of the event, persistent avoidance of the stimuli associated with the traumas, and a clinically significant decrease in the individual's ability to function.

RESULTS

Extensive assessment and diagnoses in Southern Florida following Hurricane Andrew revealed that 89 percent of the children interviewed had severe PTSD and more than 80 percent of the adolescents, the adults, and the disaster workers interviewed had severe PTSD. Also, at least half of the health care workers and the teachers or educators had severe PTSD. Many residents decided to leave the community, thereby increasing the stress of rebuilding for remaining families, and the majority of the survivors expressed frustration about not receiving emergency aid promptly. One study notes that within six months of Hurricane Andrew 46 percent of the 241 sample population in Dade County had a friend or family member relocate to another county or another state (Norris et al. 1998).

In Southern Florida over 30 percent of the survivors interviewed by the first author indicated that they had established positive meaning in their experiences of the hurricane. In general, it was helping others that fostered positive meaning for survivors in the midst of all the trauma and tragedy. One victim explained, "Although I felt vulnerable to Mother Nature, talking and working with friends and fellow employees [was the] most meaningful," while another victim realized "Helping friends and neighbors is most important in life." It is significant that respondents who found meaning in their trauma measured much lower on the Reaction Index Scale, indicating lower levels of post-traumatic stress disorder. They also reached acceptance, which is an essential step in the move toward resolving an existential crisis. The acceptance stage, as defined by Kubler-Ross (1969), is neither happy nor sad. It is devoid of feeling; a passive acquiescence to the tragic triad of human existence: pain, guilt, and death (Frankl 1962).

SIX MONTH FOLLOW-UP RESULTS

Survivors experienced a multitude of coping difficulties. Although three months posthurricane the survivors reported going through normal reactions to a massive trauma such as grieving for their losses, struggling to address daily obstacles, helping one another and receiving help from others, six months later they were overwhelmed by feelings of uncertainty and despair. Some began to rely on substances to alleviate or numb their pain and suffering, saying to themselves, "There is no use, I might as well get drunk." Others became short-tempered and irritable and began physically and verbally abusing one another. Domestic violence increased, as did spousal and child abuse. Responses such as, "She irritates me so much, I can't take it anymore," were common for situations of child abuse. Those who did not have a spouse or children reported abusing their pet dogs and cats. However, those survivors who had positive meaning associated with the disaster, about 22 percent of those interviewed, reported coping in a healthier manner.

Analysis of variance revealed strong correlations between PTSD and education ($p < .001$), PTSD and severity of damage to home ($p < .001$), education and helplessness ($p=005$) employment and helplessness ($p=003$), and PTSD and meaning ($p=003$).

ONE-YEAR FOLLOW-UP

According to authorities, nearly 12,000 people still had no place to live one year after Hurricane Andrew. Others whose homes were destroyed had moved into mobile homes provided by FEMA, even though mobile homes were 21 times more likely to be destroyed by hurricanes than regular houses. The Cutler Ridge area was 50 percent rebuilt, except for the shopping mall. Miami hotels, which served as homes for many displaced residents, did well. Overall, the tourism industry revived rather rapidly in Dade County.

The survivors were additionally traumatized by the practices of insurance companies, federal agencies, looters, robbers and construction workers. The American Psychological Association (APA) had issued a warning to Hurricane Andrew survivors that the anniversary dates of disasters can reactivate thoughts and feelings from the actual event and that survivors may experience a resurgence of symptoms such as anxiety, depression, helplessness, frustration, and loss of control.

One year after Hurricane Andrew, post-hurricane stress manifested itself and remained just as apparent in Floridians as it did across the landscape with gnarled street signs and empty shopping malls. Haunting memories of Hurricane Andrew, its impact, and the fear of yet another hurricane tormented many residents of South Dade County. Many survivors found themselves drinking heavily, fighting with family members or coworkers, and panicking over a thunderstorm. Some still had nightmares, woke up screaming at night, could not concentrate, and could not engage in their prehurricane hobbies.

Spousal and child abuse increased in Dade County and the divorce rate rose by a reported 30 percent. Results from the one-year follow-up interviews of close to one hundred survivors were consistent with the above findings. The number of domestic violence suits filed in 1992 in Dade Circuit Court reached 4,586, about double the number from the previous year. One survivor said, "My husband drinks more and more now after the hurricane, and when he drinks he is violent toward me."

The schools in Dade County had experienced a tremendous increase in the frequency of suicide attempts. According to Joseph Jackson, supervisor of psychological services for the Dade County schools, there were 19 suicide attempts among young children in less than one year after Andrew; this is compared to only two suicide attempts one year before the hurricane. Some very small children had regressed in their toilet training and verbal skills. Some remained fearful to sleep alone, afraid of loud noises and all storms. The Association for Trauma Outreach and Prevention's Mental Health Outreach Project (MHOP) designed special art and play therapy groups to work with the traumatized children who were unable to express their feelings through language. Play therapy and art therapy provided a nonthreatening and fun way to talk about a difficult issue that surrounds them all. Children also feel and internalize the trauma of their adult parents and care givers. Therefore, double trauma was expected in some children's cases.

Homestead Air Force Base, once home to 8,000 active military and civilian workers, had only about 200 people working there, as officials planned its rebirth as a military reserve post and general aviation center. The tent cities and more than 29,000 troops and reserve units deployed at the peak of the recovery were gone, along with the long lines for water, food, mail, and gas. Out of the 47,000 houses and apartments destroyed in Dade County, only 15,000 had been repaired. Of the 101,000 dislocated residents, only two-thirds had returned. Officials estimate it will take until the turn of the century for the population to return to pre-Andrew levels.

As for employment, of the 60,000 jobs lost in Dade County following the hurricane, only one-third had returned. Fortunately, countrywide employment had actually increased by 4.5 percent since Andrew, and sales tax proceeds had soared due to the rebuilding efforts. Claims numbering 7,236 for disaster unemployment assistance were submitted and $12.4 million was disbursed.

Although the last hurricane of Andrew's size was Donna in 1960, this first anniversary had left Floridians especially uneasy, anxious, and even paranoid. FEMA reported taking steps to ease fears and uncertainty by educating and preparing the residents. A statewide campaign on hurricane preparedness was launched at this time.

Floridians and FEMA have developed a better understanding since Andrew, assuring that following a natural disaster, joint damage assessment teams would be on the ground within 10 hours. Stricter local and state requirements for preparation have helped revamp FEMA (Calhoun and Plymale 1995). FEMA has since learned to work very closely with state disaster agencies and has found quicker means by which to provide aid to disaster survivors. FEMA was expected to stay in Southern Florida for at least two or three years after the Andrew. They have spent over $2.1 billion on the recovery from Hurricane Andrew, with about $3 billion allocated. Another $5 billion will be spent by other federal agencies on economic development, agriculture, and social services. One year after the hurricane, FEMA reported that more than 90 percent of the nearly 47,000 requests for housing assistance had been settled.

COPING WITH HURRICANE ANDREW: RESPONSIBILITY, TIMING, AND PREPAREDNESS

In the aftermath of a natural disaster shock, disbelief, and strong emotional expressions are normal. Post-traumatic stress disorder (PTSD), depression, and certain psychosomatic illnesses can also follow. Although basic needs such as food, clothing, and shelter must be met first, emotionally coping should follow.

The desire to help others can be a strong and initially constructive force in survivors. This feeling is derived from a strong sense of helplessness and a desire to do something about it. Becky Spillers, a Hurricane Andrew survivor and farmer living near the Homestead area commented "Initially I felt devastated, but then I found out everyone was in the same situation, so I began helping my neighbors, and then felt so much better. We then helped one another in our neighborhoods, we all felt so much stronger." Survivors can benefit from acceptance of their trauma and finally release, redefine, and transform their experience by helping one another and by learning a positive lesson.

Finally, another important factor in coping is preparedness. After Hurricane Andrew many survivors confessed that they were not prepared, did not take the warnings seriously, and that instead they prepared to have a hurricane party. Research findings reveal that preparedness is a key factor in determining postdisaster recovery (Kalayjian 1995).

RECOVERY RITUALS: RESILIENCE AND MEANING-MAKING

As discussed earlier, survivors cope with trauma and loss in a myriad of ways. Some suffer from anxiety, shock, feelings of helplessness and hopelessness, and intense anger. Post-traumatic stress disorder, depression, and psychosomatic illnesses such as constant headaches and nausea can all arise due to traumas like Hurricane Andrew. Others fall into denial. They are unable to grasp or accept what has occurred, and therefore are incapable of responding proactively by transforming their feelings of loss into meaning-making. Still, others channel their grief into helping others around them. Nevertheless, what is clear is that failure to cope with grief through appropriate and therapeutic outlets has grave personal and social consequences.

As mentioned earlier, in the months after Hurricane Andrew Dade Country experienced a significant increase in looting, crime, violence, and overall chaos. Many victims began drinking heavily and resorting to drug use, domestic violence increased, the number of divorces rose by thirty percent, and local schools saw 19 suicide attempts among school children (Gelman and Katel 1993; Sokol 1993), much more than in previous years. Many of these reactions arose out of a deep feeling of helplessness. To cope, victims chose to self-medicate through alcohol, drugs, or violence. "I'm running away from it," explains Raul Gonzalez, 53, who began consuming pints and fifths daily after Hurricane Andrew (as quoted in Sokol 1993). Gonzalez, like many other survivors, was plagued by insomnia and nightmares after the hurricane. Nightmares particularly affected younger children, who reported having recurring dreams about storms approaching and waking up screaming. Fighting between family members and spousal and domestic abuse reports rose after Hurricane Andrew. In Dade County, the total number of domestic suits filed in Dade Circuit Court in 1992 (4,586) was double the amount from the previous year (Sokol 1993). Psychologist John Carnes explained, "[I] think of anger as being the flip-side of insecurity. Survivors then, when they realize the full extent of the damage, will very often vent that anger at an agency or a representative, sometimes, that might even be their children or their spouses" (as quoted in Mauro 1992, 44).

With few outlets for their grief, anger, and frustration, some victims chose to pick up and leave Dade County altogether, the site and perceived root of all their pain. Frustrated with living in overcrowded tent camps, slow progress in rebuilding their homes, and little help from insurance companies, many survivors chose to start over in other parts of Florida or in another state. For those who remained in Dade County, this exodus had a tremendous impact on the community and local reconstruction efforts. Even one year after Andrew, parts of Dade County struggled to regain the population numbers it lost due to the hurricane. One study observed how in South Dade, where Hurricane Andrew hit the hardest, the population decreased by nearly 60,000 between 1992 and 1993 (Smith and McCarty 1996, 272). By 1994 South Dade's population was still

26,000 lower than it was before Hurricane Andrew. Between 1992 and 1993, Dade County as a whole declined by nearly 32,000 (Smith and McCarty 1996, 272).

One journalist poignantly observes when interviewing survivors, "Everyone has a 'but' when grief is reconciled" (Allen 1993, 42). This suggests that survivors were optimistically stating "But thank God I suffered less" during times when many, living in tent camps months after the disaster, waiting to reenter their homes, had glimpses of hope. While many of the circumstances can be subjectiv[e, those that chose to stay in the aftermath of a natural disaster were making a clear choice to remain in the community and work together for survival, regeneration, and continuity. Rather than uproot and disrupt their lives even further, survivors chose to pick up the pieces with an optimistic and enduring faith. They created continuity, collective healing, and reconnection.

In the Impact and Recoil phases of recovery, therapists agree that for survivors "there is a split level of responsibility: to first take care of their own family and then rebuild their lives to be more secure than their prehurricane status" (Mauro 1992). Yet to accomplish this, survivors first need to take care of themselves. Only then can they look after others and rebuild their community. Therefore, effective and appropriate outlets for survivors need to be available. Survivors need to have outlets where they can tell their stories of survival and feel that they have been heard (Crabbs and Heffron 1981).

After Hurricane Andrew many relied on their faith as a way to cope; victims turned to their church leaders and church community for support, even if the actual church they used to gather at no longer existed. One cardboard sign on a devastated lawn read, "God saved us from Andrew's fury." Only in this way were many able to derive hope and strength within themselves amidst all the mess. In this sense, Hurricane Andrew was understood as a test for humankind. At an interfaith worship service, Miccosukee Indian chairman Billy Cypress told followers: "Throughout history, man has always found a way to come back from disaster . . . There is a tomorrow. There is no darkness unless man makes the darkness himself" (as quoted in *St. Petersburg Times,* November. 27, 1992). In this way, Cypress sought to reassure survivors of the strength within, and the choice they have about how they want to perceive and cope with the aftermath.

It was this kind of strength within that helped form the base for the more positive coping rituals that some survivors chose to practice. Despite the darkness and despair, some survivors were able to come together and heal collectively. Alvin Chapman, a former Knight-Ridder chairman, understood Hurricane Andrew as having a biblical origin. He labeled Andrew "the introducer," for "He introduce[d] death, devastation and sadness to our community . . . but Andrew also introduced . . . compassion, concern, brotherly love and people helping people" (as quoted in *St. Petersburg Times,* November 27, 1992). One example of survivors coming together to heal collectively was a Thanksgiving celebration, which took place after Hurricane Andrew. Three months after Andrew, Dade County looked just as it did when the hurricane hit in August. Yet victims were still able to come together to prepare a large meal that celebrated their survival, focused on hope for the future, and stressed the importance of interpersonal relations and meaning-making.

With so much PTSD affecting survivors, some chose humor and optimism. Valerie, a 20-year-old, explained, "I laugh at everything . . . I feel if I laugh I won't cry" (as quoted in Allen 42). It is this sort of choice—to opt for humor and the positive—that not only works to reestablish and strengthen a faith in humanity, but also sets a powerful example for the rest of the community. Children in particular have been shown to suffer from severe PTSD in the aftermath of disasters (Jones et al. 2001). Hurricane Andrew was no exception, with many young children reportedly suffering from severe nightmares, anxiety, and levels of stress about the possibility of another disaster and their families' situations (Jones et al. 2001). When parents and adults in a community, especially in the sordid, crowded tent camps, opt to laugh, they create a positive shift in the community that certainly has a positive effect on children—revealing a powerful coping mechanism. Survivors can choose to select therapeutic outlets for coping and meaning-making. This will replace fear and uncertainty with a reassurance in self and in community and a faith in the human spirit and survival.

After Andrew, while statements of despair and helplessness were visible, it was messages of hope and humor that felt ubiquitous. On pieces of cardboard, walls, and garage doors, statements like "Nice Try Andrew, we'll be back," "We can't be beat," and "Hurricane yard sale. Half price" prevailed (Ulbrich 1992).

Another ritual of expression after Hurricane Andrew was a graffiti-art movement that not only allowed survivors to express themselves—providing a viable and important outlet for them in their grief, but served as a collective voice and healing outlet for the community. Short poems like "Andrew's dead/ we're alive/ forget the feds/ we'll survive" became a voice of the community by echoing an enduring spirit that will survive despite all the problems (Ulbrich 1992). Using artistic and aesthetic expressions as a way to heal and find meaning continued long after Hurricane Andrew. Many artists took pieces of wreckage from the storm—pieces that for many were painful reminders of life before the storm—and created works that sought to find positive meaning even in tragedy. Artists such as Pablo Cano used a Kentucky Fried Chicken sign, which he found after Andrew to create a piece that now resides in the permanent collection of the Museum of Art in Fort Lauderdale, Florida (Gresko 2006). For Cano, as for other artists, using art in this way helps the country to remember, but more importantly, to come together. "It's like, for me, like God painting. He takes a big brush and swipes it across the land. It's a tremendous canvas that we are all a part of" (quoted in Gresko 2006). Thus, art serves to remind us that we are all together in this, that we are all affected in some way by grief, and that together we can heal and move on. Amidst all the wreckage and pain, we can find beauty again, extended from our inner beauty.

CONCLUSION: LESSONS LEARNED AND MEANING-MAKING

A natural disaster has both a terrible and terrific way of illustrating that there are forces far greater than us at work. For humankind, nature has both a marvelous and devastating way of reminding us how small we are—that we are not at the center of everything. However, being small and lacking degrees of control in these cases do not have to be demeaning or defeating; instead, it can be empowering and inspiring with an ability to move humans and society in perhaps an unforeseen, alternative direction. Cypress channeled this thought when he proclaimed to followers, "Throughout history, man has always found a way to come back from disaster . . . There is a tomorrow. There is no darkness unless man makes the darkness himself" (quoted in the *St. Petersburg Times,* November 27, 1992). It is the darkness experienced in disaster that allows us to appreciate the light within ourselves and in those around us. As Lukas asserts: "A negative input I receive may be painful and traumatic, but a positive output I send into the world keeps me well even in pain" (Lukas 1991).

Pain and suffering caused by massive losses after natural disasters may cause a fruitful tension, making the community aware of what could be, appreciate what it is, and prevent what ought not to be. These tensions may help the community to come together and act responsibly and collectively. Massive traumatic losses not only create a crisis in the community; they create opportunity for survivors to understand their obligation to one another and to Mother Earth, and also help communities feel such obligation. Above all, crises carry the potential to help community members care for each other and exhibit this caring in a humanistic way. It may well be a paradox that traumatic disasters that disrupt the way of life of a community may lead to a spiritual evolution as long as the community can learn from and find positive meaning in communal crises.

REFERENCES

Allen, D.L. 1993. "Hurricane Andrew, A Reporter's Dispatch. The Story of Three Families: In the Wake. of the Storm, How Are People Doing Psychologically?" *Psychology Today* (January/February): 38–41, 92.

Booth, C. 1993. "Roofers from Hell." *Time* 41 (9): 45.

Calhoun, P., and Plymale, I. 1995. "The Storm that Stayed." *Fund Raising Management* 25 (12). Available at: http://www.ophsource.org/periodicals/ophtha/medline/record/MDLN.10123822.

Crabbs, M.A., and Heffron, E. 1981. "Loss Associated with a Natural Disaster." *Personnel and Guidance Journal* 59 (6): 378–82.

Erikson, K.T. March, 1976. "Loss of Community at Buffalo Creek." *American Journal of Psychiatry* 133 (3): 302–5.

Frankl, V.E. 1962. *Man's Search for Meaning.* New York: Simon and Schuster.

Gelman, D., and Katel, P. 1993. "The Trauma After the Storm." *Newsweek* 121 (14). Available at: http://www.newsweek.com/id/119364?tid=relatedcl.

Gresko, J. 2006. "Florida Artists Turn Hurricane Trash to Treasure." *Cincinnati Post* (June 9): A15.

Jones, R.T., Frary, R., Cunningham, P., Weddle, I.D., and Kaiser, L. 2001. "The Psychological Effects of Hurricane Andrew on Ethnic Minority and Caucasian Children and Adolescents: A Case Study." *Cultural Diversity and Ethnic Minority Psychology* 7 (1): 103–8.

Lukas, E. 1991. "Trauma and Meaning-Making." Presentation at 8th World Congress of Logotherapy, San Jose, CA.

Kalayjian, A.S. 1995. *Disaster and Mass Trauma: Global Perspectives on Post Disaster Mental Health Management.* Long Branch, NJ: Vista Publishing.

Kubler-Ross, E. 1969. *On Death and Dying.* New York: International University Press.

Mauro, J. 1992. "Hurricane Andrew's Other Legacy." *Christianity Today* 25 (6): 42.

Norris, F.H., Perilla, J.L., Riad, J.K., Kaniasty, K., and Lavizzo, E. 1999. "Stability and Change in Stress, Resources, and Psychological Distress following Natural Disaster: Findings from Hurricane Andrew." *Anxiety, Stress, and Coping* 12: 363–96.

Park, C.L., and Ai, A.L. 2006. "Meaning Making and Growth: New Directions for Research on Survivors of Trauma." *Journal of Loss and Trauma* 11: 389–407.

Shelby, J.S., and Tredinnick, M.G. 1995. "Crisis Intervention with Survivors of Natural Disaster: Lessons from Hurricane Andrew." *Journal of Counseling and Development* 73 (5): 491–97.

Smith, S.K., and McCarty, C. 1996. "Demographic Effects of Natural Disaster: A Case Study of Hurricane Andrew." *Demography* 33 (2): 265–75.

Sokol, M. 1993. "Then and Now: Storm Still Taking Toll on People's Emotions Series: Hurricane Andrew 1 Year Later. *St. Petersburg Times* (August 24): 1A.

St. Petersburg Times. 1992. "Hurricane Victims Give Thanks for Life." (November 27): 9B.

Ulbrich, J. 1992. "Sign of the Times: Floridians Display Humor and Tragedy." *Chicago Tribune* (August 31): 2.

U.S. Census Bureau. 2007. *American FactFinder.* Available at: http://www.census.gov/.

Chapter 6

WEATHERING THE STORMS LIKE BAMBOO

The Strengths of Haitians in Coping with Natural Disasters

Guerda Nicolas,
Billie Schwartz, and
Elizabeth Pierre

The bamboo symbolizes the Haitian people . . . The bamboo is really weak, but when the wind comes, it bends, but it doesn't break. Bamboo takes whatever adversity comes along . . . that's what resistance is for us Haitians; we might get bent . . . but we're able to straighten up and stand.
—Bell and Danticat, *Walking on Fire,* 23

Haiti as a country has faced many political, economic, and environmental storms over the centuries and these storms have significantly impacted the lives of the people residing in Haiti. In addition to these storms, Haitians have been faced with the occurrence of many natural disasters and they are in desperate need of support. While support from outside of Haiti is certainly beneficial and helps to reduce the stress of their circumstances, it is also important for the people of Haiti to be able to access their own resources and tap into their own strengths when dealing with their many challenges. Therefore, it is important to think about questions such as: what are the strengths of the country and its people in coping with these disasters? and what role do history and social support systems such as family, religion, and community play in facing these challenges? These are some of the main questions that are addressed in this chapter. Specifically, a description of the following issues is provided: (1) Haiti's history of political instability; (2) Haiti's misfortune with natural disasters; (3) a description of the intersections of trauma and natural disasters; and (4) the cultural strengths of Haitians in coping with natural disasters.

AN OVERVIEW OF HAITI'S POLITICAL HISTORY

Haiti is a small island, equivalent to the size of Maryland and often referred to as "the pearl of the Antilles" (Coupeau 2002; Hickey 1982). The French developed the western part of the island whereas the Spanish developed the Eastern part, which is now the Dominican Republic (Hickey 1982). St. Domingue was eventually called Haiti (which means great mountains or great land) by its original inhabitants, the Arawaks and Tainos, and this name has remained throughout its existence (Heinl and Heinl 2005).

Haiti was appropriately named the pearl of Antilles because it was both lush and verdant with forests (Coupeau 2008). Haiti was also the first island to produce sugar, and the mining provided precious stones. In essence, Haiti was rich with many natural resources that yielded wealth for the French colonists, and eventually became one of the most prosperous colonies and the leading producer of both sugar and coffee by 1791 (Hickey 1982). Unfortunately, this wealth was enjoyed by the French colonists and not by the black slaves, whose arduous work had provided the prosperity (Coupeau 2008). This chasm between the white (the haves) and black (the have-nots) populations of Haiti led to discontentment, frustration, and ultimately a revolution led by Francois Toussaint (Hickey 1983).

Francois Toussaint, who became Toussaint Loverture (his name was changed to Loverture because of his ability to escape effortlessly from traps), was an ex-slave who became a general and led the revolt against the French (Knight 2000). Haiti was certainly a small nation compared to France, yet the tenacity of Loverture and those on his side was powerful, and that is what overthrew Napoleon Bonaparte and his army (Knight 2000). This unlikely victory reverberated throughout the world and instilled fear among leaders (Knight 2000). Unfortunately, but not surprisingly, Loverture was eventually captured, sent into exile, and died in France (Knight 2000). Jean-Jaques Dessalines succeeded him and declared Haiti as an independent nation in 1804. However, it would take some time for other nations to acknowledge Haiti's independence; it took the United States 60 years (Coupeau 2008).

As Haiti attempted to reconcile differences among leaders and establish its own government, Dessalines was assassinated, and from 1806–1820 the country became divided into two: (1) the predominantly mulatto population lived under the rule of General Alexandre Petion; and (2) the predominantly dark skinned people lived under the rule of King Henri Christophe (Coupeau 2008). This division was the beginning of the turmoil in leadership that Haiti would undergo in subsequent years.

Some of the most unstable political times for Haiti have been within the last 30 years. President Francois "Papa Doc" Duvalier reigned as dictator of Haiti from 1957–1971 (Coupeau 2008). President Duvalier remained in power by killing people he suspected to be enemies (Farmer 2006), and this continued under the rule of his son Jean Claude "Baby Doc" Duvalier who was president from 1971–1986 (Heinl et al. 2005). Both regimes resulted in Haitians fleeing Haiti to save themselves and their loved ones; the large majority of them immigrated to New York City and Miami (Stepick and Portes 1986).

Although the Haitians who fled Haiti expected to experience safety and a sense of security in the United States, they were viewed as an economic threat, were not granted political asylum, and the Immigration and Naturalization Services (INS) made a concerted effort to assure that Haitians were ineligible for permanent residence (Stepick and Portes 1986). In response, various community organizations and churches lobbied on behalf of Haitians for better conduct towards them. In addition to the stress they encountered upon arrival to the United States, it is also important to recognize the trauma they experienced in relocating to a new country (and particularly to big cities) where many of them did not know the language or the system by which America operates (Stepick and Portes 1986). Haitians' plight in the United States was further exacerbated in the early 1990s when they were targeted by the Centers for Disease Control (CDC) as the group responsible for carrying the HIV virus (Glick-Schiller and Fouron 1990). This false accusation spread throughout the country (and eventually the world) and resulted in many Haitians losing their jobs and support network, and having the general population within the United States afraid of associating with them. Haitians throughout the United States protested against the CDC's claim that they were carriers of the HIV virus and this fight eventually resulted in the removal of Haitians from the at risk list for AIDS (Glick-Schiller and Fouron 1990).

The government in Haiti remained relatively unstable after President Baby Doc's ousting in 1986, having five brief administrations from 1987–1990 (Coupeau 2008). Unexpectedly in 1991 Jean Bertand Aristide, a priest turned political figure, ran for office and won one of the first open and democratic elections in Haiti. This event provided a sense of hope that the war-torn and impoverished nation would become a safe and prosperous place, not only for its inhabitants but for the world (Farmer 2006). Aristide strived to regulate the economic system and redistribute the wealth that had been hoarded by a small minority. President Aristide's political stance instilled fear among other foreign leaders, including the United States. Unfortunately, seven months later hope quickly expired when a military coup, with United States knowledge and involvement, ousted President Aristide from office (Coupeau 2008). It was this fear that led to two other coup d'états when President Aristide was in power from 1994–1996 and then from 2000–2004. The last coup led President Aristide into exile in Central Africa, leaving Haiti once again in great distress (Farmer 2006).

HAITI'S PLIGHT WITH NATURAL DISASTERS

Along with political devastation, Haiti has also be been battered by natural disasters throughout its history. The island lies in the middle of the hurricane belt and is subject to strong storms from June to November (i.e., hurricane season) and these storms have resulted in severe wind damage, flooding, landslides, and coastal surges (World Bank 2008). Hurricanes have been a part of Haiti's history, with the first hurricane documented in 1508, since it is surrounded by water. The first official devastating hurricane was an unnamed hurricane in 1935 that resulted in 2,150 deaths (National Hurricane Center Publication 2008). Hurricane Hazel followed in 1954, contributing to the death of over 1000 people. Hurricane Flora (ranked as the 6th most deadly hurricane) hit Haiti in much greater magnitude in 1963, killing over 8,000 people. The country received a reprieve in the 1970s and 1980s, but was hit once again by Hurricane Gordon in 1994, killing over 1000 Haitians. Then Hurricane Georges in 1998 killed over 400 people and destroyed 80 percent of the crops in the country.

The hurricanes and tropical storms have persisted and some of the most devastating ones have occurred in 2004, 2005, and 2008. Hurricane Jeanne (ranked as the 12th deadliest hurricane of all time) hit Haiti in September 2004, resulting in the death of over 3,000 people, mostly in the town of Gonaives (Arie 2004). In 2005, Hurricane Wilma, not predicted to cause much damage in Haiti, led to 11 deaths in the country. In the summer of 2008, Haiti was struck with three more hurricanes in less than one month (Casselman 2008). First Hurricane Fay hit Haiti, followed by Gustav, then tropical storm Hanna, and the streak ended with Hurricane Ike. Collectively, these storms led to over 800 deaths, 10,000 people without homes, and damages estimated at tens of millions of dollars.

Despite Haiti's history of being impacted by tropical storms and hurricanes, there is very little governmental infrastructure in place to respond to these events. In fact, the Haitian Red Cross is the only national group in Haiti that responds to these occurrences. This is due in part to the support of the American Red Cross that maintains a 15 person office in Port-au-Prince that works with other Haitians in carrying disaster response activities such as evacuation, search and rescue, acute emergency care, distributing supplies, and so on. However, given the number of tropical storms and hurricanes that impact the country yearly, one disaster response network (that is not fully staffed) is clearly not enough to handle the devastating impact of these events.

With all of this devastation, there is fear and uncertainty about the future of the country. Michelle Pierre-Louis, the prime minister of the country, reported, "the whole country is facing an ecological disaster . . . We cannot keep going on like this. We are going to disappear one day. There will not be 400, 500 or 1,000 deaths. There are going to be a million deaths" (The Guardian 2008). In fact, Robert Zoellick, the president of the World Bank, reported that Haiti as a country is at "tipping point" and requires immediate attention and intervention from the world. Thus, he warned that the old Haitian saying "*bourik chaje pa ka kanpe*" (an overloaded donkey cannot stand up) may be applicable to the situation in Haiti with respect to the effect of natural disasters. Understanding the factors that lead to the vulnerability of the country may be one step in rectifying the overall impact of these tropical storms and hurricanes in Haiti.

CAUSES OF NATURAL DISASTERS IN HAITI

A number of causes have been documented as possible explanations for Haiti's high vulnerability to storms and hurricanes. Some of these include poverty, inadequate infrastructure, deforestation, and an unstable political system. Each of these areas merits their own detailed examination, which is beyond the scope of this chapter. Below is a summary of one of these factors, deforestation, as an example of the ways that such a factor can increase the country's vulnerability to storms and hurricanes (Arie 2004).

The lack of Haiti's once dense forests limits the extent to which trees can absorb the rain from tropical storms. As a result, rain is able to rush down the mountains and hills of Haiti, destroying anything in its path (Arie 2004). For example, in 1980 Haiti had 25 percent of its forests in existence, enabling the country to avoid devastation despite the heavy rain of Hurricane Emily (a category 3 storm). However, only 1.4 percent of the forests remained in 2004 and they are believed to have decreased even more in the last two years. As a result, tropical storms such as Jeanne and Gordon (which were not the same caliber as hurricanes) can cause excessive flooding (due to the lack of tree cover resulting in flooding), leading to devastation in the country. In May of 2004, more than 2,600 people were killed as result of flooding in the towns from three days of significant rain (approximately 18 inches).

Therefore, as just one example, the lack of trees (combined with the susceptibility to major tropical storms and hurricanes) in Haiti results in damaged crops and ultimately perpetuates the cycle of poverty (for those people who rely on farming as their source of income) in the face of tropical storms (Arie 2004). Although the Haitian government cannot prevent the storms from hitting Haiti, it can put systems in place that help to limit the extent to which the storms can devastate the island when they occur. For example, putting programs in place to help replace the forests that have disappeared could help to prevent such extreme and dangerous flooding from occurring. Therefore, part of the reason that Haiti is so vulnerable to disaster in the face of tropical storms and hurricanes is that the country does not have systems in place to help reduce or limit the potential damage that can occur when storms strike the island.

TRAUMATIC IMPACT FROM NATURAL DISASTERS

Disasters are commonly viewed as mass traumatic events, involving groups of people, often connected to economic and housing hardship. In the broadest sense, trauma is defined as the response a person has to what is considered a disaster, whether it is on a large scale or a more personal level (Allen 1996). A recent review of disaster studies highlights that natural disasters, technological disasters, and mass violence, including terrorism in the United States and other developed countries, and in developing countries, can have severe impacts on those affected (Norris et al. 2001). There are various forms and degrees of trauma, but it is the uncontrollable and unpredictable elements of events that often trigger traumatic responses to certain events (Nicolas et al. 2006). The current understanding of trauma needs to be broadened even further to take into account the type of responses and support that people receive when they experience traumatizing incidents, such as natural disasters. Specifically, this response trauma is broadly defined as stressors associated with a lack of support from governmental agencies following a disaster or traumatizing event (Allen 1996). Nicolas and colleagues (2008) assert that response trauma can be as traumatizing as the traumatic incident itself, if not more so, and thus must be taken into account in the assessment and treatment of individuals impacted by disastrous events. This is particularly true for Haitians, who are living in a country with limited resources for coping with natural disasters.

While hurricanes are often referred to as natural disasters, their impact is rarely natural. For example, the traumatic impact from a disaster is often associated with factors such as poverty, inequalities, and housing crises (among other factors) as opposed to the actual storm. Thus, there is a risk of providing inadequate treatment to a client impacted by a disaster without an integration of the sociocultural and political factors that are often attached to the traumatic experience of a natural disaster (Blaikie et al.

1994; Kalayjian 1995). A detailed account of the impact of natural disasters and the symptoms associated with the impact of such stressors is found in other chapters in this book. It is important to note, however, that several factors contribute to the impact of a natural disaster beyond the actual event itself and the symptoms of the individuals must be understood from a sociocultural, historical, and political perspective. Therefore, given the lack of coordinated governmental efforts in Haiti to address the devastating impact of natural disasters (as described in the previous section), it is important to consider the sociocultural, historical, economic, and political factors that are inevitable aspects of the natural disasters, as well as the strengths of the Haitian people in coping with these events.

THE SOCIOCULTURAL TRADITIONS
AND CUSTOMS OF THE HAITIAN PEOPLE

Knowledge and awareness about Haitians and Haiti predominantly comes from popular media, which unfortunately is often negative in nature. Given the stressful and essentially disastrous experiences of Haitians over the years, it is clear that as a people they have undergone extremely difficult times, politically, economically, and through natural disasters. However, as documented by many, Haitians have considerable cultural pride and are resilient when faced with distressing situations (Carroll 2007). In this section of the chapter, a summary of the main cultural strengths of Haiti and its people is provided with a specific focus on: (1) cultural traditions and customs; (2) family; (3) religion; and (4) community. An understanding and appreciation of these strengths may be useful to mental health providers and researchers working with Haitian clients who have been impacted by natural disasters, and systems that are not able to adequately deal with natural disasters.

Haitian Cultural Values

Through its difficult history, many Haitians have taken pride in believing that they are capable of overcoming many obstacles and that they have the inner strength to cope with most challenges. This belief system is largely rooted in their historical victory in defeating Napoleon's army and in freeing themselves to become the first black independent country in the Western Hemisphere. In addition to the cultural pride that many Haitians take from their historical bravery, there are many other cultural strengths characteristic of the Haitian people. First, regardless of their situation and level of poverty, Haitians will always extend kindness and hospitality to strangers. It is not unusual for Haitians to extend their only means and resources to complete strangers who are guests in their home. Directly connected to this is Haitians' tendency to use food to connect with, educate, and soothe themselves as well as others. The majority of Haitians are skillful cooks, who often will utilize food as an opportunity to connect with and provide comfort to those in need. Second, as a people, Haitians take the law very seriously and are, for the most part, followers of the law. Despite the portrayal of violence in Haiti in the media, the crime rate in Haiti is much lower than in other countries. Finally, Haitians have a strong work ethic and are often acknowledged for their dependability. Few obstacles hinder Haitians' desire to go to work and fulfill their obligations. In a similar vein, education is highly valued by Haitians, and they are willing to exceed what is necessary to ensure the upward mobility of their children, and firmly believe that the road to such mobility is through academic success. These strengths are connected to the people and are integral parts of their lives.

Cultural Elements

Haiti as a country has a strong African root, which significantly contributes to the culture of the people, including its language, music, and religion. The culture of Haitians is distinct from other ethnic groups (i.e., Latino cultures) and other Caribbean cultures. Within the fabric of Haitian culture are the artistic and musical impressions that are distinct to the Haitian people. For example, the well-known Haitian style music of compass (also known as Konpa or Kompa) is an important aspect of the Haitian culture. This musical style combines music and dance through the application of African drumming, guitars, saxophones, horn, and Creole lyrics to create music that is unique. Kompas music groups such as Tabou Combo, T-Vice, and Carimi are well known not only to the Haitian community but also to the world.

A description of the cultural strengths of Haitians would be incomplete without including the cuisine. Like the arts and religion, the traditional food of Haiti is influenced by African, Taino, and French cultures. Although food items such as rice and beans, fried pork (*griyo*), cornmeal (*mayi moulen*), bean sauce (*sòs pwa*), and fish (*poisson*) may be found in other Caribbean and Latin cultures, the herbs and spices used to created these dishes maintains the authenticity of these cuisines to the Haitian culture.

In summary, Haiti is a country that is rich in culture and cultural traditions. There are numerous strengths that have been found to be associated with Haitians and increasing awareness of these strengths is instrumental in providing culturally competent services to Haitian clients who have been exposed to a natural disaster. Although many writers have noted the cultural strengths of Haitians, few have documented the components that comprise such strengths. In addition to the cultural values, traditions, and elements, other factors such as family, religion, and community connection are important cultural strengths of Haitians that allow them to cope with the impact of natural disasters.

Family Support

Prior to the 20th century, the *lakou,* an extended family—usually defined along male lines—was the principal family form in Haiti. The term *lakou* referred not only to the family members, but also to the cluster of houses in which they lived. Members of a *lakou* worked cooperatively and they provided each other with financial and other kinds of support. Similarities in these family experiences can be seen in current Haitian families. Haitian families are not only extended and flexible (i.e. multi-generational and fluid in members), but more importantly, they also provide the fundamental foundation of Haitian life (Nicolas et al. 2008). Families (one's relatives) and households (with whom one lives) include parents and children, but also grandparents and grandchildren, uncles and aunts, cousins, and even non-blood relatives from one's hometown in Haiti (Stepick 1998). Additionally, Haitian families constitute a transitional community as they link individuals in different countries not only in Haiti and in the United States, but also in the Bahamas and Canada (Stepick 1998).

Family members support and assist each other, both instrumentally and emotionally, regardless of the distance and the individual hardship such support entails (Stepick 1998). For example, Haitians living in the United States often send goods and money to their family members who remain in Haiti. This type of support is particularly important in the face of natural disasters, when residents in Haiti are able to count on financial support, among other kinds, to help them get through the crisis situation (Nicolas et al. 2008). Thus, families are a supportive unit that is cohesive beyond oceans, borders, and natural disasters. It is incredibly important to Haitian life and should remain at the center of the discussion on strengths. In addition to family, religion has been shown to be an important aspect of the Haitian culture that warrants further investigation.

Religious Support

The literature on Haitian religion is plentiful and diverse and provides an illustration of the function of religion for Haitians in Haiti and abroad (Bibb and Casimir 1996). Although historically Catholicism was the official recognized religion in Haiti, there is an increased diversity in religious affiliations among Haitians (Bibb and Casimir 1996). In a recent study of Haitian immigrants in the United States, Nicolas and DeSilva (2008) found that Catholicism and Protestantism are the two primary religious affiliations reported by the participants. In addition, Voodoo is prevalent and has a tremendous impact on the lives of Haitians (EchodHaiti 2004). In fact, in 2003, Voodoo was formally recognized as a religion in Haiti (Bellegarde-Smith 2003). Although religion serves many functions for the individual who practices it, the overall impact of religion and spirituality transcends individuals to families and communities. For example, research has found a high connection between family and church attendance, suggesting that religion is probably a shared experience among Haitians (Nicolas and DeSilva 2008). Religion has also been shown to be associated with coping in dealing with poverty, illness, and death (Bibb and Casimir 1996; Stepick 1998). Thus, in times of psychological distress such as experiences from natural disasters, religion can serve as a protective force by providing individuals with a sense of community and a support network (Bibb and Casimir 1996; Stepick 1998).

Hence, when dealing with the devastation of natural disasters some Haitians may look towards religion as a way to cope. By having a religious or spiritual leader, people can feel as if they are getting the help they need to survive in the face of having nothing. Additionally, Christian congregations and other churches can offer support not only by providing spiritual guidance and support, but also a means of monetary and material services. Thus, it is clear that religion and the church are integral aspects of Haitians' lives that need further exploration to fully understand its influence and impact in the lives of Haitians and their communities.

Community Support

Within the United States there is the constant struggle to define sense of community and neighborhood, laboring over the specifications of notions such as boundaries and membership. Haitians, however, are more likely to have a distinct concept of community based on their way of life. The influence of neighborhoods and communities has received considerable attention as researchers attempt to understand the positive and negative impact of these systems on individual lives (Cantillon, Davidson, and Schweitzer 2003; Colombo, Mosso, and de Piccoli 2001). According to Regis (1988), the development of sense of community for English-speaking Caribbean immigrants is based in part on perceived commonalities, which include sharing a common interest in educational and economic advancement, similar experiences of adjustment and acculturation to the American way of life, shared experience of being different from Americans, and being grouped in the same category by Americans. This sense of community that immigrants develop towards each other is consistent with two of the community elements described by McMillan and Chavis (1986): membership and shared emotional connection. For Haitians, communities, in essence, combine both family and religion in creating a sense of community support for the people (Stepick 1998).

Social networks extending out from the family provide emotional and material resources as well as knowledge to each other. A norm of generalized reciprocity operates within the Haitian community (Stepick 1998). In the cities of Haiti, and around North America, people will call each other cousin, which denotes good friendship and a sense of equality. This also applies to community members that have been good neighbors for a long time (Stepick 1998). This closeness among neighbors is not only a source of support and strength; it may also be seen as a source of reference for childcare and a network for jobs. Everyone has social networks of friends and relatives, and these networks serve the purpose of exchanging goods and services as well as for conviviality (Stepick 1998). For example, social networks provide transportation to and from work and for shopping and other errands. Networks are also used to form credit associations and for informally borrowing and lending money. Among Haitians, plates and pots of cooked food are constantly exchanged across households as people express and reinforce their social ties to others in their networks of family and friends (as cited in Stepick 1998, 21; Richman 1992). Hence the Haitian community works together to take care of their own, even in troubled and desperate times. However, this sense of community may change drastically upon migration to another country such as the United States.

In examining the social support network of Haitian immigrant adults, Nicolas and colleagues (2007) found that the sense of community for Haitian immigrants in the United States is markedly different than in Haiti. For example, the participants in the project report having few family members living in their neighborhood and feeling that they did not and could not necessarily rely on their neighborhood to provide them with a sense of belonging or membership, fulfillment of their needs, or a shared emotional connection (Nicolas et al. 2007). The results from this study suggest that the social support that Haitians are accustomed to in Haiti may be lost upon migration to the United States. Nevertheless, a sense of community and obtaining and providing support to members of the community is a significant characteristic of the Haitian people that should be integrated in the understanding of the social support network of this group. This is particularly true when thinking about the experience of Haitians who have endured natural disasters and a lack of support from their government in dealing with the disaster; they can rely on their community connections to help buffer against the significant impact of natural disasters.

SUMMARY AND CONCLUSIONS

Despite the negative portrayal of Haiti and its people often depicted in the media, it is a country that is steeped in cultural traditions and strengths. An understanding of the cultural strengths of Haitians is necessary as we seek to provide services to Haitian clients in Haiti and abroad. In this chapter, we have sought to provide not only a summary of the impact of natural disasters but also an overview of the strengths of Haitians and their cultural resources as potential sources of support when dealing with natural disasters. This is a particularly important area of study given the lack of support that is offered through the Haitian government.

Haiti is a country stricken with poverty, weak infrastructure, and a history of ineffective political leadership. As a result it is vulnerable to natural disasters because of its physical location in the world, the lack of resources available to help buffer against the effects of these disasters, and the lack of preparedness for these disasters. Such vulnerabilities have significant ramifications for the country when its people are trying to cope with natural disasters. However, despite multiple devastations, Haitians continually prevail where resources such as family, religion, community, and culture help to increase their resilience. This history and these strengths, together, are the roots that continue to sustain Haiti and that allow it not only to regrow but to flourish in the midst of the storms.

REFERENCES

Allen, I. 1996. "PTSD among African Americans." In *Ethnocultural Aspects of Post-traumatic Stress Disorder: Issues, Research, and Clinical Application,* ed. Marsella, A. J., Friedman, M. J., Gerrity, E. T., and Scurfield R. 209–38. Washington, DC: American Psychological Association.

Arie, K. 2004. "Talking Point: Why is Haiti So Prone to Disaster?" Available at: http://www.alertnet.org/thefacts/reliefresources/109655418734.htm.

Bell, B., and Danticat, E. 2001. *Walking on Fire: Haitian Women's Stories of Survival and Resistance.* Ithaca, NY: Cornell University Press.

Bellegarde-Smith, P. 2003. *Vodou Is Fully Recognized as a Religion in Haiti.* Available at: http://www.hartford-hwp.com/archives/43a/522.html.

Bibb, A., and Casimir, G. 1996. "Haitian Families." In *Ethnicity and Family Therapy,* ed. M. McGoldrick, J. Giordano, and J. Pearce, 97–111. New York: The Guilford Press.

Blaikie, P., Cannon, T. Davies, I, and Wisner, B. 1994. *At Risk: Natural Hazards, People's Vulnerability and Disasters.* London: Routledge.

Cantillon, D., Davidson, W.S., and Schweitzer, J.H. 2003. "Measuring Community Social Organization: Sense of Community as a Mediator in Social Disorganization Theory." *Journal of Criminal Justice* 31: 321–39.
Carroll, D. 2007. *Live from Haiti.* Available at: http://livefromhaiti.blogspot.com/2007/02/pearl-of-antilles.html.
Carroll, R. 2008. "We Are Going to Disappear One Day." *The Guardian.* Available at: http://www.guardian.co.uk/world/2008/nov/08/haiti-hurricanes.
Casselman, B. 2008. "World News: Gustav Hits Haiti, Threatens Gulf as Course Worries Energy Industry." *Wall Street Journal* (August 27): A10.
Colombo, M., Mosso, C., and de Piccoli, N. 2001. "Sense of Community and Participation in Urban Contexts." *Journal of Community & Applied Social Psychology* 11: 457–64.
Coupeau, S. 2008. *The History of Haiti.* Westport, CT: Greenwood Press.
Desmangles, L. 2003. *Haitian Culture: Vodou, a Haitian Perspective.* Available at: www.studiowah.com/arttours/culture/religion/aboutvodou.html.
EchodHaiti. 2004. *Culture Revolution of 2004: Identity.* Available at: http://www.echodhaiti.com/culture/identity.html.
Farmer, P. 2006. *The Uses of Haiti* 3rd ed. Monroe, ME: Common Courage Press.
Glick-Schiller, N., and Fouron, G. 1990. "Everywhere We Go, We Are in Danger: Ti Manno and the Emergence of a Haitian Transnational Identity." *American Ethnologist* 17 (2): 329–347.
Gopaul-McNicol, S. 1993. *Working with West Indian Families.* New York: Guildford Press.
Heinl, R., and Heinl, N. *Written in Blood: The Story of the Haitian People 1492–1995.* New York: University Press of America.
Help for Haiti. 2008. *New York Times* (October 13, Late Edition).
Hickey, D. 1982. "America's Response to the Slave Revolt in Haiti." *Journal of the Early Republic,* 2 (4): 361–79.
Kalayjian, A. S. 1995. *Disaster & Mass Trauma: Global Perspectives on Post Disaster Mental Health Management.* Long Branch, NJ: Vista Publishers.
Knight, F. 2000. "The Haitian Revolution." *American Historical Association* 105 (1): 103–15.
Laguerre, M. S. 1989. *Voodoo and Politics in Haiti.* New York: St. Martin's Press.
Master, J. 2008. *The 31 Deadliest Tropical Cyclones for the Atlantic Ocean.* Available at: http://www.Wunderground.com/hurricane/deadly.asp.
McMillan, D.W., and Chavis, D.M. 1986. "Sense of Community: A Definition and a Theory." *Journal of Community Psychology* 14: 6–23.
Nicolas, G., DeSilva, A.M., Bejarano, and Desrosiers, A. 2007. "A Descriptive Evaluation of Religiosity among Haitian Immigrants: An Empirical Study." *Journal of Haitian Studies* 13 (2): 60–72.
Nicolas, G., DeSilva A. M, Grey, K. S, and Gonzalez-Eastep, D. 2006. "Using a Multicultural Lens to Understand Illnesses among Haitians Living in America." *Journal of Professional Psychology: Research and Practice* 37 (6): 702–7.

Norris, F., Perilla, J., Ibanez, G., and Murphy, A. 2001. "Sex Differences in Symptoms of Post-traumatic Stress: Does Culture Play a Role?" *Journal of Traumatic Stress* 14: 7–28.

Pan American Health Organization. 2004. *The Crisis in Haiti: Who Can Provide the Best Response?* Available at: http://www.disaster-info.net/newsletter/95/haiti.htm.

Partlow, J. 2008. "Across Haiti, a Scene of Devastation; Hundreds Dead, Thousands Homeless and Aid Delivery Difficult in Wake of Ike and 3 Other Storms." *Washington Post* (September 10): A08.

Portes, A., and Grosfoguel, R. 1994. "Caribbean Diasporas: Migration and Ethnic Communities." *Annals of the American Academy of Political and Social Sciences,* 533: 48–69.

Regis, H. 1988. "A Theoretical Framework for the Study of Psychological Sense of Community of English-speaking Caribbean Immigrants." *Journal of Black Psychology* 15: 57–76.

Richman, K. 1992. *They Will Remember Me in the House: The Pwen of Haitian Transnational Migration.* Doctoral dissertation, University of Virginia.

Stepick, A. 1998. *Pride against Prejudice: Haitians in the United States.* Needham Heights, MA: A Simon & Schuster Company.

Walser, R. D. 2002. "Disaster Response: Professional and Personal Journeys at the Pentagon." *The Behavior Therapist* 25: 27–30.

Ward, O. 2008. "Storms Batter Haiti: Aid Groups Struggling to Help Flood Victims after Torrential Rains Leave Hundreds Dead." *Toronto Star* (September 9): AA01.

Washington Post. 2008. "The Storms in Haiti: A Desperately Poor Country Is Devastated by Three Weeks of Violent Weather." (September 9): A22.

World Bank. 2008. *IDA at Work: Disaster Risk Management, Preparing for Natural Disasters in Haiti.* Available at: http://siteresources.worldbank.org/INTSDNETWORK/Resources/IDA_Disaster_Risk_Mgt.pdf.

Wright, F. 2000. "The Haitian Revolution." *The American Historical Review* 105 (1): 103–15.

Zéphir, F. 1996. *Haitian Immigrants in Black America: A Sociological and Sociolinguistic Portrait.* Westport, CT: Bergin & Garvey.

Chapter 7

RESILIENCE AND HEALING AMONG HELPING PROFESSIONALS AND PEOPLE OF SRI LANKA

Post Tsunami

Merry Evenson and
Jenny Dougherty

Give a man a fish and you feed him for a day; teach a man to fish and you feed him for a lifetime.

—Chinese Proverb

INTRODUCTION

This chapter examines resiliency and the healing process in helping professionals and the people in Sri Lanka after the devastation of the tsunami in 2004. Resiliency is the capacity to spring back, rebound, successfully adapt in the face of adversity, and develop social competence despite exposure to severe stress. Resilience refers to the qualities that foster a process of successful adaptation and transformation despite risk and hardship. Clark (1995) gives the following example:

> Imagine three dolls lying side by side. One doll is made of china, another is made of metal, and the third doll is made of rubber. A person strikes a hammer against each doll. The china doll shatters into a million pieces, never to be fully repaired. The metal doll is dented, but doesn't break. The rubber doll barely shows any marks and bounces back to its original shape (2).

Clark's example succinctly demonstrates the concept of resilience. Some individuals are shattered by the environmental, behavioral, and personal characteristics that are part of their lives, while others seem more vulnerable to life experiences and exhibit problematic behavior. Yet other individuals cope with their life experiences, exhibit positive behavior and seem to flourish in their abilities to thrive. The characteristics of the rubber doll and its ability to rebound successfully after pounding form the backdrop for this chapter.

The chapter focuses on helping professionals specifically and on nonprofessionals more generally. Risk factors that inhibit healthy development and work against the ability to bounce back after a tragedy of the magnitude of the 2004 tsunami are identified. Additionally, the authors address protective factors in the helpers' lives that work to enhance the ability to resist stressful life events while adapting to the situation and developing competence in coping effectively. This chapter identifies the personality characteristics and qualities of individuals who are able to go beyond helping themselves and to help others cope with a life-changing catastrophe.

A discussion of the research is included throughout the chapter and illustrates that resiliency is a long-term process of human development based on nurturance, caring relationships, and trust, as well as the development of long-term goals. Several previous research studies have identified the role of existential or spiritual well-being, religious practices, and meaning-making as contributing to the development of resilience. The instillation of hope has been cited by previous researchers as a critical therapeutic factor for mental health practitioners to consider when working with clients recovering from traumatic experiences (Feinauer, Middleton, and Hilton 2003; Valentine and Feinauer 1993; Warfield and Goldstein 1996).

Personal examples and the stories of Sri Lankan professional helpers disclosed over the course of a two-week group counseling experience and training during the summer of 2005 are interwoven throughout the previous research studies cited in this text. The helpers' personal examples of tragedy and coping strategies over the course of their lives and through their experiences with the disaster demonstrate the essence of resilience. These personal stories conveying their ability to thrive are discussed in detail. Gender and cultural differences are identified through the stories of the Sri Lankan professional helpers. The authors found that the results of studies done with males and females in the United States closely matched the anecdotal experiences shared in the counseling groups that were part of the Sri Lanka experience.

COUNSELORS TRAINING HELPING PROFESSIONALS POST-TSUNAMI

December 26, 2004, marked the date of one of the largest natural disasters in recent history for Sri Lanka, an island off the tip of India. For the

20 million people of Sri Lanka, the tsunami marked devastation for a country that has been battered for decades with civil war. The tsunami was essentially an earthquake that occurred deep in the Indian Ocean, sending waves as high as 30 to 50 feet ashore. Sri Lanka was the area most affected by the tsunami second to India. Before embarking on the stories of resilience and survival of the people of Sri Lanka, it is important to discuss how a group of Americans found themselves in the middle of this amazing country six months after the tsunami hit.

We are both counselor educators at Texas Woman's University in Denton, Texas. One of our former students, a Sri Lankan living in Dallas, called to say that her family and the people of Sri Lanka were struggling after the devastation of the tsunami. She was planning a trip to Sri Lanka to assist them and wondered if we would be willing to help train some counselors there. We organized a group of students and recent graduates to join us. So six months after the disaster, a team of six of us from Texas set out to provide information and training for two weeks in the summer of 2005. The group had expertise in processing trauma, providing basic counseling skills, teaching group counseling skills, marriage and family therapy, and play therapy.

We flew into the capital of Sri Lanka, Colombo, in July 2005. We divided up in pairs, two of us traveled to Hikkaduwa (about two and a half hours from Colombo), two went to the city of Galle (an additional hour away), and two went to the city of Matara, where the orphanage was (about three hours further away). We conducted training for helping professionals in these areas, specifically addressing how to help others recover in their communities and get beyond the devastation of the tsunami. We were surprised when 50 counselors showed up for training the first day in Hikkaduwa, 30 attended in Galle, and about 10 attended in Matara. In some of the locations, the number of counselors grew as the week progressed, so that by the end, we had conducted intense counseling skills training for a total of about 100 counselors.

Our goal was to provide mental health training to helping professionals in Sri Lanka where there were a few trained counselors, social workers, or marriage and family therapists. Instead of trained professionals, we mainly found many kind-hearted and compassionate local caregivers who wanted to help others, who called themselves counselors. Upon arriving and realizing the unprocessed trauma suffered by our participants as a result of the tsunami, we had to modify our training to some extent to meet the specific professional and personal needs of these individuals.

Much of the training focused on teaching core counseling skills, basic listening skills, understanding empathy, observing body language, group counseling skills, and a variety of topics addressed in counseling including grief, substance abuse, and sexual abuse. The group in Hikkaduwa turned out to be the largest, so we divided that group in half. We taught core counseling skills with an emphasis on healing and recovering from trauma. The focus of one of the training groups was to teach the counselors how to conduct and run a counseling group. We then ran an experiential counseling process group with the counselors to help them heal from the trauma each of them experienced personally before encouraging them to work with others. An hour each morning and afternoon was spent in didactic training to address group counseling skills while the remaining hours were spent engaged in the counseling process group with individual members. The trainees took turns sharing personal issues from the tsunami as well as traumatic experiences from earlier in life.

SRI LANKAN CULTURE AND THE TRAINING

We correctly anticipated challenges because of language barriers. Sri Lanka has three national languages: Tamil, Sinhala, and English. English and Sinhala are both spoken in Colombo, the capital. Sinhala is spoken on the southern coast, and Tamil on the eastern coast. Sinhala was the language spoken in the regions of Sri Lanka where we were doing our training. Most of the helping professionals who came for the training were Sinhalese-speaking, with a few speaking a little English. Competent local translators were arranged in advance for each team. Each training team had an interpreter except the one team that had a training counselor from Sri Lanka, who provided her own translations. When a larger number of trainees showed up than expected in Hikkaduwa, we broke into two groups and recruited translators from the ranks of counselors in training. Despite our initial concerns about the language differences, it turned out to be a manageable problem.

Western thought evaluating resilience tends to focus on resilience of the individual. However, this perspective tends to overlook important religious and cultural considerations in Sri Lanka. Of Sri Lanka's 20 million natives, 70 percent are Buddhists. As the predominant religion of this island nation, reflecting on the collectivist tenets of Buddhism may provide better understanding regarding how survivors of the 2004 tsunami found meaning and the ability to bounce back by helping and supporting others in their communities devastated by the disaster.

The concept of collectivism and social interest was a recurring theme we heard shared by the professional helpers who participated in our training. Many of the trainees came to learn from our training program because of a desire to help and assist their fellow survivors. Over and over the training counselors heard stories of communities coming together and a desire to do more for others.

RESILIENCE OF THE COUNSELORS IN MAKING SACRIFICES TO RECEIVE THE TRAINING

These were immediate lessons in resilience and resourcefulness from the counselors seeking training. They were genuinely interested in doing something for others. Most were unpaid volunteers who traveled a long distance to attend the training. Because of their own personal family struggles, many could not even afford the bus fare for transportation to attend the training and had to catch a ride wherever they could find one.

One of the trainees obtained a van and drove five men and three female helping professionals from Colombo for the training. The five young men did not even have a place to stay, but the driver worked to locate a house to accommodate the young men. The home did not have a bathroom, so the counselors in training spent their evenings, after a long day's training, putting in a bathroom for the family in exchange for the week's accommodation. We remember seeing the five men from our group swimming in the ocean outside our hotel one afternoon. We spoke to them, assuming they were relaxing and resting after the long day of training; however, we discovered later that their afternoon swim was not simply to relax and cool off, but served as their bath for the day. The three females that traveled with the van were able to find a place to stay for seven hundred rupees a night, the equivalent of seven dollars, while they were in Hikkaduwa for the training. They did not have the money for this, but one of the other trainees located the housing and covered the costs himself.

The person who provided the transportation for this group was the recruited translator for one of the groups for the week. He was a young married man who had a wife and five small children. He was a native Sri Lankan who had been living and working in Denmark for the past 18 years. His native language was Tamil but he was also fluent in Sinhala and English. After the tsunami hit, he took a year's leave of absence from his job in Denmark and brought his family to his native country to assist others by building houses.

This man, along with many other counselor trainees, went from our training to another volunteer job of helping to build houses at the conclusion of the training late each afternoon. They either helped build houses until late every evening or they worked on the home they were staying at, building a bathroom, for example, or working on some other task in exchange for their room for the week.

RESILIENCY DETERMINANTS AND RESILIENCY PROCESS

Resiliency determinants and resiliency process are two distinct concepts that have been identified in literature. Resiliency determinants refer to a combination of personality traits and environmental influences that provide individuals with protection from the detrimental psychological effects of trauma and enable them to lead satisfying and productive lives (Barnard 1994; Bogar and Hulse-Killacky 2006). Resiliency is conceptualized as an ongoing lifelong experience of bouncing back after trauma (Valentine and Feinauer 1993). More research has focused on factors influencing the development of resilience and positive outcomes for postdisaster survivors than on the lifelong process of being able to bounce back.

RESILIENCY DETERMINANTS

Resiliency factors have been identified by both practitioners and researchers to include various psychological, behavioral, and environmental factors. Several researchers have identified existential well-being and meaning-making as important factors contributing to the recovery of individuals from traumatic or abusive experiences (Feinauer, Middleton, and Hilton 2003; Valentine and Feinauer 1993; Warfield and Goldstein 1996). Individuals reported that the ability to find meaning in their lives beyond their traumatic experiences provided them with coping skills and assisted in combating feelings of shame, guilt, betrayal and powerlessness. The ability to find meaning enabled them to move past their trauma and focus on the healing process rather than on the injustice or pain resulting from their experience.

Practitioners interested in identifying and recognizing factors leading a client to develop resilience may wish to utilize and/or explore a formal psychological assessment developed by Baruth and Carroll (2002) to identify resiliency factors in individuals. The Baruth Protective Factors Inventory (BPFI) is a 16-item Likert scale inventory assessing four protective factors that the developers saw repeatedly referred to in literature delineating resiliency factors. The four protective factors in this inventory include: (a) compensating experiences, (b) fewer stressors, (c) supportive environment, and (d) adaptable personality. The development of this assessment illustrates the desire of researchers to translate identified elements of resiliency into measurable constructs that can be assessed and enhanced through the therapeutic process.

Examples of the relevance of the Baruth and Carroll protective factors could be found with the Sri Lanka trainees. One young man in his midtwenties told that he had 17 people that he felt responsible for. They lost their homes, loved ones, and all their possessions. He did not have a home large enough for all of them or the finances to build a home for all of them. He compensated by working, helping out with food, watching over them, providing guidance and support, and advising them on a daily basis.

Another example was the woman from a small fishing village who attended the counseling training. She was in her 40s and felt the need to help a family of children whose parents were killed in the tsunami. She helped them to apply for funds to have a house built. She recently discovered that a couple from Great Britain was going to be providing the funds to build them a house. She considered this a success story, and saw them as now having a chance to make it. Both of these counselors experienced great personal stress because of the tsunami, but possessed resiliency characteristics that allowed them to go beyond themselves and support others.

RESILIENCY PROCESS

The majority of research studies assessing resilience are outcome studies rather than longitudinal analyses. As a result, the subtle process of resilience is frequently overshadowed by the specific adaptive and psychological functioning of the individual at the time the research was conducted. The Discovery Health Channel and APA Practice Directorate (2002) recognized resilience as a "process of adapting well in the face of adversity, trauma, tragedy, threats, or even significant sources of stress"— such as family and relationship problems, serious health problems, or workplace and financial stressors. They describe resilience in a manner similar to Clark as a "bouncing back" from difficult experiences. This description considers resilience as a process involving several factors. It is noteworthy that resilience has consistently been identified as consisting of behaviors that can be learned rather than traits individuals inherit or have from birth.

Some of the helping professionals in Sri Lanka said that after the tsunami many people had sought their help. They described these people as being dependent on them for almost all of their needs. They described these individuals as frozen and stunned from all of the devastation and virtually immobile. They reported giving them small assignments to do, encouraged interactions with others who were handling things more actively, and even modeled the interactions that they themselves were taking. In short, without even realizing it, the helping professionals were attempting at teaching resiliency behaviors.

Resiliency process addresses actions an individual can take or has taken rather than characteristics an individual has. As mental health practitioners work with individuals postdisaster or trauma, emphasizing the process of recovery can assist in normalizing the post trauma experience and instill hope in the survivor. Although literature on resiliency process is comparatively scarce, the studies that exist emphasize the action-oriented nature of the ongoing formation of resilience. Examples of actions that have been identified as assisting in the healing process include: utilizing coping strategies such as writing, prayer, and depersonalizing the experience; committing time and energy to activities such as helping others, academic or career interests and pursuits, dedication to religion or spirituality; and achieving closure by integrating the trauma into their lives rather than merely attempting to forget about the experience.

From our experience in Sri Lanka we learned that many of these helpers were committing extensive energy to helping others. Many were in school or working to further their education and participating in the training we were offering was another example of this. One of our objectives was to help them process the trauma that each of them had experienced and to begin to heal from this. We accomplished this by teaching group counseling and by conducting personal process counseling groups for them to experience the benefits of the group process firsthand.

In another exercise to help them process the trauma, we asked them to write or talk about just what they said and did at the time of the tsunami. We then had them talk about all the senses involved—what they saw, felt, smelled, tasted, and heard. We then had them write or talk about the total impact of the tsunami, and how it was affecting or changing their lives. We emphasized the importance of feelings and encouraged them to examine and discuss all of their feelings about what had happened.

We used similar exercises on processing trauma with the children in the areas that we visited. Instead of having them write about the trauma of the tsunami, we had them draw and talk about their feelings and experiences. They talked about the huge wave they saw, the bodies they witnessed, the black water of the ocean that they never knew was this black, the horrible smells they experienced and tasted from the water, and the noise of dogs barking and people screaming and other noises they experienced before, during, and after the trauma of the tsunami. The processing of the trauma, although painful, seemed healing for those who participated.

Perhaps the most extensive study evaluating factors, outcomes, and the process of resiliency over time is the 1955 Kauai Longitudinal Study. An interdisciplinary team of public health, medical, and mental health professionals studied the development of all babies born on the Hawaiian island of Kauai. Several books and research articles have been published tracking resiliency in the lives of the 698 children in the study at 1, 2, 10, 18, and 32 years of age. The researchers evaluated the roots of resiliency in children who successfully coped with biological and psychosocial risk factors (Werner 1992).

The implications of this research for current mental health practitioners working with individuals post-trauma were extensive. The researchers asserted that the most "precious lesson that we choose to learn from this study is hope" (Werner 1992, 265). Practitioners communicated hope by promoting self-esteem and self efficacy and encouraging supportive relationships. Additionally, the researchers learned that a strong faith and involvement in church activities provided meaning for the at-risk youth on their way into adulthood. This correlation between finding meaning through religion and/or spirituality is supported by researchers and mental health practitioners time and again.

RELIGIOUS IMPLICATIONS WITH RESILIENCE

In Sri Lanka the followers of Buddhism view Buddha as a person who achieved enlightenment. The accomplished followers of Buddha's teachings are monks. For those who don't become monks, the most effective way to gain enlightenment is to accumulate merit through moral actions. They believe that if they work dutifully, support the monks, and are compassionate to other living beings, they may hope to achieve a higher birth in a future life, and from that position accumulate sufficient merit and knowledge to achieve enlightenment. Other meritorious activities include social service, reverence of Buddha at shrines, and pilgrimage to sacred places.

Gifts to monks rank among the most beneficial merit-making activities. Buddhists in Sri Lanka invite monks to major events, such as deaths in the family or celebrations, and publicly give them food and provisions. In return, the monks perform the reading of the scriptures. This accumulates merit both for the family and for the deceased family members.

After the tsunami, Sri Lankans referred to the funerals and offering of food as alms giving. They said that after a death, the family gets together and cooks a large meal to share with friends, family, and others. They invite the monks to their home to preach the Buddhist scriptures and share their food. They will then transfer merits to both the family and the person who dies, hoping to help them be in a better place in their next life. They do this after the death and funeral, again seven days later, three months after that, and every annual anniversary after the death. One Sri Lankan said that the person who has passed away can't do their own good deeds so the family and others do this for them to help them be in a better spot in the next life.

The idea of becoming a counselor or provider of social services seems to rank high in Sri Lankan religious beliefs as a means of earning merit. If an individual is able not only to bounce back from his or her own trauma after a disaster of this magnitude but also work toward helping others heal, this would contribute to the idea of resilience as well. The resilient people seemed to follow their religious beliefs faithfully, hoping for the enlightenment of others as well as themselves. This contributes to their concept of collectivism and social interest, working together toward the best interests of all.

SPECIAL POPULATIONS

When considering resiliency determinants and process, several populations have been extensively explored in literature. Additionally, the team of practitioners who traveled to Sri Lanka witnessed firsthand the influences of previous traumatic encounters experienced throughout the lives of the tsunami survivors, including prior sexual abuse, and the abundance of substance abuse problems afflicting this island nation. Considerable research has focused on survivors of sexual abuse, substance abuse recovery for individuals and their families, gender differences and cultural considerations influencing both the process of resiliency development and the behavioral and psychological outcomes. Stories provided by the professional helpers we encountered are woven throughout this portion of the chapter to provide specific examples of the impact of the tsunami and the development of resilience in this community.

SURVIVORS OF SEXUAL ABUSE

Feinauer et al.'s study (2003) of the adjustment of adults sexually abused as children explored existential and spiritual well-being as an important factor in survivors' recovery from abuses experienced in childhood. Participants reporting severe sexual abuse as children, including physical contact, physical coercion and/or intercourse, experienced less existential well-being as reported on the Adapted Measure of Existential Well-Being than adults who reported no abuse as children. Existential factors, such as having a sense of personal uniqueness, having purpose, and finding meaning in a hostile world were found to protect the victim from internalizing the shame associated with the abuse. Thus, Feinauer et al.'s hypothesis that a sense of existential well-being would provide adult survivors of childhood sexual abuse with a coping mechanism and increased resilience was supported.

Spirituality and meaning-making were cited in another study of resilience factors associated with survivors of childhood sexual abuse. The researchers found that the participants in the study reported a "remarkable philosophy of life" (Valentine and Feinauer 1993, 222). Participants reported having full-time employment, successful relationships with others, and finding a purpose in life. The ability to find supportive relationships outside the family, religion or spirituality, recognizing personal power, believing in oneself, and finding a purpose in life were stated by survivors as being crucial to peace and happiness (Kalayjian 1995; Valentine and Feinauer 1993).

The theme of spirituality and meaning-making as part of the resiliency process for adult survivors of childhood sexual abuse was again highlighted by Bogar and Hulse-Killacky's research (2006). The authors emphasized the importance of mental health practitioners conceptualizing resiliency as a process that occurs over a lifetime. This conceptualization encourages clients to see their recovery as ongoing, with expected hills and valleys of high and low periods, and communicates hope to the survivors that they can heal from their past traumatic experiences. Additionally, mental health practitioners can build their treatment plans from this conceptualization by focusing on clients' strengths rather than solely addressing their problems and past traumatic experiences.

To illustrate the idea of meaning-making and finding a purpose in life, we give the following example. On the second day of group counseling a young female counselor tearfully shared her personal story of the impact of childhood sexual abuse. She said when she was 10 years old, her mother left her and her four siblings at home to work in the Middle East. Her mother used to come home quite regularly but then stopped suddenly and did not return home for a three-year period. The young counselor said she and her siblings were terrified because they did not hear from her at all during the entire three-year period and feared she had been killed. As it turned out, the mother had gotten into some trouble with her employer and had to go into hiding over there for three years and eventually did let her family know she was okay. Despite the sense of relief she felt, the young counselor reflected on the trauma resulting from the absence of her mother and the fear that she would never return.

The counselor said she became the caretaker of her siblings starting at age 10. She reported being backed into a corner and later described this as being sexually abused. While she never used the words abused or molested, she described herself as "an object to others." Her fellow Sri Lankan group members readily understood her to mean that she had been sexually violated by others. The words molested, abused, or raped are not used in Sri Lankan culture. She reported turning to several sources to assist in overcoming her feelings of pain and shame, some positive and others harmful. She reported that that she was constantly looking for love from others that she did not have from her parents. She reported that she then became an object to other people too.

Positive coping skills that helped her deal with her early childhood trauma included her gifts of dance and music. Additionally, she cited her religious dedication and described her current work as a warden in a bible school.

This young woman's sense of resilience developed from caretaking for her younger siblings and her religious faith. They are now being played out in her ability to reach out to protect and assist other children.

Through the group experience, the young woman was free to reflect on her feelings of shame and pain. The level of empathy and understanding among the group members was demonstrated nonverbally throughout her story. A determination to assist others has enabled this woman to bounce back first from childhood sexual abuse and now the tsunami. Her resilience and her ability to work on her own issues, and share her pain with others, demonstrated her desire to contribute to the healing of others experiencing similar painful experiences and shame.

SUBSTANCE ABUSE

Researchers examining the effects of substance abuse on children and families of alcoholics have identified several risk factors, including parental depression, unhealthy family functioning, punitive parenting, violent and unpredictable interactions, and greater incidence of both psychological and life stress (Barrera, Hageman, and Gonzales 2004). Factors contributing to the sense of resilience among families of alcoholics included sibling attachments; nonalcoholic mother-child relationships; relationships with other adults including grandparents, aunts, uncles, teachers and mentors; and internal belief systems. The sibling attachments found in alcoholic families were the most important resiliency determinate in families of alcoholics.

The emphasis on spiritual well-being as a factor in the recovery and resilience of alcoholics is evidenced by the conceptual model of spirituality infused in the Alcoholics Anonymous 12-step rehabilitation program. Alcoholics Anonymous creates a fellowship among participants that leads to the development of a safe and supportive environment that allows vulnerability, openness, trust, and the exploration of spirituality (Warfield and Goldstein 1996). Warfield and Goldstein asserted that the spiritual component of Alcoholics Anonymous is essential to the alcoholic's recovery. One Alcoholics Anonymous member put it this way, "when positive spirituality dominates our lives, we have no need to alter our moods with addictive substances or behaviors" (Warfield and Goldstein 199).

One Sri Lankan counselor shared his personal experience with substance abuse. He described how his father died in his arms prior to the tsunami. In vivid detail, as though reliving the experience, he shared how his father gasped for air and then died and how deeply haunted he has felt ever since. To cope with his pain he reported turning to drug abuse. While he no longer abuses drugs, he was struggling at the time of the training with the realization that others in his community had not accepted the fact that he had changed, and still view him as an addict. He approached the group with the desire to enlist their guidance in helping him show others his change. The group supported and encouraged him to believe in himself and to mourn for the loss of his father, as the drug abuse had robbed him of the opportunity to experience this. In another example of resilience, this young man reported a strong desire to work with others struggling with drug and alcohol abuse.

GENDER ISSUES

Differences exist in the coping strategies for adolescent girls and boys. Some researchers suggest that adolescent girls experience greater vulnerability to life stress than adolescent boys (Barrera et al. 2004). When struggling with problems, boys tend to direct their behavior towards others while girls tend to turn inward. Research indicates that more girls than boys report sexual and physical abuse, emotional stress, poor body images, struggles with eating disorders, and that they have attempted suicide. Boys, on the other hand, tend to externalize their problems and have reported committing delinquent acts, engaged in unprotected sex, and have consumed excessive amounts of alcohol and other drugs (Barrera et al. 2004). Despite cultural differences from the groups studied by Barrera, the stories told in the group setting in Sri Lanka tended to support the fact that the females reported more sexual and physical abuse issues, as well as emotional stress, and that the males dealt with their problems externally through drugs and alcohol or other means of delinquency-type acting out.

The risk-taking behaviors frequently reported by adolescents may be prevented by identifying and enhancing protective factors such as self-esteem, a close relationship with a parent or another adult, and educational aspirations. Clark (1995) compared protective factors to a car's air bags. Such airbags are always available, but only used during a crash situation. Another way to look at protective factors is to compare them to health insurance. Most policies cover a variety of illnesses, including emergency procedures. Just because you are covered for an appendectomy on your policy doesn't mean you are going to have one. Like health insurance, protective factors need to be in place prior to their need.

Additional protective factors in developing resiliency were divided by Clark into individual-related protective factors, family-related protective factors, peer-related protective factors, school–related protective factors, and community-related protective factors. Some of the factors that work toward building resilience in all of the above helping professionals include having: (a) problem-solving skills, (b) intellectual ability, (c) self-esteem with self-efficacy, (d) social/interpersonal skills, (e) strong ability to use faith, (f) value in helping others, (g) appropriate coping skills, (h) having a close relationship or bond with at least one person, (i) positive peer relationships, (j) achievement aspirations, and (k) belonging to a supportive community. The counselors in training seemed to have a large number of the above factors working toward resilience. They somehow developed a number of individual, environmental, and social safeguards that enhanced their abilities to resist stressful events while coping with the situation and developing competence in dealing with it.

A man in his late 60s helped to clarify some of the gender issues relative to resiliency among the people in poor Sri Lankan fishing villages. He said that much of the need for change with this very poor region of the county centers on the women of Sri Lanka. He described the majority of the males in this specific region as usually attending school through the 8th or 9th grade while on the average females usually dropped out of school in the 5th grade to care for their siblings and families. He described the women as hard working, and frequently both the breadwinners and the nurturers of the children. On the surface and to the world, the men are leaders and decision makers, but, according to him, the women hold the real power. He said that many of the Sri Lankan men in these deprived areas may earn money, but little of it goes to the family. Instead, the men frequently use the money on their own recreation, hobbies, betting, alcohol, or drugs.

Many females in the most economically deprived fishing villages of Sri Lanka start having their own families as young as 13 and 14 years of age. When these young women cannot find work in Sri Lanka, they travel to the Middle East to become maids, leaving their children at home alone with their husbands. The children usually are not well cared for, and their father is often absent. As a result, rapes, molestation, and abuse of the children occur. He said that once the mothers are out of the home, others often come in and take advantage of their absence. His belief is that the key to helping the children of these poor fishing villages in Sri Lanka is to stay in school longer to get a better education so they can get better jobs in their own country. Another key is to find employment opportunities in Sri Lanka for the women. After the tsunami, many females and mothers were killed, so even more children were left at home unsupervised, and report of an increased number of rapes has been occurring as a result.

The man who described this situation did not fit the norm of the Sri Lankan male he depicted above. He retired a few years ago from a very good job in Colombo. He had recently come out of retirement to help build 25 homes after the tsunami hit. He described a donor from Texas who contacted him to coordinate an effort to build homes in a community outside of Hikkaduwa as a volunteer job. The Texas donor was a teacher and a single parent who donated $80,000 for a housing project shortly after the Tsunami hit. She donated $30,000 to buy the land to build on and $50,000 to actually build the homes. The $50,000 represented $2000 per home. It was his job to be the building superintendent of the 25 homes. Masons and plumbers were hired to assist with the building, but the rest of the work was being done by unpaid volunteers. He continued to live in Colombo, but drove the three hours to Hikkaduwa for the week to coordinate and supervise the building project. He managed to find time to come and attend the counseling training during the day, and would return to the building site immediately after the training each day until the evening.

The resiliency and level of support that this man had to help others, even at this stage in his life, was impressive. It was heartwarming to witness not only the commitment of this counselor but also the dedication and spirit of the many counselors-in-training who joined him to volunteer as home-builders by night.

CULTURAL CONSIDERATIONS

In the wake of international disasters, relief teams from around the world rally to assist global neighbors. Understanding the customs and traditions concerning grief, trauma, loss, and healing are essential considerations for relief teams and mental health practitioners postdisaster. Godakanda (2006), a Sri Lanka native, wrote of her experience conducting therapy groups for tsunami survivors and her personal experience working to keep the Sri Lankan culture in perspective throughout her work. Despite being a Sri Lankan native, Godakanda spoke frankly about the conscious effort she made to keep Sri Lankan cultural considerations in the forefront of her mind after having spent more than a decade living in the United States. The personal reflection and necessity of reminders to continually observe, respect, and integrate cultural sensitivity and reactions in her work is a call to action for all mental health practitioners working on a global stage.

Godakanda illuminated some key issues when working with the Sri Lankan people. Communication style was one of the issues. For example, nonverbal communication styles, including eye contact, pace of conversation, body language, and facial expressions, are more essential to conversation than the spoken word. Principles of collectivism are exemplified by the importance of the extended family and the tendency of emotions to be other-focused rather than self-focused. Religious ceremonies and rituals assist individuals in coping with anxiety and dealing with grief (Godakanda 2006).

THE LIFELONG PROCESS
RESILIENCY EXEMPLIFIED

The people who participated in the Sri Lankan counselor training personify the lifelong process of resiliency. They overcame great odds just to travel to our location. From there, they struggled to find adequate shelter. They embraced a desire to help others and reach outside of their own personal struggles resulting from the tsunami.

Each of the stories detailed in this chapter reflect prior traumas experienced by the counselors in training, including drug abuse, sexual assault, and family tragedy. Through the religious dedication, and desire, even necessity, to care for others, these individuals developed the resiliency to bounce back in life after experiencing the trauma of the tsunami. The support the counselors in training offered to one another during our week-long training further assisted each of them in their development of resilience and ability to find the strength to support and assist others in their communities.

IMPLICATIONS FOR MENTAL
HEALTH PRACTITIONERS

Mental health practitioners are encouraged to see resilience as a process rather than a targeted outcome. "Resilience refers to the capacity to meet life's challenges; it does not mean that one is happy or free from emotional turmoil" (Monaghan-Blout 1996). It is essential for mental health practitioners to conceptualize resilience as a lifelong process, which was clearly personified during our training experience. The individuals we met who shared prior personal tragedies were struck again by tragedy in the form of the tsunami, yet again they found the resiliency to move forward and assist others.

This conceptualization of resiliency as a process parallels the therapeutic relationship as a process itself. Practitioners striving to manage their client's expectations would be prudent to share the concept of resilience as a lifelong process of meeting life's challenges rather than an end goal of achieving happiness. Those we worked with needed the support they received during the training experience. Their desire to continue the process of meeting life's challenges was verified by their participation in the training.

Although much research has focused on determinants of resilience, other researchers have cautioned against conceptualizing resilience merely as personal attributes. Instead, resilience may be best understood as an individual's capacity to negotiate through the challenges of life based on the relationship between personal attributes, past experiences, and current life circumstances (Bogar and Hulse-Killacky 2006; Monaghan-Blout 1996). Bogar and Hulse-Killacky called for future research into resiliency to focus on the process of developing resilience.

Rather than treating it as a constant that functions across the lifespan, Monaghan-Blout asserted that more sophisticated research designs and statistical analyses are needed in future research to describe the process of resilience. As evidenced by the stories presented here, resilience was not always a constant throughout the lives of these individuals. Many of the counselor trainees reported harmful behaviors, including sexual risk taking and substance abuse, along their journey through recovery from traumatic experiences prior to developing the level of coping skills they currently exhibited.

A concept reiterated throughout literature is the importance of meaning-making in the development of resilience and the ability to bounce back postdisaster or trauma. Making meaning out of the disaster through roots in spirituality, faith, or religious practice was reported by survivors as significant to their recovery.

CONCLUDING THOUGHTS

As we reflect back on this experience, we continue to feel amazed by the genuineness, warmth, and compassion for others that we witnessed in the Sri Lankan people. Perhaps one reason for our amazement is that we were conceptualizing resilience from our western viewpoint. The individuals we met in Sri Lanka clearly lived by the social interest and collectivist teaching of Buddhism and other eastern philosophies. Their philosophy is to assist others quietly and spiritually for the betterment of all. The insurmountable loss that the people of that country experienced is difficult to explain. We hope the experiences and stories of resilience of the Sri Lankan people will serve as examples of the courage, strength and personal qualities and progressive process that is required to bounce back after a tragedy of the magnitude of the tsunami.

REFERENCES

Barnard, C. P. 1994. "Resiliency: A Shift in Our Perception?" *The American Journal of Family Therapy* 22: 135–44.

Barrera, M., Hageman, D., and Gonzales, N. 2004. "Revisiting Hispanic Adolescents' Resilience to the Effects of Parental Problem Drinking and Life Stress." *American Journal of Community Psychology* 34: 83–94.

Baruth, K. E., and Carroll, J. J. 2002. "A Formal Assessment of Resilience: The Baruth Protective Factors Inventory." *The Journal of Individual Psychology* 58: 235–44.

Bogar, C. B., and Hulse-Killacky, D. 2006. "Resiliency Determinants and Resiliency Process among Female Adult Survivors of Childhood Sexual Abuse." *Journal of Counseling and Development* 84: 318–27.

Clark, P. 1995. "Risk and Resiliency in Adolescence: The Current Status of Research on Gender Differences." *Equity Issues* 1 (1): 2–13.

Discovery Health Channel & APA Practice Directorate. 2002. *The Road to Resilience.* [Brochure]. Washington, DC: American Psychological Association.

Feinauer, L., Middleton, K. C., and Hiton, H. G. 2003. "Existential Well-Being as a Factor in the Adjustment of Adults Sexually Abused as Children." *The American Journal of Family Therapy* 31: 201–13.

Godakanda, H. 2006. "Cultural Considerations." *Family Therapy Magazine* (March/April): 26–29.

Kalayjian, A. S. 1995. *Disaster & Mass Trauma: Global Perspectives on Post Disaster Mental Health Management.* Long Branch, NJ: Vista Publishers.

Monaghan-Blout, S. 1996. "Reexamining Assumptions about Trauma and Resilience: Implications for Intervention." *Psychotherapy in Private Practice* 15 (4): 45–68.

Valentine, L., and Feinauer, L. L. 1993. "Resilience Factors Associated with Female Survivors of Childhood Sexual Abuse." *The American of Family Therapy* 21: 216–24.

Warfield, R. A., and Goldstein, M. B. 1996. "Spirituality: The Key to Recovery from Alcoholism." *Counseling and Values* 40: 196–205.

Werner, E. 1992. "The Children of Kauai: Resiliency and Recovery in Adolescence and Adulthood." *Journal Adolescent Health* 13: 262–68.

Chapter 8

A DISASTER OUTREACH PROGRAM FOR TSUNAMI SURVIVORS IN SRI LANKA

The Biopsychosocial, Educational,
and Spiritual Approach

Ani Kalayjian,
Nicole Moore,
Judy Kuriansky, and
Chris Aberson

It is through creating, not possessing, that life is revealed.
—Vida D. Scudder

ABSTRACT

This chapter describes the Mental Health Outreach Program (MHOP) for tsunami survivors using a bio-psychosocial, educational, and spiritual approach. The MHOP model is built on the principle that an important element in the healing and rehabilitation of postconflict/disaster survivors and communities is to have their voices heard, to process feelings and to build community resilience. The approach is based on extensive trauma recovery work done in countries around the world. Teams of trauma experts traveled to a community in northeastern Sri Lanka, where survivors were suffering not only from the tsunami but also from years of civil war. Groups of survivors, either self-selected or identified by the officials where they were living, participated in group sessions and were assessed for levels of post-traumatic stress disorder (PTSD), based on their scores on the revised Reaction Index Scale (RIS/R).

The results showed a high level of PTSD, and the level of PTSD was correlated with the ability to discover clear-cut goals and satisfying life purpose, and with the ability to find meaning, purpose, or a mission in life. The implications of these findings are discussed, including the importance to survivors of information about the nature of the event and reassurance about the normalcy of their feelings. The present outreach experience and study reinforces the importance of identifying at-risk individuals postdisaster and suggests the usefulness of a biopsychosocial and spiritual model of intervention for psychoeducational purposes.

INTRODUCTION

On the morning of December 26, 2004, an earthquake registering 9.0 on the Richter scale struck 12 countries in the regions of Southeast Asia and Africa. The colossal earthquake shook the earth's layers off the western coast of the Indonesian island of Sumatra and set off shock waves felt more than 3,000 miles away on the coast of East Africa (Elliott 2005). Less than an hour later, a major tsunami resulted in massive destruction, extensive loss of lives and livelihood. The regions most devastated included southern India, Indonesia, Thailand, and Sri Lanka.

In Sri Lanka, 39,000 people, out of a population of 20 million, were drowned by crashing walls of water or killed by uprooted houses, boats, vehicles and debris (Elliott 2005). In addition, approximately 800,000 people were displaced and 518,000 people lost their homes. They relocated to friends' and relatives' residences or were housed in temporary shelters comprised of public buildings, schools and makeshift camps (Prasad 2005). The availability of psychological services in Sri Lanka is limited. There are reportedly 40 psychiatrists in a country of 19.9 million people, mostly concentrated in the southwestern part of the island near the capital of Colombo (Ziffer 2005). Batticaloa, a town on the northeast coast hit hard by the tsunami and the area selected for this outreach by the Director of the Mental Health Outreach Program (MHOP), has a population of over 2.5 million people and only one psychiatrist.

MHOP is one of the programs of the Association for Disaster & Mass Trauma Studies, a nonprofit organization based in New York with chapters in other countries. One of the goals of MHOP is to provide mental health interventions for survivors of disasters in order to reduce negative psychological after-effects of trauma. The project has provided psychosocial relief after catastrophes such as earthquakes, floods and other disasters in Armenia, the Dominican Republic, Japan, Pakistan, Turkey, the United States, and other countries. After the impact of the tsunami in Sri Lanka, the MHOP team was actively engaged in the Batticaloa district, providing psychosocial support to empower survivors and support their ability to help themselves. The MHOP model is built on the principle that an important element in the healing and rehabilitation of postconflict/disaster survivors and communities is to have their voices heard, to process feelings and to build community resilience.

In this chapter, the authors present the outcome of the application of the MHOP model in Sri Lanka after the tsunami, discuss the psychosocial and spiritual impact of the tsunami on survivors, describe important steps in developing a culturally sensitive outreach program, and offer lessons learned from biopsychosocial, psychoeducational and spiritual programs that can be applied to other disasters.

LITERATURE REVIEW

Statistics from the Red Cross Society suggest that Asia is the most disaster-prone area of the world, partly because of its geographic location in relation to earthquakes (Kokai et al. 2004). While natural disasters can cause a wide range of psychological distress, studies of psychological outcome in this region are limited, partly due to the fact that psychiatry and psychology are not well recognized in these countries (Kokai et al. 2004).

There is limited research on the psychological effects of tsunamis in particular, but there is growing evidence about the mental health outcome of similar natural disasters, such as earthquakes in Asia, Armenia, and Turkey, and hurricanes in the United States (Kalayjian 1995; Kokai et al. 2004). These reports show that the impact of mental health on survivors by conditions such as those that occurred as a result of the Asian tsunami can be significant and long-lasting (Norris et al. 2005; Norris and Kaniasty 1996). These conditions include the magnitude of the disaster, high prevalence of injury and deaths, severe economic decline, and destroyed social networks. The severity and duration of these effects would necessitate a long-term recovery plan.

Previous studies have also shown that victims of natural disasters may suffer a wide range of psychological difficulties. These can include depressive symptoms (including major depressive disorder and dysthymia), a range of anxiety disorders, and other adjustment disorders (Doherty 1999; Elhai, North, and Frueh 2005; Norris et al. 2005; Stevens and Slone 2005). Clinical and subclinical post-traumatic stress disorders (PTSD) are among the most common psychiatric and psychological disorders to develop in survivors after a natural disaster (Lantz and Buchalter 2005). Commonly experienced PTSD symptoms include fear, helplessness, hyperarousal, emotional numbing, re-experience of the trauma through images and flashbacks, and avoidance of people, places, and things that recall the experience (Rosen et al. 2001). Some individuals may reduce social involvement with others and lose interest in previously enjoyed activities. These symptoms may become chronic and interfere with the ability to function in society (Davidson 2001; Yehuda 2002).

In some cases, survivors may not display symptoms immediately, but suffer from delayed-onset PTSD, which develops six months or more following the traumatic event (Davidson 2001; Yehuda 2002). Maladaptive behavior patterns, such as substance abuse disorders, can also manifest and exacerbate the primary effects of the trauma. The manifestation of these conditions supports the importance of early identification of traumatic symptoms (Brown, Stout, and Mueller 1999; Miller et al. 2004; Rosen et al. 2001; Stewart 1996). Given these findings one can predict that in severe disasters such as the Asian tsunami, many survivors would suffer from an array of psychiatric problems.

It has been recognized that interventions treating trauma-related psychiatric difficulties in survivors must be explored within the local cultural context, since the manifestation of symptoms may differ (Doherty 1999). Thus, international NGOs and other projects must be sensitive to the particular cultural, moral, religious, communal, economic, and familial context of the local population.

Socioeconomic status (SES), as manifested in education, income, literacy, or occupational prestige, was found to affect PTSD outcomes significantly in 11 samples of studies of disaster victims. In 10 (91%) of these samples lower SES was consistently associated with greater postdisaster distress. The effect of SES has been found to grow stronger as the severity of exposure increases (Freedy, Resnick, and Kilpatrick 1994).

RISK FACTORS FOR PTSD

Research has shown that half of the people affected by natural disasters will be resilient and bounce back after a few months (Stevens and Slone 2005). In addition, Bonanno (2004) suggested that resilience occurs more commonly than once thought when people are faced with loss or trauma. Although the factors that lead to resilience are not clear, coping skills, scale of the traumatic event, demographic characters, personal and social resources, and the existing life stress before the trauma may predict resilience (Bonanno and Mancini 2008). However, despite this resilience and the fact that a majority of survivors will not develop clinical levels of psychiatric disorders, the trauma can result in nonspecific distress and chronic problems related to daily living (Norris et al. 2005). Health problems (somatic complaints and verified medical conditions) surface frequently, with an increase in reported sick days from work, elevations in stress levels, sleep deprivation, and a decline in immune functioning (Norris et al. 2005). Therefore, along with the potential risk factors, religion and capacity for meaning-making will be examined in this research.

It is imperative, therefore, for mental health workers to be able to identify people most at risk for developing psychopathology and to focus on helping these people overcome adversity. An extensive literature review reveals that several factors—being female, having a previous history of trauma related events, and having a PTSD diagnosis—contribute to increased service use (Elhai et al. 2005). Stevens and Slone (2005) noted that studies of natural disasters identified the following risk factors for PTSD: gender and family variables (women and girls more affected than men or boys), individual functioning, lack of social support, and increased exposure to the disaster. According to Davidson (2001, 2004), women were two times (10–14% PTSD) more likely to develop PTSD than men (5–6% PTSD).

Other risk factors that have been found to predict PTSD and adverse outcomes include bereavement, injury, or life threat to self or another family member, panic or similar emotions during the disaster, horror, separation from family, loss of property and displacement (Pynoos et al. 1987; Stevens and Slone 2005; Vogel and Vernberg 1993). These can be seen to apply to the situation in Batticaloa, Sri Lanka, since everyone in the community was subjected to grave threat, experienced panic or similar extreme emotions, as well as bereavement. In some cases, survivors lost all their family members or property.

Another major factor determining risk and the outcome for recovery is the extent of social support (Stevens and Slone 2005). Stevens and Slone state "disasters occurring in developing countries cause more numerous and severe mental health consequences than disasters in developed countries" (27). This is partly because these areas have limited amounts of resources to assist people, which makes the damage of any existing system and structure of social support more dangerous and an impediment to recovery. In Batticaloa, the high number of deaths destroyed the social support systems as communities were torn apart by the tsunami, families and friends were displaced, and people were required to move to other areas or to live in refugee camps. Destruction of bridges and roads exacerbated the separation and loss of connections between people (Stevens and Slone 2005).

The role of other demographic factors has been disputed. Findings are contradictory about whether age is a determinant to developing psychopathology, whereby some studies suggest that younger age is a risk factor, with affected children at risk of developing adult-like PTSD, depression, anxiety disorders, and a range of developmental delays (Doherty 1999; Elhai et al. 2005). Intelligence and education level have also been proposed as potential risk factors for psychopathology postdisaster, but research in this area has also produced ambiguous findings (Elhai et al. 2005; Litz et al. 2005).

In addition, there are studies that examined the effect of cultural, eth-nic, or religious background after traumatic stress events. According to de Silva (2006), Hispanic veterans of the Vietnam War reported about twice as many stress symptoms as whites. Various researchers have also exam-ined the ethnic and cultural differences and reported that vulnerability to stress seems to exist when compared to numerous people with different culture and race. In addition, Hatthakit and Thaniwathananon (2007) ex-amined the Buddhist survivors of the 2004 tsunami in Asia, and reported that Buddhist concepts, such as Law of Nature and Law of Karma, tend to influence the view of the survivors after disaster in a positive manner. Therefore, it is likely that the concept and practice of each religion has an influence on the aftermath of disasters.

An example of the spiritual rituals used in the tsunami group intervention is mindfulness. This practice involves focusing attention on the breath to access inner resources for healing. A meta-analysis of 20 empirical studies proved its effectiveness in alleviating suffering associated with physical psychosomatic symptoms (many of which were reported by the tsunami survivors) and psychological distress (Grossman et al. 2004). The process is becoming more mainstream but is very consistent with the cultural prac-tices of the region, which avoids direct expression of emotions and instead turns inward to attain a quiet mind. The practice is akin to a type of med-itation, and consistent with mind-body techniques which are becoming more popular throughout the world. Focused breathing used in the tsunami group intervention is a recognized part of such mind-body techniques, as is imagery to direct the mind to positive outcomes. The effectiveness of this approach has been shown in one study, where such mind-body tech-niques were used with youngsters in Kosovo to treat post-traumatic stress disorder in the postwar situation (Gordon et al. 2004). Assessment of 139 participants in a six-week program that included meditation and breath-ing techniques showed significant decreases in post-traumatic stress scores after completion of the program, proving that such skills are effective in reducing these symptoms in a war-traumatized population.

Another common religious activity is prayer. The word prayer is derived from the Latin precari, which means to entreat. Prayer may be defined as an intimate conversation with a higher being for the purpose of implor-ing or petitioning for something or someone. Prayer is the most common practice in all religious systems. "Generally prayer, understood as a human communication with divine and spiritual entities, has been present in most of the religions in human history" (Eliade 1987). "Prayer serves many functions including invocation, adoration, thanksgiving, confession, or re-pented sin and petition. Petition may be both for one's needs and in prayer of intercession, for the needs of others. It may be a request for material or spiritual benefit" (Grant 1995).

Praying is practiced in all faiths and by people of all societies. Prayer may be performed using words. These prayers may be ones that were created by others and memorized. Praying can also be done without words. These prayers are usually mental, and require meditation. Prayer can be either directed or nondirected. Directed prayer is used when one prays for a specific and positive outcome. Nondirected prayer is used when one prays to have the ability to accept the outcome. The main ingredient in prayer is concentration, or detachment from all thoughts other than those that are the focus of the prayer. Saying prayers for another individual is known as intercessory prayer. These prayers maybe intended either for someone in close proximity or someone at a great distance. Intercessory prayers transcend the boundaries of time and space (Dossey 1993).

Prayer can be a mind-body healing intervention. The mind is responsible for what one thinks or believes, and it can have either a positive or negative effect on one's health (Cousins 1998). However, the mind can have significant influences on one's healing. Prayer has played a vital role in healing for various cultures throughout history. Many of the religious traditions, including Christianity, Hinduism, Buddhism, and Islam, confirm the interconnection between the self and the source of all beings (Dossey 1996).

Prayer is the ancient healing practice. It is the simple act of turning the mind and heart to the revered. There does not have to be a belief in one higher god. In Christianity, Judaism, and Islam there is a belief in one god, as opposed to Hinduism, which has belief in many gods. The most passive forms of prayer fall into the general area of meditation, although there are degrees of activity here as well. Meditation is used in all religious traditions to calm the mind. Other common meditation techniques are attention to breath, concentration on a fixed image, guided imagery, and mindfulness.

Dr. Herbert Benson from Harvard Medical School researched the health benefits of prayer and meditation. Dr. Benson identified and named the relaxation response. The relaxation response "is a scientifically definable state in which metabolism, breathing, and heart slow, blood pressure drops, and brain waves become less active" (Benson 1996). This study proved that the relaxation response was most effectively elicited through different forms of prayer. He states that a "person's belief system", or what he called the faith factor is actually responsible for producing healing by itself (Benson 1996). Meditation has been shown to produce very beneficial physical effects. Meditation can produce a series of physical reactions that could be characterized as a relaxation response. Meditation can lower respiratory rates, heart rates, blood pressure, and skin temperature, as well as having a positive effect on alleviating pain, nausea, vomiting, and insomnia (Benson 1996). Prayer and/or meditation seem to have a very positive, physical effect. In essence prayer/mediation creates a relaxation response.

As the majority of people affected by the tsunami were exposed to a multitude of risk factors, it is anticipated that they will suffer higher rates of PTSD and other mental illnesses than prior to the natural disaster. The present study aims to further specify risk factors associated with psychopathology after natural disasters.

Based on these findings, the following hypotheses were made:

1. Scores for the majority of participants on a scale of post-traumatic stress disorder (the RIS/R) would indicate moderate to severe levels of PTSD

2. Less educated people would have higher scores on the RIS/R scale compared to more educated people

3. Those participants who were more exposed to the event would have higher scores on the RIS/R scale

4. With regard to religion, Hindus would have lower scores on the RIS/R scale compared to other religions, specifically, Christians

5. There would be a correlation between the scores on the RIS/R scale and the ability to find meaning in life after the tsunami as well as the ability to find clear-cut goals

NEED FOR PSYCHOSOCIAL INTERVENTION

The extent of possible primary and secondary maladaptive outcomes to disasters such as the Asian tsunami suggests the need for extensive multilevel interventions for those affected. Failure to provide psychosocial intervention for affected individuals can be financially, socially, and psychologically costly in the long run.

A multitude of guidelines for psychological response to disasters has been devised by various researchers and agencies to assist in international intervention efforts (Cohen 2000; Doherty 1999; Dudley-Grant, Mendez, and Zinn 2000; Weine et al. 2002). Such guidelines address the contextual challenges faced by communities during or after trauma, establish values on which mental health workers should base interventions and establish core curricular elements of interventions in order to improve future training (Weine et al. 2002). For example, proper training of mental health workers, establishing social support groups, and promoting community education about the trauma is suggested to serve as a protective function for those affected (Doherty 1999; Dudley-Grant et al. 2000; Norris and Kaniasty 1996; Weine et al. 2002). A goal of MHOP is to provide psychosocial support within the context of preventive healthcare in order to limit incidences of mental health problems after such a crisis.

METHOD

Participants

Two hundred and fifty survivors of the Asian tsunami (about two-thirds females and one-third male) participated in the MHOP program. Participants were self-selected, selected by the camp directors or by the SHADE psychosocial team, according to the criteria that those participating be identified as receptive or needing psychological assistance. As the MHOP presence became more visible, participants volunteered because of word of mouth and referrals from past participants. Several groups were run specifically for those survivors who were identified by camp staff as having lost family members.

Two to four groups were held daily, consisting of 10 to 30 people, for a period of two to three-and-a-half hours each. Adult groups consisted of individuals of varying age, socioeconomic status and family constellation (whether or not family members had died). In some cases, several members of the same family were present. Children's groups were also held, which were diverse in terms of age, socioeconomic status and family constellation (presence of siblings and whether or not family members had died).

Thirty-four people filled out the revised Reaction Index Scale (RIS/R). Due to incomplete scales, responses of 24 subjects were used for the present analysis. Of the 24 respondents, 63 percent were men and 37 percent were women. The majority had high school education (58%) with the remaining having either grammar school (29%) or no education (13%). Most were unemployed at the time of the evaluation (83%). Prior to the tsunami, the majority of the men were employed as fishermen and the majority of women were housewives. With regard to marital status, half were single and half were married. The majority (37%) of the respondents were between 30 to 39 years old, followed by 21 percent of the group who were 20 to 29 years old, 21 percent who were 40 to 49 years old, and 17 percent who were under 20 years old. The most common religion was Hindu (67%), followed by Christian (21%) and Roman Catholic (8%), with one respondent who did not indicate religious affiliation.

CULTURAL SENSITIVITY

The program placed emphasis on cultural sensitivity, a factor that is widely recognized as important in international settings. Cultural sensitivity was accomplished by consultation with professionals in the trauma and psychological fields who were native Sri Lankans, contacts with professional organizations, personal contacts, meetings at the United Nations about the tsunami relief efforts, and inclusion of a native Sri Lankan as part of the MHOP team. Special consideration was given to the impact of religion on coping, culture-specific forms of communication, willingness to share feelings with strangers, the impact of political upheaval, and cultural views on the cause of natural disasters.

In Sri Lanka, prayer was a powerful tool for coping. Most people, no matter if they were Muslim, Christian, or Hindu, prayed to a higher power during this tragic time. They may have prayed for understanding, strength, health, or their loved one who had passed. Prayer was also a piece that the team used in the six step Biopsychosocial-Spiritual model. Prayer was sometimes used as a therapeutic step to work with the people to process and help them find meaning in their lives. In particular, prayer can provide a refuge, solace, strength, comfort, and guidance (Drugay 1992). Prayer offers meaning to life. Involvement in meaningful activities is a crucial factor in preservation of the self (Tobin 1999). In the breathing and movement exercises, meditation and/or mindful breathing was taught. Prayer and meditation were therapeutic interventions that can produce overall positive health outcomes both physically and mentally.

CHOICE OF LOCATION

The choice of location, Batticaloa, a town on the northeast coast of Sri Lanka, was made on the basis of the following criteria: it was an area underserved by other nongovernmental organizations or services, given that a majority of local professionals and governmental organizations were located in the more southern areas of the island; the extent of devastation; and a history of over 25 years of conflict between the government and a rebel force called the Liberation Tigers of Tamil Eelam (LTTE), otherwise known as the Tamil Tigers.

Local people who were proficient in English and Tamil were identified to serve as translators. These individuals needed to possess strong communication skills and empathy, and made a commitment for a one-year period to work with the MHOP teams and insure continuity of care. Translators included an administrator of the YMCA, a local basketball coach, and a 25-year-old computer technician who had been living in one of the camps. An additional trained translator was a female school guidance counselor.

INSTRUMENT

The post-traumatic stress reaction index scale (RIS) developed by Calvin J. Frederick and revised by Ani Kalayjian (1995) was used to gather the assessment data. This instrument was chosen for its clarity and conciseness. It is a two-part questionnaire that consists of 39 items, with the first section including 20 items whereby participants rate their emotional responses to the tsunami, scored on a scale of 0 (indicating none of the time) to 4 (indicating much of the time) with sum scores inverted. The second section of the questionnaire consists largely of demographic questions and several open-ended questions indicating level of exposure, purpose in life, and lessons learned. Following the scoring of the RIS/R, the percentages of mild, moderate, and severe PTSD were calculated. Scores from 12 to 24 were defined as mild PTSD, scores of 25 to 39 were termed moderate, scores of 41 to 59 were categorized as severe, and scores of 60 and higher were deemed as very severe. The assessment measures were translated into Tamil by accepted procedures and back-translated prior to deployment.

COLLABORATION

MHOP collaborated with several local and international organizations. This is consistent with World Health Organization guidelines for disaster outreach that all international interventions have a public health focus, long-term presence, and coordination with local organizations (Cohen 2000). The three collaborating entities were: (1) The Association for Disaster & Mass Trauma Studies' MHOP that provided teams of mental health professionals, training expertise and assessment skills; (2) The UNITED SIKHS, a volunteer civic service organization whose mission is to assist communities in need, provided housing, logistical arrangements and coordination with the local and national organizations.

The latter collaboration included meeting in the early stages of planning between the project leader with Ambassador Bernard Goonatilleke, Permanent Representative of Sri Lanka to the United Nations, who gave his support for the project, as well as various collaborations in Sri Lanka. These included coordination with: (1) the minister of health in Colombo, who gave the approval for the effort; (2) UNFPA staff at headquarters in Colombo, specifically a Sri Lankan psychologist; (3) the local psychosocial coordinator in Batticaloa; (4) the local psychiatrist, who was the only psychiatrist serving about two million people living on the East Coast; (5) the local psychosocial group, SHADE, consisting of volunteers without extensive formal psychological training but with techniques of listening and empathy that were identified as key to the psychosocial effort; and (6) the district officer of the Consortium of Humanitarian Agencies.

MHOP TEAM MEMBERS

Volunteers were solicited to be part of the MHOP team through a variety of methods. These included personal contacts by the project's founder and team members, announcements in professional newsletters and websites, including those of professional organizations such as the American Psychological Association, and dissemination of information about volunteer opportunities at multiple informational meetings at the United Nations.

Volunteers completed an application form to assess their levels of professional experience, education and their purpose for volunteering. The project director organized the teams and conducted orientation and training prior to their deployment. The majority of volunteers came from the United States and a few others came from Germany, Australia, and Africa.

The initial MHOP team consisted of psychologists with extensive training in disaster work, a family counselor, and epidemiologists from university and clinical settings as well as a documentarian. This team established the program and logistics, while subsequent teams consisted of three to five mental health professionals who were expected to commit to a term of service in the field for a period of three weeks to three months depending on their professional and personal availability. The teams submitted progress reports to the project director both during and after their term of service. These reports were used to assess the progress of the project and make any necessary adjustments.

DEBRIEFING FOR TEAM MEMBERS

Trauma work can lead to distress in volunteers and team members. As a result, debriefing sessions, considered important for maintaining the mental stability of the volunteers and team members, were conducted in the evenings for team members to share experiences and receive support. The meetings also included meditation and deep diaphragmatic breathing sessions.

THE CLINICAL INTERVENTION

The six-step Biopsychosocial-Spiritual model of intervention was utilized (Kalayjian 2002). The steps were not necessarily covered in sequential order since the team members had to respond to the organic evolution of issues brought up by the participants. In some situations, groups were held separately for men and women, but on most occasions the group included both genders (who sat on opposite sides of the room). The group discussions took place in various locations in the camps, such as meeting rooms, classrooms, auditorium stages or open areas, and subsequently were held in survivors' homes.

RESULTS

Levels of post-traumatic stress were determined based on the scores of the revised Reaction Index Scale (RIS/R). Twenty-five percent of respondents' scores indicated a level of mild PTSD, 29 percent indicated a moderate PTSD, 17 percent indicated a level of severe PTSD, and the scores of 29 percent of respondents indicated a level of very severe PTSD. These results confirm hypothesis 1, that the level of PTSD in the participants would be high, that is, reach the level considered diagnosable according to the cut-off point for the RIS/R scale. Seventy-five percent scored at least moderate or higher levels of PTSD on the RIS/R scale and 46 percent of respondents revealed severe or very severe PTSD.

The RIS/R scores showed no gender difference with regard to the PTSD scores; Men ($M = 40.7$) and women ($M = 46.8$) indicated similar levels of PTSD, (t (22) $= 0.7$, ns, $d = 0.31$). Age was not related to PTSD level, r (24) $= -.21$, ns. However, there was a trend suggesting that older individuals experienced less PTSD than younger individuals and that age might be significant factor with a larger sample.

Hypothesis 2 was supported in that education was negatively related to PTSD level, such that the more educated the subject the lower the scores on the RIS/R scale, r (24) $= -.53$, $p < .05$.

Hypothesis 3 was not supported in that the level of exposure to the tsunami was not related to the scores on the RIS/R scale; specifically, neither damage to home or office, r (24) $= -.31$, ns, nor observation of losses, r (11)$= .34$, ns, were related significantly to the RIS/R scores.

Hypothesis 4 was not supported in that there was no difference in the RIS/R score (i.e. ability to find meaning, goal or mission in life as a result of the tsunami) with regard to religion. Christian/Roman Catholics (M s $= 47.1$) indicated the same level of PTSD as did Hindus ($M = 42.6$), t (21) $= 0.5$, ns, $d = 0.22$.

Table 8.1 shows the correlation between the scores on the RIS/R that indicate the level of PTSD, ability to find pleasure in tasks of daily living, the discovery of clear-cut goals in life and the ability to find meaning, purpose, or a mission in life. The results show that level of PTSD was correlated with the ability to discover clear-cut goals and a satisfying life-purpose and with the ability to find meaning, purpose or a mission in life (i.e., scores on the RIS/R scale were lower for individuals who rated higher on their ability to find meaning in life since the tsunami and on discovering clear cut goals). This supports hypothesis 5. The table also shows that PTSD was marginally related to how participants rated their ability to face daily tasks since the tsunami.

Table 8.1 also shows that according to the subjects' ratings of their experience as they imagined they felt before the tsunami, those individuals who found more pleasure and satisfaction in their daily tasks before the tsunami indicated greater PTSD. However, ratings of their ability to find clear-cut goals and of their ability to find meaning, purpose, or a mission in life before the tsunami was not related to PTSD scores. Following the tsunami, participants indicated significantly fewer clear cut goals in life, less ability to find meaning or purpose, and marginally less pleasure in facing daily tasks than existed before the tsunami.

Three DSM IV-R factors derived from the RIS/R scale—avoidance/numbing, reexperiencing trauma and arousal—were found to be related to subjects' ratings of their ability to find meaning in the tsunami. Participants who found more meaning in life after the tsunami experienced less avoidance/numbing, $r(24) = -.87$, $p < .001$, less reexperiencing, $r(24) = -.62$, $p < .01$, and less arousal, $r(24) = -.74$, $p < .001$.

According to answers on the questionnaire (see Table 8.2), types of interventions that participants reported useful in coping with the tsunami included outside health professionals' support (26.3%), family members (21.1%) and religion (5.3%).

DISCUSSION OF CLINICAL OBSERVATIONS

The tsunami and its subsequent aftermath traumatized the population, causing immense psychological strain, which was compounded by a lack of facilities for dealing with mental health issues, as well as a lack of understanding or knowledge of what a tsunami is and why it occurred.

Clinical observations of the use of the six-step Biopsychosocial and Spiritual Model with these groups of tsunami survivors suggested the effectiveness of this model in this particular context. The participants' sharing of their experience in each of the following steps is described below: expression of feelings; empathy and validation; meaning discovery and expression; information dissemination; and breathing and relaxation exercises.

Expression of Feelings: Participants were encouraged to express their feelings at present as well as at the time of the event. Predominant feelings expressed included nightmares and flashbacks about the event as well as

Table 8.1
Correlation between PTSD, Finding Meaning in Life, and Facing Daily Tasks

		M	SD			**After**		**Before**	
PTSD		43.0	20.2	PTSD	Facing:	Discovered	Ability	Facing:	Discovered
	PTSD	43.0	20.2						
After	Facing my daily tasks is:	3.4	2.3	−.37 @ (24)					
	I have discovered:	4.0	2.4	−.68* (24)	.01 (24)				
	Ability to find meaning, purpose, or a mission in life	4.8	2.4	−.75* (24)	.46* (24)	.70* (24)			
Before	Facing my daily tasks is:	3.7	2.4	.65* (15)	.27 (15)	−.79* (15)	−.55* (15)		
	I have discovered:	5.1	2.0	.05 (16)	−.53* (16)	.59* (16)	.12 (16)	−.29 (15)	
	Ability to find meaning, purpose, or a mission in life	5.6	1.6	−.24 (16)	.07 (16)	.58* (16)	.56* (16)	−.06 (15)	.64* (16)

Pre-post difference	Change	T	d
Facing my daily tasks is:	−1.3	2.0@	1.4
I have discovered:	−1.6	2.9*	2.1
Ability to find meaning, purpose, or a mission in life	−1.4	2.4*	1.7

Note: * $p < .05$, @ $p < .10$. Sample sizes for each analysis in italics. Pre-post change scores reflect only those participants who completed both measures.

Table 8.2
Sample Questions for Ability to Find Meaning in Life

	None of the time	Little of the time	Some of the time	Much of the time	Most of the time
I believe that my exposure to the tsunami was an extreme stressor that could cause emotional problems in most people.	0.0	25.0	29.2	25.0	20.8
Fears of personal experiences with the tsunami continue in my mind.	4.2	16.7	45.8	12.5	20.8
I re-experience disturbing scenes about the tsunami either physically or emotionally.	4.2	20.8	33.3	4.2	37.5
Uncomfortable thoughts about my experiences in the tsunami attack seem to invade my mind in spite of efforts to keep them out.	0.0	12.5	29.2	29.2	29.2
Dreams about my tsunami experiences keep coming back.	4.2	16.7	37.5	16.7	25.0
I see or think of something that makes me feel as if my tsunami experiences are about to happen again.	8.3	20.8	37.5	8.3	25.0
I keep an interest in activities that were important before the tsunami attack, such as sports (e.g. bowling, golf, going to football games, etc.). Please specify.	37.5	16.7	16.7	20.8	8.3
Fears about the tsunami have left me numb or emotionally unfeeling.	20.8	16.7	20.8	8.3	33.3

I am now more detached and less involved with other people than I was before the tsunami.	25.0	33.3	12.5	4.2	25.0
I express emotions and feelings as freely as I did before the tsunami.	12.5	20.8	0.0	29.2	37.5
I seem jumpy, edgy, and more easily startled than before the tsunami.	16.7	33.3	8.3	16.7	25.0
I sleep well.	20.8	12.5	25.0	33.3	8.3
I feel bad or guilty that I didn't do more to try to prevent what happened or went through less than others.	4.2	29.2	0.0	20.8	45.8
I remember things as well as I did before the tsunami.	16.7	12.5	16.7	20.8	33.3
My concentration is as good as it was before the tsunami.	12.5	16.7	4.2	25.0	41.7
I tend to avoid activities that might make me remember my experiences of the tsunami.	8.3	33.3	8.3	25.0	25.0
When something resembles the tsunami, or reminds me of the tsunami, feelings of distress increase in me.	25.0	12.5	8.3	29.2	25.0
Feelings of distress about the tsunami occur.	0.0	29.2	33.3	4.2	33.3
I am relaxed and without tension when I think of the tsunami.	16.7	20.8	16.7	29.2	16.7
It is as easy for me to make decisions as it was before the tsunami.	0.0	37.5	41.7	16.7	4.2

losing family members. Feeling bad or guilty much or most of the time was expressed by two-thirds of participants (specifically, not doing more to prevent the deaths of loved ones or going through less stress than others). Participants especially expressed guilt over not being able to save their children, spouses, relatives, or friends. One woman stated, "The guilt of living is too much. It would have been better if everyone died." A distraught father said, "I could not grab my boy in the lagoon. I had him by his shirt, but the force of the water pulled him out to sea."

The majority of the participants (79%) reported experiencing nightmares and flashbacks (at least some of the time), particularly of the last image of their loved ones in the sea with hands waving as they were being swept into the water. Fears were reported by a similar number of survivors. Statements like "I am afraid to go back to my home" or "I am afraid of the sea" were frequently expressed.

Other feelings expressed in the groups included anger (toward themselves, family members for dying, forces of nature, and the government for slow response in distributing relief and rebuilding the community), uncertainty as to whether another tsunami would occur, sadness over loss of loved ones and livelihood, and anxiety over the future (where to live, what work would be available, schooling). Many of these fears were similar to those expressed by survivors of other disasters, both natural and human-made.

Participants showed a willingness to tell their stories and be heard. Themes were universal, but each story also had unique components. For example, in one refugee camp, people may have lost one family member, but in another camp many people were the sole survivors of two generations and suffered multiple losses that some found unendurable, while others were resigned to accept as part of their destiny or karma.

Empathy and Validation: Many survivors of natural disasters have common feelings of survivor guilt, fear, and sadness. The MHOP team offered reassurance to the participants that their reactions were normal. Sharing feelings with the group and the reassurance of the commonality of reactions is particularly important in a culture such as in Sri Lanka, where expression of feelings is not common. Feelings of the survivors were validated by team members using statements such as, "I can understand," or "It makes sense that . . ." Team members further gave information about how survivors from around the world have coped in the wake of natural disasters. Using Eagan's concept (1982) of "accurate empathy," the team expressed awareness of the individual's circumstances; this consisted of understanding both the content and affect expressed by the group members and encouraging participants to engage in dialogue, leading to movement through recovery and acceptance.

Given that the level of verbal expression is sometimes limited in such cultural contexts, nonverbal expressions of empathy were also employed. Therapeutic touch, such as holding the survivor's hand or gentle hugging after a particularly emotional release, was also used in a culturally appropriate manner. This was done with great care for its appropriateness and acceptability to the individual. The group participants were encouraged to interact with one another both within and outside the group. This was done to encourage mutual support and identification with one another's experience. It has been reported that trauma ruptures an individual's link with the group, potentially resulting in an intolerable sense of isolation, disarray and helplessness (Dasberg 1976). However, the MHOP team observed increased rapport among the participants, including those of diverse religious and socioeconomic backgrounds.

Meaning Discovery and Expression: Survivors were asked, "What lessons, meaning or positive associations did you discover as a result of this disaster?" This question is based on the principles of logotherapy that positive meaning can be discovered even in the face of the worst catastrophe (Frankl 1962). These questions were also asked in the third stage, after spending considerable time dealing with their feelings. Each member of the group was invited to focus on their strengths in being able to survive and the new meanings about life that arose out of their tsunami experiences. The survivors in Sri Lanka mentioned positive lessons learned that are similar to those from other trauma experiences (Kalayjian 1995). These include, as one man stated, "Interpersonal relations are much more important than material possessions."

Another major lesson learned centered on the importance of feeling united with others without prejudice and in peace. This is consistent with the fact that participants in this particular region of Sri Lanka are of various cultural and religious backgrounds (Hindu, Muslim, and Christian), yet they assisted each other after the disaster without regard for religion, ethnicity, or other differences. As one woman said, "It did not matter what religion or gender you were, everyone was trying to help each other." Additionally, though people in this region had been living under civil war tensions (between the government and rebel groups) for many years, the common enemy provided a basis for their leaning on each other in the disaster. Some participants said that they learned that they could not rely on the government (either because of lack of response to the disaster or because of constant civil war), but rather could look to their own resources and to community members.

Feelings of heroism also emerged in the groups. Survivors reported helping one another to safety. For example, people screamed to warn others to run away from the water; telephone warning calls were made; and assistance in terms of shelter was given to relatives and friends. Some participants did not feel heroic, but rather felt guilty for not saving others or not doing enough, in which case the MHOP facilitators emphasized that everyone did the best they could under difficult circumstances that were beyond their control. The team acknowledged the courage, creativity, and survival skills of each person, and explained how these skills can remain with them through life, and can be applied to other situations.

Information Dissemination: The team provided didactic information to the survivors in response to their needs, given that survivors in all groups were particularly anxious and uninformed about the nature of a tsunami. They expressed questions such as, "What exactly happened?" and "Can such an event happen again?" The facts about a tsunami were given in a handout (e.g., as a disturbance in the ocean caused by an earthquake, landslide or volcanic eruption that in turn causes so much pressure that the water moves in a dramatic and violent way, and that a warning system is being planned) (Elliott 2005). Other practical tips and information were given on how to move back to one's home or readjust to work. Anecdotal feedback from the participants indicated that this information helped alleviate some fears of the unknown and gave some hope for the future.

To understand the tsunami, some religious people looked to their belief systems. As one Muslim man stated, "Allah is punishing us for the bad things people are doing." A Hindu woman said, "I do not know what we did to make the sea angry." Such lack of knowledge of the facts of a disaster can lead to fear of the unknown. As one man asked, "Will the wave occur always in December and if the sea is rough will there be another wave?" It is suggested that education about such an event and large-scale programs for information dissemination would empower people by giving them an understanding of the natural disaster, help dispel myths and mystery, help people become aware of warning signals and systems and prepare for any disaster, as well as make better-informed decisions about coping.

Consistent with the hypothesis 2 about education levels and PTSD symptoms, as well as with previous research findings (Kalayjian 2002), well-educated people seemed to cope better with the tsunami. This is consistent with the fact that those with higher education had a better cognitive understanding of the nature of a disaster and potential reactions as well as more resources and opportunities necessary to rebuild their livelihood than those with lower education.

Breathing and Movement Exercises: Experiential, therapeutic, and mindful breathing exercises were also taught for relaxation and the desensitization of fears (like that of the sea) and the reduction of symptoms. The underlying premise is that if the startle-response or alarm-reaction adversely affects the respiratory patterns (e.g., gasping, thoracic breathing, breath holding), then normalizing the respiratory patterns with diaphragmatic breathing will lead to an improvement in health and performance, as well as a lessening of the negative effects of the human stress response. The participants appeared to respond positively to instruction about these simple exercises and demonstrated proudly to the team over subsequent days that they were doing them properly.

DISCUSSION OF THE RESULTS OF THE ASSESSMENT

Overall, the results indicated that more than 75 percent of the participants were suffering from moderate to severe levels of PTSD. While this does not reflect the general levels of distress in the population, the findings do reflect that the selection process of the participants was effective in identifying people who could benefit from such psychosocial support. The devastating effects of the tsunami transcended gender, age, religion, ethnic background, and socioeconomic class. All participants in the groups witnessed death, dismembered people, and/or body parts. As one man stated, "I was surrounded by limbs. I cannot escape these images." In some cases, parents had to choose which of their children to save, as one woman stated, "I could only hold one child and hold on to a tree. I had to let go of my son." As one teenager stated, "I close my eyes at night to be wakened up by the blast of the boiling black sea, it is sucking me and my family."

The study results show that participants' educational status related to the level of PTSD experienced is consistent with prior research that has shown that socioeconomic status, as manifested in education, income, literacy, and occupation, affects outcomes for disaster survivors such that lower SES is most often associated with a poor outcome (Freedy et al. 1994; Norris 2005).

While it was hypothesized that religious outlook would affect individual responses, this was found to not be significant. However, this can be explained by the small sample size, as differences were noted anecdotally. Several Hindus believed that the tsunami was destined to happen and called it Karma, while several Christians and Muslims considered the tsunami to be a punishment from God.

CULTURAL APPLICABILITY

Although cultural norms suggest that people in this area do not express feelings as much as Westerners or would not respond to foreigners' interventions, the survivors were not only willing but took initiative in relating deep and personal feelings. In addition, participants conveyed appreciation for the team members' presence and intervention. The following sentiment was stated frequently: "If you can come here all the way from the other part of the world to help us, and you don't even know us, we then can find ways to help ourselves as well as each other."

The level of trust the participants felt with the team was evident by participants' sharing of their innermost feelings and psychological problems, including suicidal ideation. This depth of sharing occurred despite differences in culture, language and religion.

Certain cultural issues became evident. For example, in the Tamil culture there is no word for depression, and therefore, symptoms were somaticized. This was evident in statements like, "I feel sad, I do not want to eat or get out of bed," or "I have a headache, and my chest is tight." These feelings and emotions exist in the Tamil culture, and it was part of the team's goal to explain that they are experiencing normal emotions and feelings for an abnormal situation.

LIMITATIONS AND RECOMMENDATIONS
FOR FURTHER RESEARCH

There were both logistical and practical circumstances that limited the extent to which assessments could be carried out in large numbers. Despite the small sample size for the objective measurements, clinical assessments were conducted with several hundred people by each MHOP team.

The plan to administer a pre- and postassessment protocol was not possible due to practical circumstances, including logistical problems caused by the ongoing conflict. On one occasion, a team member was held up at gun point by a rebel; on another occasion, the entire team had to be relocated overnight due to pending outbreaks of violence due to the resurgence of civil war tensions.

Limitations common in cross-cultural research were encountered in this project, including language and cultural differences, finding private and quiet space to hold group sessions and participants having limited time to devote to groups (since other daily self and family care necessities took precedence).

Further research is recommended to include a larger sample size and to address logistics necessary to conduct full assessment protocols. Since the present results indicated high levels of distress in the self-selected sample, an epidemiological survey of the psychological needs and levels of distress is recommended as well as screening methods to identify high-risk individuals. A study of a six-month follow-up of survivors is currently being done by the director of MHOP.

As in any disaster, care for relief workers must also be recognized both during the relief assignment and upon returning home. A study examining the impact of volunteering and participating in disaster relief by the volunteers is currently being conducted by the authors of this chapter.

CONCLUSION

The MHOP experience and study results reinforce the importance of identifying at-risk individuals post-disaster and suggest the usefulness of a Biopsychosocial and Spiritual Model of intervention for psychoeducational purposes. Elements of such a model can be integrated into other extensive psychosocial and educational postdisaster interventions. Assessment tools and clinical techniques can valuably be refined and provided for training professionals as well as for training local mental health workers.

REFERENCES

American Psychiatric Association. 2000. *Diagnostic and Statistical Manual of Mental Disorders*. 4th ed., rev. Washington, DC: Author.

Benson, H. 1996. *Timeless Healing: The Power and Biology of Belief*. New York: Scribner.

Bonnano, G.A. 2004. "Loss, Trauma, and Human Resilience: Have We Underestimated the Human Capacity to Thrive after Extremely Aversive Events?" *American Psychologist* 59 (1): 20–28.

Bonnano, G. A., and Mancini, A.D. 2008. "The Human Capacity to Thrive in the Face of Potential Trauma." *Pediatrics* 121 (2): 369–75.

Brown, P.J., Stout, R.L., and Mueller, T.M. 1999. "Substance Use Disorder and Post-traumatic Stress Disorder Comorbidity: Addiction and Psychiatric Treatment Rates." *Psychology of Addictive Behaviors* 13 (2): 115–22.

Cohen, R.E. 2000. *Mental Health Services in Disaster: Manual for Humanitarian Workers*. Washington, DC: Pan American Health Organization.

Cousins, N. 1998. *Head First: The Biology of Hope and the Healing Power of the Human Spirit*. New York: Penguin.

Dasberg, H. 1976. "Belonging and Loneliness in Relation to Mental Breakdown in Battle: With Some Remarks on Treatment." *Israel Annals of Psychiatry & Related Disciplines* 14 (4): 307–21.

Davidson, J.R.T. 2001. "Recognition and Treatment of Post-traumatic Stress Disorder." *Journal of the American Medical Association* 286 (5): 584–88.

Davidson, J.R.T. 2004. "Long-Term Treatment and Prevention of Post-traumatic Stress Disorder." *Journal of Clinical Psychiatry* 65 (suppl 1): 44–48.

de Silva, P. 2006. "The Tsunami and its Aftermath in Sri Lanka: Explorations of a Buddhist Perspective." *International Review of Psychiatry 18* (3): 281–87.

Doherty, G.W. 1999. "Cross Cultural Counseling in Disaster Settings." *The Australasian Journal of Disaster and Trauma Studies* 1999 (2): 1–15.

Dossey, L. 1993. *Healing Words: The Power of Prayer and the Practice of Medicine*. San Francisco: Harper.

Dossey, L. 1996. *Prayer Is Good Medicine: How to Reap the Benefits of Prayer*. San Francisco: Harper.

Drugay, M. 1992. "Influencing Holistic Nursing Practices in Long-Term Care." *Holistic Nursing Practice* 7 (1): 46–52.

Dudley-Grant, G. R., Mendex, G. I., and Zinn, J. 2000. "Strategies for Anticipating and Preventing Psychological Trauma of Hurricanes through Community Education." *Professional Psychology: Research and Practice* 31 (4): 387–92.

Eagan, G. 1982. *The Skilled Helper*. Monterey, CA: Brooks/Cole Publishing.

Elhai, J. D., North, T. C., and Frueh, B. C. 2005. "Health Service Use Predictors among Trauma Survivors: A Critical Review." *Psychological Services* 2 (1): 3–19.

Eliade, M. 1987. *The Encyclopedia of Religion*. Vol. 11. New York: Macmillian Reference Books.

Elliott, M. 2005. Sea of Sorrow. *Time* 165 (2): 22–45.

Frankl, V. E. 1962. *Man's Search for Meaning*. New York: Simon & Schuster.

Freedy, J. R., Saladin, M. E., Kilpatrick, D. G., Resnick, H. S., and Saunders, B. E. 1994. "Understanding Acute Psychological Distress Following Natural Disaster." *Journal of Traumatic Stress* 7 (2): 257–73.

Gordon, J. S., Staples, J. K., Blyta, A., and Bytyqi, M. 2004. "Treatment of Posttraumatic Disorder in Postwar Kosovo High School Students Using Mind-Body Skills Groups: A Pilot Study." *Journal of Traumatic Stress* 17 (2): 143–47.

Gorrsman, P., Niemann, L., Schmidt, S., and Walach, H. 2004. "Mindfulness-Based Stress and Health Benefits: A Meta-Analysis." *Journal of Psychosomatic Research* 57: 35–43.

Grant, F. C. 1995. *The Encyclopedia Americana*. Vol. 22. New York: Library of Congress Cataloging in Publication Data.

Hitthakit, U., Thaniwathananon, P. 2007. "The Suffering Experiences of Buddhist Tsunami Survivors." *International Journal of Human Caring* 22 (2): 59–66.

Jernazian, L., Kalayjian, A. S. 2001. "Armenia: Aftershocks." In *Beyond Invisible Walls: The Psychological Legacy of Soviet Trauma,* ed. Lindy, J. D., and Lifton, R. J. 170–95. New York: Brunner-Routledge.

Kalayjian, A. S. 1995. *Disaster and Mass Trauma: Global Perspectives on Post Disaster Mental Health Management*. Long Branch, NJ: Vista Publishers.

Kalayjian, A. S. 1999. "Forgiveness and Transcendence." *Clio's Psyche* 6 (3): 116–19.

Kalayjian, A. S. 2000. "Coping Through Meaning: The Community Response to the Earthquake in Armenia." In *When a Community Weeps: Case Studies in Group Survivorship*. ed. Williams, M. B., and Zinner, E. S. Taylor & Francis Publishers.

Kalayjian, A. S. 2002. "Biopsychosocial and Spiritual Treatment of Trauma." In *Comprehensive Handbook of Psychotherapy*. Vol. 3: *Interpersonal, Humanistic, Existential,* 615–34. New York: Wiley & Sons.

Kalayjian, A. S., Kanazi, R. L., and Aberson, C. L. 2002. "A Cross-Cultural Study of the Psychosocial and Spiritual Impact of Natural Disaster." *International Journal of Group Tensions* 31 (2): 175–86.

Kokai, M., Fujii, S., Shinfuku, N., and Edwards, G. 2004. "Natural Disaster and Mental Health in Asia." *Psychiatry and Clinical Neurosciences* 58 (2): 110–16.

Kowalski, K. M., and Kalayjian, A. S. 2001. "Responding to Mass Emotional Trauma: A Mental Health Outreach Program for Turkey Earthquake Victims." *Safety Science* 39: 71–81.

Lantz, M. S., and Buchalter, E. N. 2005. "Post-Traumatic Stress Disorder: When Current Events Cause Relapse." *Clinical Geriatrics* 13 (2): 20–23.

Litz, B., Gray, M., Bryant, R., and Adler, A. 2005. *Early Intervention for Trauma: Current Status and Future Directions.* Available at: http://www.ncptsd. va.gov/facts/disasters/fs_earlyint_disaster.html.

Miller, M. W., Kaloupek, D. G., Dillon, A. L., and Keane, T. M. 2004. "Externalizing and Internalizing Subtypes of Combat-Related PTSD: A Replication and Extension Using the PSY-5 Scales." *Journal of Abnormal Psychology* 113 (4): 636–45.

Norris, F. H. 2005. *Psychosocial Consequences of Natural Disasters in Developing Countries: What Does Past Research Tell Us about the Potential Effects of the 2004 Tsunami?* Available at: http://www.ncptsd.va.gov/facts/ disasters/fs_earlyint_disaster.html.

Norris, F. H., Byrne, C. M., Diaz, E., and Kaniasty, K. 2005. *The Range, Magnitude, and Duration of Effects of Natural and Human-Caused Disasters: A Review of the Empirical Literature.* Available at: http://www.ncptsd. va.gov/ facts/disasters/fs_earlyint_disaster.html.

Norris, F. H., and Kaniasty, K. 1996. "Received and Perceived Social Support in Times of Stress: A Test of the Social Support Deterioration Deterrence Model." *Journal of Personality and Social Psychology* 71 (3): 498–511.

Prassad, R. R. 2005. "Women Emerge Stronger after the Tsunami." *Global Politician.* Available at: http://www.globalpolitician.com/2608-sri-lanka.

Pynoos, R. N., Frederick, C., Nader, K., Arroyo, W., Steinberg, A., Eth, S., et al. 1987. "Life Threat and Post-traumatic Stress Disorder in School-Age Children." *Archives of General Psychiatry* 44: 1057–1063.

Rosen, C. S., Chow, H. C., Murphy, R. T., Drescher, K. D., Ramirez, G., Ruddy, R., et al. 2001. "Post-traumatic Stress Disorder Patients' Readiness to Change Alcohol and Anger Problems." *Psychotherapy: Theory, Research, Practice, Training* 38 (2): 233–44.

Stevens, S., and Slone, L. June, 2005. *Tsunami and Mental Health: What Can We Expect?* Available at: http://www.ncptsd.va.gov/facts/disasters/ fs_ear lyint_disaster.html.

Stewart, S. H. 1996. "Alcohol Abuse in Individuals Exposed to Trauma: A Critical Review." *Psychological Bulletin* 120 (1): 83–112.

Tobin, S. 1999. *Preservation of the Self in the Oldest Years.* New York: Springer.

Vogel, J. M., and Vernberg, E. M. 1993. "Children's Psychological Responses to Disasters." *Journal of Clinical Child Psychology* 22: 464–84.

Weine, S., Danielim, Y., Silove, D., Van Ommeren, M., Fairbank, J.A., and Saul, J. 2002. "Guidelines for International Training in Mental Health and Psychosocial Interventions for Trauma Exposed Populations in Clinical and Community Settings." *Psychiatry: Interpersonal and Biological Processes* 65 (2): 156–64.

Yehuda, R. 2002. "Post-traumatic Stress Disorder." *The New England Journal of Medicine* 346 (2): 108–14.

Ziffer, D. 2005. *Help for Sri Lanka's Wave of Mental Illness.* Available at: http://www.theage.com.au/news/asia-tsunami/help-for-sri-lankas-wave-of-mental-illness/2005/04/09/1112997220286.html.

Chapter 9

CROSS-CULTURAL COUNSELING ISSUES

Transpersonal and Clinical Counseling Training
for Recovery Workers and Psychologists
in Post-Tsunami Indonesia

Beth Hedva,
Elisabeth Arman, and
Harold Finkleman

If the individual's spirit is awakened, he or she could access a
renewed courage, righteousness, and self-respect . . .
—Dr. Ramses Seleem, *The Illustrated*
Egyptian Book of the Dead (64)

ABSTRACT

Aceh, with a population that is 98 percent orthodox Muslim, is a province located in the northern most tip of Indonesia's island of Sumatra. This paper describes an integration and application of transpersonal and clinical counseling training at Tarumanagara University, Jakarta, and in Banda Aceh. Aceh was only five minutes from the epicenter of the earthquake that caused the tsunami disaster on December 26, 2004. A pre- and post-training t-test analysis of symptoms of Acehnese survivors who became post-tsunami volunteer recovery workers verify the efficacy of the first author's *Spiritually Directed Therapy Protocol,* which integrates spirituality and intuition into Western clinical psychology and counseling practices.

The extent of trauma encountered by victims of the south Asian tsunami has helped to expose both the *need for* and the *success of* integrating spirituality and intuition into western clinical psychology. It also resulted in a reasonably large scale opportunity to examine the capacity of helping professionals to learn and utilize counseling approaches that bring those often contrasting (spiritual/clinical) worlds together (Hedva 2005).

It was in the cross cultural environment of Indonesia—a string of 3,000 tropical, mountainous, and volcanic islands with a culturally diverse population of 200 million people speaking 250 languages and dialects—where some of the limitations of contemporary western psychology were confronted. Spiritual practices—both modern and ancient—presented themselves as natural opportunities for helping victims to deal with many issues.

Aceh is located in the northwestern tip of Indonesia's island of Sumatra. Aceh was only 160 miles from the epicenter of the Indian Ocean earthquake (International Medical Corps 2004) that triggered the tsunami that claimed over 226,000 lives, 170,000 of which perished in Aceh (*Tsunami Facts* 2005). In Aceh the tsunami also destroyed 690 hospitals and health clinics, 2,135 schools and universities, hundreds of miles of road, bridges, houses, and communities, leaving over 550,000 refugees stranded (Fritsch 2005).

As a result of the scale of the December 2004 trauma and the desire to deal with the spiritual dimensions, in January 2005 Beth Hedva, the first author, was invited, as a specialist in transpersonal counseling psychology and cross-cultural psychology, to enhance and upgrade the training of psychologists working with survivors in Aceh. The invitation came from the Indonesian Psychology Association, and the International Council of Psychologists Board Director-At-Large, Dr. Monty Satiadharma of Tarumanegara University.

At my 2005 training session, I learned the extent to which Aceh was suffering from double trauma. In addition to tsunami losses, Aceh had also endured casualties from 30 years of conflict between the Indonesian Government's TNI (Military Police and army troops), and the GAM rebels (Free Aceh Movement) (Human Rights Watch Briefing Paper 2003). Human rights violations, including the extrajudicial executions of 35,000 Acehnese civilians, was sadly commonplace for three decades (Tsunami Facts 2005). That is roughly three deaths a day, every day, for those 30 years. With the loss of facilities in Aceh due to the tsunami and the civil war still brewing (Firdaus 2005), I first provided training programs in Jakarta at Tarumanagara University and the University of Indonesia's Psychology Expo.

The success of the first programs in Jakarta drew requests to provide training within Aceh itself. One of the psychologists who took the *Using Transpersonal and Clinical Counseling Skills to Support Recovery From Trauma* training at Tarumanagara University was Lisa Arman (the second author), who at the time was a member of the psychology faculty at Atma

Jaya University. She was working as a volunteer recovery worker with Peduli Aceh, an Atma Jaya program in cooperation with SEFA—*Save Emergency for Aceh,*[1] a well established Achenese NGO. SEFA had been offering emergency services to orphans and victims of the civil war since 1999 (Firdaus 2005). After the tsunami, SEFA immediately extended their role to support victims and survivors of the disaster (Eko 2005).

Together with SEFA, Lisa, who acted as translator and cofacilitator, and Harold Finkleman (the third author), a consultant and lecturer in Communication Psychology, I planned my return to Indonesia to coincide with the anniversary of the disaster. We arrived in the city of Banda Aceh on January 17, only weeks after the GAM rebels had turned over their stockpile of 840 weapons in exchange for the departure of a total of 24,000 Indonesian Military TNI (*Indonesian Rebels Disband* 2005).

Under the auspices of SEFA, we conducted a five-and-a-half day training for participants from eight different local Muslim NGOs. The 24 participants were all helping professionals—university students, social workers, counselors, teachers, psychologists, and recovery workers, mostly between the ages of 20 to 30. All of the participants were, themselves, survivors of both the tsunami and civil war. Some participants were still living in refugee housing; all had lived their whole lives in Aceh. This means they grew up under various forms of martial law, including impact from extrajudicial executions of family or friends.

At the time of our training, Aceh was still under reconstruction. One year later, 300,000 had returned to their homes; 75,000 were reported to be living with relatives or neighbors; 67,000 were still living in refuge tent camps and 50,000 were living in newly built barracks (Aceh.net 2005).

SPIRITUALLY DIRECTED THERAPY PROTOCOL FOR SUPPORTING RECOVERY IN ACEH

Ninety eight percent of Aceh's population is Orthodox Muslim, blended with a strong mystical indigenous cultural tradition. A deep spiritual foundation is integrated into every aspect of life. Under normal circumstances, the local population might turn to prayer and reading the Quran, or to a beloved spiritual leader, an Imam, cleric, indigenous healer, or *dukun* (a spiritual healer who uses traditional medicine together with the forces of magic), long before they would consider seeking psychotherapy. As transpersonal approaches relate to each individual's unique spiritual resources and mind-body-spirit experience, it was possible that religion might become an issue of conflict during our training (in addition to the SEFA staff, our team included a culturally and ethnically diverse group of non-Muslim individuals). In fact, hearts and minds opened quickly and the transpersonal approach was well received.

Conventionally, the current treatments of choice coming out of North America are medication management and cognitive-behavioral models, including relaxation techniques, breath retraining, and exposure therapy (which is a form of classical desensitization), combined with psychosocial interventions and play therapy for children.

The degree of traumatic reaction may vary depending on the scale of the event, and on the personal history or background of the victims. Ancient and indigenous approaches to community health and wellness, like initiatory rites of passage, show us how to respond to even the most radical of changes by facing them as a spiritual test, and I have integrated this approach into my trauma-recovery training programs. There are five stages of initiation that correlate to five distinct stages of recovery from trauma (Hedva 2001):

- *the shock of trauma* (the shock of separation, where we are cut off from our old way of life)
- *crisis and triage* (feeling emotionally overwhelmed by physical and psychological ordeals, reframed as spiritual tests and trials)
- *loss and mourning* (consciously confronting death, symbolically or actually, and responding to survivor's guilt)
- *intuitive quest for meaning* (creating personal value and meaning out of the traumatic experience within the greater context of one's insight into or intuitive understanding of one's greater "life-purpose")
- *personal and community renewal* (integration of the person's sense of purpose, as he or she takes on a new and meaningful role in his or her community, and makes valuable contributions that bring forth personal fulfillment and benefit to one's community simultaneously)

Each of these stages of recovery may benefit from employing spiritually directed therapy methods that blend transpersonal approaches with clinical counseling techniques.

All the conventional clinical and counseling practices, including cognitive behavioral therapy techniques, can be combined with transpersonal and cross-cultural healing practices. Studies have shown that spirituality, when blended with conventional psychotherapy methods, is more effective in treating schizophrenia and depression, for example, than just medication and psychotherapy (D'Sousa 2004).[2]

We each have within us the ability to access an infinite source of healing within the psyche that may guide us toward psychological health, wellness and self-renewal. Self-reflection that awakens inner guidance, together with skilled clinical and counseling technique and best psychological practices, all combine to encourage individual healing in ways that are consistent with each person's unique cultural background, history and healing traditions.

The program the first author developed included conventional psychological practices in tandem with Eastern healing practices and contemporary transpersonal approaches including:

Eastern Breathing Practices

Mental Focus, Body Awareness, and Intuition Expansion

Eastern Style Energy Work

Guided Image and Symbolic Process (including expressive art therapies, psychodrama, or play therapy for children)

Mindfulness, Meditation, Dream Incubation and Ritual Practices, including time for traditional Muslim prayer;

Conventional psychosocial and cognitive-behavioral interventions, including imaginal exposure therapy, and play therapy for children.

This became the foundation for the first author's *Spiritually Directed Therapy Protocol* (Hedva, 2006) which specifically blends transpersonal, clinical, and counseling skills to support a cross-cultural approach to emotional healing and self-renewal as a model for an integrative method to psychological health and community wellness.

5-STEP SPIRITUALLY DIRECTED THERAPY PROTOCOL

1. Connect with spiritual healing resources within oneself, and be present with others.

   Use breath / energy work, mental focus, and intuitive awareness to ground and be present physically, emotionally, mentally, and spiritually.

2. Assess and evaluate needs.

   1. physical safety and
   2. emotional safety (a) degree of shock (b) crises, (c) grief/mourning, (d) intuitive insight, (e) resilience and/or psychopathology

3. Listen empathetically

   1. Build and rebuild interpersonal connection and psychosocial support systems

2. Acknowledge, appreciate, and allow for memories to emerge and be expressed

3. Encourage expression and normalize traumatic stress reactions as is appropriate relative to the degree of shock, mourning/expression of loss, or insight and resilience.

4. Train others to connect with inner spiritual healing resources and intuition.

1. Provide tools: breath/energy work, mental focus, intuitive awareness, and creative process and

2. instruct on how to allow for and identify intuitive insight, greater meaning or meaningful inner guidance for self-renewal and emotional healing

5. Empower individuals to support community renewal

1. Train survivors to use both inner and outer resources and

2. develop individualized cognitive-behavioral action plans (including emergency disaster plans in times of disaster trauma) that integrate inner guidance and spiritual resources with concrete strategies for self-care and meaningful community involvement

---

Hedva, B. 2006. *Spiritually Directed Therapy Protocol Workshop Training Manual.* rev. ed. 2009. Portions of this article are abridged versions of sections of Dr. Hedva's Spiritually Directed Therapy Protocol Manual and Training Materials, prepared for this article with the permission of Finkleman Communications, Ltd. Canada, AB.

Connect with Spiritual Healing Resources within Oneself and Be Present with Others

Use breath / energy work, mental focus and intuitive awareness to ground and be present physically, emotionally, mentally, and spiritually. Transpersonal psychology suggests that before you can help others, you need to attend to your own well being. Self-care is as close as your next breath. According to ancient, indigenous, Eastern, and Asian spiritual traditions, each breath infuses us with oxygen, and also with a subtle spiritual energy or vital life force that relaxes the physical body, emotionally soothes the tender heart, clears the mind as well as awakens and renews the human spirit. (Chow 2004; Ramakrishna 1905).[3]

Practice taking some full, gentle, deep breaths for the next five minutes as you are reading, and observe how your body feels. As you breathe you connect with spiritual healing energies. Take time to send yourself positive, healing energy. Begin with a deep breath and hold the thought that you are connecting with a universal vital healing force with every breath you take. Many Asian traditions incorporate the use of breath and mental focus or meditation to clear the mind and create inner calm, build strength of body, and open to spiritual resources.

Breath can be used to relax or conversely, to energize the nervous system, depending on whether you breathe slowly, or more rapidly. Each breath, when slow, steady, and even, each rise and fall of the chest, is like a gentle massage that relaxes the muscles, and at the same time acts as a natural tranquilizer, calming the mind, and soothing the nervous system.

ASIAN BREATHING PRACTICES FOR CONTACTING VITAL ENERGY

Never force the breath. *If you get dizzy doing a breathing practice, return to a normal breath.* These various breathing techniques go by many names in many cultures and are offered here to suggest various methods in support of psycho-spiritual healing.

1. *Earth Breath—for balancing and relaxing the body.* Take a long, slow, even deep breath through the nose, feel the belly move, ribs move, and finally feel the upper chest fill with air. Exhale a long, slow, steady breath out through the mouth. This is also known as the complete breath or yogic breath. Repeat: inhale to a count of four, hold to a count of four, exhale to a count of four, pause to a count of four, until the natural inhalation follows, then breathe in and repeat, 4, 4, 4, and 4.

2. *Water Breath—for soothing and calming the emotions.* Similar to the earth breath, inhale and exhale very slowly, so slowly that there is no sound as you breathe. The air streams in like water over stones, silently filling every part of the body and mind. After a brief pause at the top of the inhalation, slowly and silently release the breath in an even, steady stream, out the mouth or out the nose, as it washes away tension.

3. *Windy Breath—for releasing stress and worry, to cleanse and clear the mind.* (Keep tissues close by for clearing the nasal passages!). Take an extended deep forceful inhale sniffing in through the nose, and exhale with an extended, forceful sniffing sound, out through the nose. The sound is like wind moving through the trees.

4. *Fire Breath—for overcoming grief, depression and anxiety, and to purify and strengthen the spirit.* To get the feel of this breath, make the sound of a sneeze through your nose. Do it again, with your mouth closed, focusing attention on the tip of your nose, and you will feel the lower belly and diaphragm muscles forcefully push air out the nose, followed by a natural and automatic inhalation through the nose once the lungs are empty. This brings oxygen and spiritual energy rushing in to fill the lungs and body. Breathe in and out in a series of rapid inhale-exhale short, powerful breaths. Keep the mouth closed on both inhale and exhale.

5. *Ujjayi/Chi-Gung Breath—for overcoming obstacles and to build awareness of spiritual energy connections.* With mouth closed, breathe in through the nose. Exhale moving air down the back of the throat (over the epiglottis), imagining a stream of subtle energies continuing all the way down, through the core of your body. The breath will sound like ocean waves moving in and out as you inhale and exhale in slow, even steady breaths.

MENTAL FOCUS: SET INTENTION AND FOCUS ATTENTION TO GROUND AND CENTER YOURSELF

When helping someone in need, let your intention be one of service, to be a healing support, and to do no harm. We direct our thoughts in many ways: through focus, study, intentional thought, concentration, conscious and unconscious attitudes, prayer, ideas and beliefs, and through creative activities, including chanting, singing, dancing, art, creative imagination, visualization, meditation, and mindfulness.

MENTAL FOCUS: METHODS TO SET INTENTION AND FOCUS ATTENTION

1. Concentration: mindfulness, affirmations, mantra, chanting
2. Meditation
3. Prayer
4. Imagination: including guided visualization, guided image, symbolic thinking
5. Dream Work: dream incubation, dream interpretation, read dream passages from the Quran
6. Creative Process: music, song, dance, movement, art, poetry, writing, drama, improvisation, play (especially with children)

7. Storytelling: sacred stories, myths and legends, as well as personal stories/histories

8. Study: take classes or courses with a teacher, cleric, imam, study the Quran, Bible, Vedas or other spiritual or inspirational reading

9. Self-Study: self-observation, self-awareness, witnessing inner thoughts, feelings, sensations, impressions and intuition

10. Attitudes and Beliefs: note or record unconscious positive and negative thoughts or ideas

11. Associations and Correspondences: hold or use traditional talismans, ritual objects, stones, aromas, herbs, colors or vibrational healing practices

12. Ceremony and Ritual

EXPAND INTUITIVE AWARENESS TO BE PRESENT PHYSICALLY, EMOTIONALLY, MENTALLY, AND SPIRITUALLY

We can train ourselves (and those we are helping) to become more intuitively aware of subtle signals, including awareness of body sensations, emotional feelings, thoughts, subtle perceptions, images, symbols or spiritual energies. Intuitive perceptions penetrate one's awareness through a metaphoric involvement of the senses (Noddings 1984). In fact, the ancient Egyptians said that humans have twelve senses (Seleem 2001) that give us feedback about the interaction between physical and more subtle spiritual dimensions of reality.

In addition to the senses of *(1) sight, (2) sound, (3) taste, (4) smell,* and *(5) touch,* which all become metaphors, consider these additional subtle senses:

6. *Feeling:* This is your gut instinct; a *felt-sense.* Your body senses what is going on around you through a signal, like an energy boost or an energy sink. You gain information about what is happening in regard to people, circumstances or events outside of you. This could be like a knot in the stomach, a headache, or a wave of relaxation for example. Parapsychologists call this clairsentience or clear-sensing.

7. *Transmission of Emotion:* Parapsychologists call this telepathy or empathy. Unlike our idea of telegraphic thoughts being sent between people, telepathy is the transmission of emotions. You sense the emotional feelings of others by empathetically knowing what someone else is feeling, hopefully as distinct from your own emotional reactions or responses.

Telepathy also implies being able to transmit, evoke, or send emotional energy to others. This is part of transference and counter-transference in clinical psychology.

8. *Thought Transference:* This includes sensing the intentions of another. We may sense intentions through impressions of thoughts and ideas, attitudes, beliefs, or assumptions that are transmitted behind the expressed words, behaviors, or interactions between people. Just think about a time when you heard someone say something, yet mean something else, that is, you sensed the words did not match the unspoken message that was being delivered. We all have the ability to read intentions. This is called clairaudience or clear listening. Spiritual traditions suggest that also we receive nourishing spiritual messages from ancestors, spiritual guides or mentors through thought transference.

9. *Clear Sight:* Seeing beyond the surface, is also called clairvoyance. This is sensing subtle energy or vibration in the form of colors, images, pictures, symbols, and holographic symbolic impressions—including dreams, visions, or visual impressions, like seeing someone's aura or subtle energy field.

10. *Intuition:* Intuition synthesizes information from the five senses, together with subtle awareness of energy, emotions, intentions and symbolic impressions. This synthesis awards us with a sense of meaning, purpose, insight and understanding. Intuition perceives patterns, and because it transcends time and space; it includes prophecy or prediction, what parapsychologists call precognition, as well as retrocognition. Intuitive insights can thus reveal past and present conditions plus future possibilities, what Hindu culture might define as *karma,* or the subtle causes and effects that impact how we live.

11. *Spiritual Discernment:* Spiritual discernment is a sense of expanded clarity and choice. One senses the right direction to go forward, without judgment or analysis (as is required in rational thinking). What is right is not a moral judgment between making a right or wrong choice. Rather, clarity comes from one's synergistic perception of the whole truth, which perceives *all* paths including automatic responses, as well as new possibilities, and options that awaken one's full human potential as a spiritual being.

12. *Realization:* This is a very refined subtle sense that is sometimes called God-consciousness, Self-Realization, Direct Knowing or Self-Actualization. Often experienced as a sense of non-dual or mystical oneness and unity with others, God and all of life, realization awakens an inner sense of infinite possibility, creativity and inner peace, independent of one's external circumstances or conditions. Mystics, prophets, spiritual teachers and saints from throughout the ages give us good models of individuals who have a highly developed sense of realization.

Realization is a sense that is natural to all of us, to one degree or another, and inspires one's sense of spiritual purpose in life. It also inspires us to embody and live to our full potential as human beings. Integration of one's full potential, or Self-Actualization informs one's actions in life, and thus becomes both the means and the end that inspires living one's life (and healing process) as a personally determined spiritual practice.

Intuition has the ability to awaken new awareness, like insight into greater meaning, sense of purpose or personal value, even in the midst of catastrophic experiences. Self-observation along with a metaphoric involvement of the senses naturally expands one's intuitive awareness (Noddings 1984). The five senses, together with more subtle senses—cognitive thoughts, emotional feelings, body sensations, subtle impressions—act as signals, intuitive messages, if you will, from an innate intelligence that abides within the human spirit.

Intuitive awareness of subtle cues, signs, and signals is the essence of a personally directed spiritual guidance. Hence the first author calls this process *spiritually directed therapy* when applied clinically. Together, both the therapist's and survivor's inner guidance and intuition direct the healing process. In practice, open your heart and witness the traumatic event the survivor shares. Listen with the ears of your heart. Behold both of you with compassion, respect, and unconditional love or appreciation, as you build a sacred container for survivors to do their healing work.

ASSESS AND EVALUATE

(1) physical safety and (2) emotional safety: (a) degree of shock, (b) crises, (c) grief/mourning, (d) intuitive insight, (e) resilience and/or psychopathology

Clinical psychology has emphasized diagnosis of psychopathology, and an extensive amount of information has been gathered about how different people respond or react to stress and trauma. During the 1980s the American Psychiatric Association (APA) began to systematize 100 years of clinical observations and quantitative research. From this data, a diagnostic manual of symptoms, entitled the Diagnostic and Statistical Manual was developed. Though it originated in the United States, the DSM IV is referenced world-wide.

For example, after the December 26, 2004 tsunami, the World Health Organization (WHO 2005) predicted that the impact on those who experienced the tsunami would fall into several categories, and each category of reaction to trauma would need a different kind of treatment:

WORLD HEALTH ORGANIZATION (2005)

1. People with mild psychological distress that resolves within a few days or weeks . . . [Are] perhaps 20–40% of the tsunami-affected population . . . *[These people] do not need any specific intervention . . .*

2. People either with moderate or severe psychological distress that may resolve with time or with mild distress that may remain chronic . . . [Are] 30–50% of the tsunami-affected population and covers the people that tend to be labeled with psychiatric diagnoses . . . *[These people would] benefit from a range of social and basic psychological interventions.*

3. People with mental disorders—mild and moderate mental disorder[s] . . . (e.g., mild and moderate depression and anxiety disorders, including [post-traumatic stress disorder] PTSD) . . . [Are] likely to rise—possibly to 20% [of the population] . . . and settle at a lower rate, possibly at 15% [of the tsunami affected populations] . . .

    . . . A misconception is that PTSD is the main or most important mental disorder resulting from disaster (trauma) . . . [I]n many non-western cultures . . . PTSD is not the focus of many trauma survivors.

4. Severe mental disorder . . . that tends to severely disable daily functioning (psychosis, severe depression, severely disabling anxiety, severe substance abuse, etc.) is approx. 2–3% in general populations . . . [and] may be expected to go-up (e.g., to roughly 3–4%) [in tsunami effected populations].

In addition to evaluating the degree of psychopathology, therapists assess the survivor's needs. The kinds of support someone needs will vary depending on one's personal history with trauma. Physical, biological and psychosocial conditions and whether a person seeks help immediately or later, determine treatment interventions. Spiritual healing resources may be of use during every stage of healing.

Immediately after a traumatic event during *the shock of trauma,* therapists need to ensure a sense of both emotional and physical safety first and foremost.

Next, during *crisis and triage,* emergency services interventions need to be specific and concrete to promote a sense of mastery for victims of trauma.

Emotional integration is the primary focus during *loss and mourning.* Emotional support is especially important, including exploring and expressing feelings.

This naturally leads to the next stage, *intuitive integration.* Interventions help survivors gain personal insights, create meaning or cultivate a sense of optimism, which fosters personal renewal, self-empowerment and resilience. *Cognitive-behavioral integration* is a valued support during the final stage, which requires that survivors become more and more self-responsible, engage in ongoing self care, and develop emergency plans. Encourage and empower individuals to support community wellness. Help survivors to develop ideas that will allow them to integrate their intuition into healing activities that will also make valuable community contributions. Psychological resilience is reinforced through participating in activities that bring forth both personal fulfillment and benefit to the community.

LISTEN EMPATHICALLY

1) build and rebuild interpersonal connection and psychosocial support systems,
2) acknowledge, appreciate and allow for memories to emerge and be expressed,
3) encourage expression and normalize traumatic stress reactions as is appropriate relative to the degree of shock, mourning / expression of loss, or insight and resilience

Transpersonal, clinical and counseling approaches to psychotherapy may work together as a spiritually integrative approach to psychological health and wellness. We touch each other with awareness first, then with energy. As a counselor, you touch with your intention, your presence, your words (and tone), your hands, your nonverbal body-cues, facial expressions and gestures, or any combination of these. When someone has been touched, some form of acknowledgment follows, from concrete feedback (physical or verbal), to more subtle expressions (changes in breathing, energy or presence). Learning to read these subtle signs is one of the ways that intuition and spiritual healing resources provide direct feedback about what helps and hurts a survivor's recovery from trauma.

As a client shares his or her experiences, you may notice subtle changes in his or her breathing, posture, or general energy field. Through the use of expanded awareness these kinds of subtle signals help us perceive intuitively how we are impacting each other, and provide information about the impact of different healing techniques, or offer direction or guidance on how to proceed.

Use Rogerian client-centered interventions to join with the survivor and build trust (Rogers 1942). Convey acceptance and warmth. Acceptance is essential to healing (Hedva 1992). We demonstrate acceptance by accepting clients unconditionally, just as they are, however they are, in whatever stage of healing or injury they may be suffering. By suspending personal judgment or criticism, and instead extending warmth and connection, we energetically transmit a sense of support and hope. Pay attention to transference *and* counter-transference as opportunities to foster growth for both you and your client. As a psychotherapist, it is important to know yourself, your personal strengths and blind spots, so you can be of service to others, and take good care of yourself at the same time. Personal barriers to trusting your client and his or her process of healing are, from a transpersonal perspective, an opportunity to grow and develop spiritually, psychologically, and clinically. Observe yourself and your reactions. Monitor your facial expressions—scowls, knit brows, surprise, disapproval, and so on. Cultivate non-judgment regardless of the nature of the client's problem, behavior, or personality. Develop immunity to being embarrassed, shocked, dismayed, or overwhelmed by another's behavior—no matter how offensive it may seem. This is especially important in cross-cultural work.

To help survivors come to accept themselves and open to their own ability to make creative choices, we begin with basics. Every human being has an existential right to be—including being just how he or she is. We help survivors come to accept themselves and their circumstances so they may begin their journey of emotional healing and self-renewal.

The Steps to Building Acceptance Include:

1. *Acknowledge* and validate the survivor's experience as it is by helping the survivor feel seen, heard and understood. Use client centered counseling techniques as the survivor shares personal stories and experiences. Cultivate the ancient healing art of story telling as you explore ideas, thoughts, and themes.

2. *Appreciate* feelings. Give the survivors a vocabulary of feelings and encourage survivors to express their feelings as is appropriate to the degree of shock or stage of healing and mourning losses.

3. *Assimilate* the felt sense. Return awareness to the body or felt-sense. Use a vocabulary of sensations to help expand the survivor's self-awareness. Within the counseling session, encourage survivors to breathe, which will help them slow down the experience and assimilate their emotions and thoughts in the moment. Truly integrating and assimilating our experiences takes time. In general, encourage the survivor to be patient with his or her healing process.

4. *Allow* feelings, memories, intuitive insights to emerge or a new awareness to awaken.

5. *Action* allows for integration of the survivor's intuitive insights while it empowers creativity and self-worth through meaningful community involvement. Personal homework can be assigned, such as practicing breathing techniques, mental focus practices, writing in a journal, further exploring and developing self-awareness, testing out new behaviors, including helping other survivors, or assisting with community renewal. Homework is a useful tool to support acceptance, resilience and self-renewal.

TRAIN OTHERS TO CONNECT WITH INNER SPIRITUAL HEALING RESOURCES AND INTUITION

1) provide tools: breath / energy work, mental focus, intuitive awareness and creative process, and
2) instruct on how to allow for and identify intuitive insight, greater meaning or meaningful inner guidance for self-renewal and emotional healing

Introduce breath work, mental focus and expanded intuitive awareness (as per the tools you use in Spiritually Directed Therapy Protocol # 1) to train survivors to connect, ground and be present physically, emotionally, mentally, and spiritually. Teach and train others from your own experience. Model what you know works, and become an example of healing for others.

Our role as recovery workers is to hold space, to be present with another, and to follow the signals that guide the survivor's healing process. Being present with another is called witnessing. The act of witnessing allows the spirit of the person you are working with to have space to expand. This helps the survivor to become aware of resolution, conflict, or whatever is being assimilated in the moment (as it emerges), during the individual's recovery from psychological injury. Psychotherapists intuitively follow subtle cues, signs, and signals that reveal the path to healing. Next, a therapist helps the survivor to become self-aware, to witness his or her own healing process by observing these same subtle cues, signs. and intuitive signals.

Expand a survivor's awareness of intuitive resources through *innerwork,* which trains him or her to witness his or her own experiences—to be present with the various feelings, memories, thoughts or sensations that may arise during recovery from trauma. There is a vast supply of spiritual practices and psychological resources that can be applied in clinical circumstances to support emotional healing. Recovery workers in the 2006 Aceh training used prayer, ceremony, ritual, dream work, self-reflection, guided image, and other symbolic processes to support healing from trauma. Indonesian psychologists who attended the 2005 transpersonal and clinical counseling training at Tarumanagara University learned and practiced guided imagery to support survivors' recovery from disaster trauma. Specific intuition development methods, including guided imagery, have been evolving over the last 40 or more years, and integrate intuition, emotions, sensations, and cognitive constellations with ego development and the growth of self-awareness.

The process *of Guided Imagery,* first introduced by Dr. Roberto Assoagioli (1965), founder of psychosynthesis, is also known as *Guided Daydream, Guided Visualization,* or *Initiated Symbol Projection* and can be used as a psycho-diagnostic, a psychotherapeutic technique, a phenomenological description of the survivors psychological process, as well a technique for intuition development. Guided image is also effective when dealing with trauma and recovery from post-traumatic stress. As a cognitive-behavioral technique, *Imaginal Exposure Therapy* helps to desensitize the survivor to the experience of trauma, while at the same time helps the survivor to access and receive intuitive guidance and healing.

Ways to Use Guided Imagery as a Clinical Tool

1. *Diagnosis:* Use guided imagery to get a sense of where a survivor is in his or her life in relationship to specific issues.

2. *Body-Tracking (intuitively tracking the felt-sense in the body):* Guided image can allow the body-voice to become clear. For example, the experience of numbness / palsy of a survivor: *"Let that numbness take another form . . . notice how you feel as you make contact with the image . . . what does it look like, sound like, feel like . . . Talk to it . . . Touch it and, notice what happens . . . Merge with it . . . look at the world through its eyes or experience . . . What does it tell you, what does it want you to know . . . what gift does it have for you . . . what does it want from you?"*

3. *Spirit Possession/Depossession; Soul Retrieval:* Guided image is a powerful tool to support healing from the spirits of trauma. It can also be used to contact spiritual healing agents (Angels, universal healing spirits). E.g. *"Notice where you experience that 'intrusion' in your body. Let it take another form . . . the form of a color, image, or impression . . . Now let's imagine that you can separate yourself from this energy . . . Call upon someone or something that has the power to help you, protect you, or heal you . . . Feel the presence of this great, infinite healing force . . . And tell me what happens next."* [Author's note: spirit possession is significant to many cultures, including Indonesia, and is described in the DSM-IV.]

4. *To facilitate regression:* To help the survivor connect with earlier experiences of strength or injury suggest, *"Get an image of when you felt that way before . . . " Who feels that way? . . . how old are you?"*

5. *Desensitization:* Imaginal exposure therapy may be used to regress to the original trauma, or anticipate the future. This allows the therapist to guide the survivor to re-experience fears, traumas, and phobias, to support both a catharsis of feelings, as well as desensitization to triggers. After desensitization, consider asking, *"What does that mean for you now in your life?"*

6. *Rehearsing:* Invite the survivor to imagine a situation, and practice doing something differently, something that would bring about success or a preferred result. This can be used both for desensitization as well as for learning new skills, enhancing peak performance, or simply to build confidence and self-esteem.

7. *Prescribe as a form of homework* Suggest using imagery as a form of meditation and relaxation. Or use imagery to receive direct guidance on what action to take to help integrate the healing experience. *"Close your eyes and ask [your guide, your heart, your body] "What can I do this week that will make a difference? . . . what will continue to support my healing? . . . show me what my next step in healing is? . . . What action can I take that will help me heal?"*

In Spiritually Directed Therapy Protocol survivors learn *inner-work* to help them move through layers of self-awareness. After an eyes-open discussion, invite the survivor to close his or her eyes, and begin to guide the exploration of body sensations, emotional feelings and subtle intuitive perceptions that may be associated with a particular memory, thought, belief or theme. This process naturally awakens intuitive realization (healing insights, greater meaning, personal guidance, direction or a new sense of purpose).

The therapist invites the survivor to transition from outer thoughts and sharing stories, by asking *"What are the sensations associated with that thought . . . Now, amplify and magnify the energy in those sensations . . . Now what are the emotions associated with that thought? . . . Now let all the energy take the form of perceptions . . . impressions . . . images . . . memories."*

To inspire spiritual healing resources you might suggest that an infinite universal healing power intercede. Suggest that this healing force take the form of a color, or healing quality. It is important to remember when guiding inner work that images are personally determined by the survivor, not the therapist, and they may take many forms beyond visual images.

GUIDED IMAGE

Visual Imagery	97 percent
Auditory	93 percent
Motor	74 percent
Tactile	70 percent
Gustatory	67 percent
Olfactory	66 percent
Pain	54 percent
Temperature	43 percent

*P. McKellar. *Experiences and Behavior.* New York: Penguin, 1968.

Sometimes the inner images may take the form of an impression of an inner mentor—a spiritual guide, or symbolic ally that is especially meaningful to the survivor. It is not uncommon for a survivor to experience a religious figure, either human or nonhuman, like an angel for example, or an ancestor, a historical figure, or even someone from myth or legend. It can also be an element from nature, animal, plant, wind, or guiding star, for example. This is especially true when working with individuals from indigenous cultures.

In addition to clairvoyant and symbolic images, it is common for clairaudient awareness or thought transference to occur in the form of a soothing, healing silent inner voice or sense of guidance. Ultimately, impressions from subtle senses often blend into a synesthesia, where colors may have flavor and taste, or an image rings true, for example, and the five senses become metaphors that take on new meaning. Sometimes synchronicity or a parapsychological event occurs that lends meaning. For example, the first author was demonstrating this inner-work technique in Aceh with a tsunami survivor. When asked, *"who has the power to soothe the grief, a source of healing, powerful enough to heal this pain,"* the survivor saw his mother (who had died in the tsunami). Suddenly loud rock style music filled the room, breaking the mood of the meditative inner-work. Though no one had touched it, the PA system switched channels. After a kerfuffle, to stop the music and get the microphones working, I inquired about the song. The second author translated, saying that it was a popular local Acehnese tune, about mother's love. This unexpected, synchronistic event brought great healing not only to the survivor who volunteered to demonstrate the inner-work process, but it also brought healing to the whole group because of what it meant to them. Many felt this event confirmed the presence of a greater spiritual power that was making its presence known, and supporting them in their healing.

This kind of process, whether through outer synchronicity or inner perceptions and insights, naturally leads to a greater intuitive awareness or *realization* of a sense of meaning, or purpose, and empowers survivors to be able to make intuitive sense out of the challenges and paradoxes of one's life. Insights may be further integrated by coaching the survivor to develop spiritual discernment, to practice making choices, take action, and take next steps toward full recovery from psychological injury.

EMPOWER INDIVIDUALS TO SUPPORT COMMUNITY RENEWAL

> *1) train survivors to use both inner resources and outer resources and*
>
> *2) develop individualized cognitive-behavioral action plans (including emergency disaster plans in times of disaster trauma) that integrate inner guidance and spiritual resources with concrete strategies for self-care and meaningful community involvement*

As survivors of trauma learn to distinguish cognitive thoughts from emotional feelings, as well as felt-sense proprioceptive feelings, and intuitive perceptions, a new greater awareness opens and guides one's healing journey. To reinforce this learning, survivors meet in small psychosocial focus groups to share stories, insights and to develop specific strategies to address particular emotional challenges and other disaster recovery issues. Each group reports to the whole group their disaster recovery strategies.

In the Aceh training, survivors shared emergency disaster plans, (including how to respond to earthquakes, volcanic activity or another tsunami), how to help children and others in the community, what breathing techniques to use if feelings of loneliness, helplessness, and worry or anxiety surfaced, and agreed to remind each other to talk to a friend or meet with a colleague from the training program to practice peer counseling techniques.

Each person created his or her own recovery-self-care / burn-out prevention program (see Table 9.1), that integrated personal inner guidance with ideas learned in the class and suggestions shared in the small groups. Individuals were instructed to practice their personal programs for a period of either 40 days or 90 days, to check in with a colleague for peer counseling during this time frame for added support, and to train others in the techniques they learned in the recovery training to support resilience and community healing

Table 9.1
Self-care / Burn-out Prevention Self-ecology: Live in Balance and Harmony

Gateway	Integrity Path of integration	Physical world	Emotional world	Mental world	Spiritual world
Impediment to healing	Feeling fragmented	Helpless	Hopeless	Lonely	Doubt and worry
Breath work	Ujjayi breath	Earth breath	Water breath	Wind breath	Fire breath
Signals that you are out of balance	Unable to stay choice-centered. Relying on habit, fear, need for approval. Use of external influences to make your decisions Manipulated by external pressures.	Unable to stay centered in the face of anger, fear, aggression or projection of negative emotions. Manipulated by threats.	Unable to stay centered in the face of others needs/ dependency, or projection of positive emotions. Manipulated by flattery.	Unable to stay centered in the face of aloofness indifference, apathy, or lack of concern. Manipulated by neglect.	Unable to stay centered in face of lies, deceit treachery, falsehood or betrayal. Manipulated by deception.
Need / learning	Need to establish equal power and capacity in each of the four worlds: Physical, Emotional, Mental, and Spiritual. Learn to distinguish between 'my will' and Thy will.	Need to take a stand and set limits. Recognize your own and others boundaries and limits without aggression toward others value-judgments.	Need to restore trust in self, others, God and the Great Mystery of life.	Need to acknowledge and bring forth one's own personal gifts, talents, inner resources.	Need to take a leap of faith Practice being an example. Find and tell the truth without blame, shame.

Burn-out Prevention	Self-care through integration	Physical self-care	Emotional self-care	Mental self-care	Spiritual self-care
	Develop Witness Consciousness through Self-observation. Use energy, breath, and mental focus to return to center. Accept and live in reality as it is. Give each world its due: physical, emotional mental, and spiritual realities. Pray. Compose your own prayers. Honor life as sacred.	Pay attention to your body's needs. Watch physical health: diet, nutrition, fasting, herbs, exercise, sports, mind-body practices (yoga/martial arts). Balance rest, sleep and activity. Notice what boosts and zaps your energy. Limit energy depleting activities. Take care of business, one step at a time. Be accountable. Use massage, baths, sauna, etc. Spend time in nature. Breathe.	Explore the origin of fears, hurts angers. Learn to release the pain of the past through counseling, family therapy, listening circle, group work, 12-steps (Alanon, AA), expressive arts therapies (art, psychodrama, gestalt, etc), peer counseling, hypnosis etc. Visit with a healer, friends or family. Constructive social involvement with others to build self-worth mastery and belonging. Breathe.	Study, explore, learn and discuss especially with those wiser than yourself: elder, mentor, spiritual teacher, coach instructor, etc. Take classes, seminars, workshops, etc. Write in your journal. Use meditation to speak with your inner teacher. Self-study. Enjoy books, reading.	Ceremony, prayer, ritual appropriate to culture. Use meditation, energy work, vision quest, dreams. Take time and space to quiet your mind and search your soul. Use intuition and intuitive tools for self- reflection (numerology, astrology, augury methods synchronicity, dreams, etc). Develop self-trust, Inner communion with Spirit.
Methods to re-AWAKEN to your true spirit	Use vibrational healing methods aromatherapy, color, sound, etc to help you center yourself.				

Self-care is essential to full recovery for survivors, and to prevent burn-out for recovery workers and volunteers.

Look at the chart above to identify different factors that may hinder health and wholeness, and what can help to re-establish inner-balance.

Copyright 2009 by Beth Hedva. You are welcome to copy, distribute, and quote this table as long as it is for personal use. For commercial or professional use contact Suzanne Paris, Rights & Permissions Coordinator, ABC-CLIO, LLC. E-mail: sparis@abc.clio.com. 805-880-6808.

ASSESSMENT OF SPIRITUALLY DIRECTED
THERAPY PROTOCOL OUTCOMES

Since all the participants were also survivors of trauma, to ascertain the effectiveness of this program the first and second authors handed out a symptoms checklist on both the first and last day of the training. The self-assessment check list offered DSM IV symptoms for depression and anxiety, including acute and post-traumatic stress indicators across six (6) dimensions:

Anxiety

Motor Tension

Autonomic Hyperactivity

Apprehensive Expectation

Mood/Affect Disturbances, including symptoms of depression and guilt

Vigilance and Scanning

After five and a half days of training, the overall mean score on each of the six (6) dimensions was lower in the post-test, except for symptoms associated with hypervigilance, as shown in Table 9.2 (Hedva 2006). Further analysis revealed significant gender differences between male and female participants and that vigilance was significantly higher for male participants in the post-test, as shown in Tables 9.3 and 9.4, (Hedva 2006).

Gender differences are not uncommon when dealing with grief and loss (Helman 2000). Permission to grieve openly in the training (ranging from acknowledgement of losses to shedding tears publicly), a year after the trauma, would be expressed differently by men than by women. During the training, scientific explanations of the neurochemistry and psychophysiology of a stress response were offered; and these kinds of explanations seemed to open the door for some men to openly discuss (or in some cases express) and accept the role of deeper emotional release. Nonetheless, men were likely more apprehensive about exposing vulnerable emotions to others, as is required in a group setting. This may have led to significant increases in symptoms of vigilance relative to increased feelings of vulnerability that emerged during the training. While women showed improvement in all dimensions, results for men were therefore mixed. Overall the Acehnese men showed a reduction in stress, on the one hand (as indicated by trends toward *decreases* in motor tension, autonomic hyperactivity and feelings of anxiety), and increased discomfort on the other hand (with trends toward *increases* in apprehension, vigilance and mood disturbance, depression and guilt).

Table 9.2
T-test scores (n = 24)

Symptom	Mean score pre => post	Correlation	Sig. $P<$
Anxiety	5.17 =>3.91	.137	.524
Motor tension	10.8 =>8.00	.505	.012
Autonomic hyperactivity	17.50 =>11.70	.367	.078
Apprehensive	7.13 =>5.67	.364	.081
Vigilance	7.79 =>8.54	.529	.088
Disturbance (mood/affect)	46.04 =>36.92	.662	.000

Table 9.3
T-test scores for females (n = 15)

Symptom	Mean scores pre =>post	T-test score ($df=14$)	Sig. (2-tailed) $P<$
Anxiety	5.27 =>3.33	1.579	.137
Motor tension	11.33 =>7.13	2.196	.045
Autonomic hyperactivity	18.53 =>9.33	2.626	.020
Apprehensive	7.00 =>4.47	1.282	.221
Vigilance	7.47 =>6.20	.834	.419
Disturbance (mood/affect)	45.07 =>29.47	2.352	.034

Table 9.4
T-test scores for males (n = 9)

Symptom	Mean scores pre =>post	T-test score ($df=23$)	Sig. (2-tailed) $P<$
Anxiety	5.00 =>4.89	1.406	.173
Motor tension	10.00 =>9.44	1.967	.061
Autonomic hyperactivity	15.78 =>15.67	1.918	.068
Apprehensive	7.33 =>7.67	.988	.333
Vigilance	8.33 =>12.44	−.632	.533
Disturbance (mood/affect)	47.67 =>49.33	1.588	.126

Let us also consider the impact of Asian cultural social mores as well as Aceh's own unique cultural history in regards to these results. Political, economic, and religious self-determination are all core values to the Acehnese people. Not that long ago, Acehnese men and women warriors cost Dutch colonizers 10,000 lives, and the local sultanate was never fully subjugated by the Dutch. It is likely that 30 years of civil war between the GAM and the Indonesian government's TNI may have contributed to the persistence of a warrior role. Additionally, direct public confrontation and expression of difficult feelings is associated with *losing face* and feelings of shame. Even though women in Acehnese culture may have the status of warrior along with men, as women proved themselves in battle historically (Yatim 1999), it may be that Acehnese women, like women in many cultures, have more permission to experience and express vulnerable emotional feelings.

Thus, the female participants' lower scores overall, compared to male participants' scores, might reflect that the women may feel a greater sense of relief that would come with congruence between inner experience and authentic self-expression, including sharing tears, grief and vulnerable feelings. It is also likely that the male participants may have been more identified with a stoic emotional style, as is typical of the traditional warrior role. In this case, conflicting contradictory feelings like discomfort (perhaps from breaking social and cultural taboos) together with feelings of relief would be expected.

In mystical traditions world-wide, moving out of the comfort of one's known or familiar social role commonly evokes an existential soul death that initiates spiritual transformation and self-renewal (Hedva 2001), or transcendence of perceived limitation (Neher 1980). It would be interesting to research whether breaking through social conditioning and taboos about expressing emotional vulnerability is a necessary step for full recovery from loss and trauma cross-culturally and cross-gender. In other words, is acceptance of the existential experience of human vulnerabilities a universal factor in healing—independent of culture and gender? And might this be the heart of what affords a shift in consciousness that awakens the transformative potential latent in healing from trauma?

LEARNINGS AND NEXT STEPS FOR INTERNATIONAL DISASTER RESPONSE AND RECOVERY FROM TRAUMA

It seems there is a universal humanitarian element that runs through all disasters: We are dependent upon one another and nature. Disasters invite humanity to cross the usual social, economic, or political divides and to share resources. Disaster reminds us of even deeper truths—there is unity amidst diversity and we are not alone in our time of need.

Whether it is the tsunami in Asia, hurricane Katrina in the southern United States, or the earthquake in Pakistan, people who face sudden and severe loss share common trauma pathology, and recovery volunteers need more than good counseling programs. They need coaching on self-care and burnout prevention. Also, further research into integrative or transpersonal training approaches to community mental health may be required to determine methods that offer genuine and respectful cross-cultural approaches to community wellness and individual mental health. Three-quarters of the world's population in our emerging global community are from Asia and Africa; and like indigenous cultures in the Americas, these populations integrate intuition and spirituality into the fabric of daily life. Though much of Western psychology tends to focus on psychopathology, what is also true is that some of us, in the face of disaster, do not regress, but actually progress and demonstrate even greater strength, compassion and goodwill. We can each learn to awaken these natural and innate humane capacities within our being to help ourselves and others in times of need.

Each time before leaving to work in Indonesia, the first author participated in ceremonies with friends and colleagues, including North American Aboriginal Elders, to help prepare me to be of service. Aboriginal peoples from the Americas teach that the shorelines are the lips of our Earth Mother, and that natural disaster, like tsunami disaster, is one of Mother Nature's ways of communicating to us and helping us to restore harmony and balance to life on Earth. In the case of Aceh, some might credit the tsunami disaster for having paved the way for peace, after 30 years of civil war, by bringing international attention to a disenfranchised part of the world community.

The influx of foreign aid, including foreign visitors and media attention, all impacted the situation in Aceh. The combination of emergency conditions that required cooperation between the Indonesian Government, foreign aid and both foreign and local rescue workers, victims and survivors, all contributed to the establishment of new protocols, successful peace negotiations in Finland and more respectful relations between the Acehnese, the Indonesian Government and the world community.

Experiences with colleagues from the International Council of Psychologists, together with the Indonesian Psychology Association, Tarumanegara University, Atma Jaya University, the University of Indonesia, and local Muslim NGOs in Aceh makes it easier to envision some of the next steps in the field of psychology.

These next steps should include building bridges of collegiality and information exchange between developing nations and more developed

nations in support of advancing a world psychology that honors the wisdom and special needs of our multicultural global community.
Let's continue the conversation on:

- How we, as psychologists, might better address humanitarian concerns locally and in the world community
- How, in both local and global programs, we might better respect Non-Western cultures and their indigenous healing practices
- How these perennial cross-cultural healing practices and spiritual traditions may be incorporated as valued (and perhaps scientifically validated) contributions to World Mental Health and Wellness in our emerging global community

REFERENCES

Assagioli, R.M.D. 1965. *Psychosynthesis.* New York: Viking Press.

Brummitt, Chris. 2005. "Indonesian Rebels Disband Armed Wing." *Globe and Mail* (December 27).

Chow, John. 2004. *What Is Yellow Bamboo?* Available at: http://www.yellow bamboo.net/john_chow_yellow_bamboo.htm.

Eko. 2005. "Double Trauma for Children in Aceh Besar." *The Jakarta Post* (March 8).

Firdaus, I. 2005. "Hopes Dim for Formal Cease-Fire in Aceh." *Boston Globe* (January 31).

Fritsch, P. 2005. "After the Tsunami, An Aceh Surprise: Good Government." *Wall Street Journal* (November 2).

Hedva, B. 1989. "A Community Model for the Uses of Intuition in Clinical Practice." Unpublished doctoral dissertation, Columbia Pacific University.

Hedva, B. 1992. *Journey from Betrayal to Trust: A Universal Rite of Passage.* Berkeley, CA: Ten Speed Press.

Hedva, B. 2001. *Betrayal, Trust and Forgiveness.* Berkeley, CA: Ten Speed Press.

Hedva, B. 2005. "Dealing with Disaster Trauma in Post-Tsunami Indonesia: Implications for Healing from Hurricane Katrina." *AAMFT News* 14 (4): 3–4.

Hedva, B. 2006. "A Year after the Tsunami: Trauma Recovery Trainings in Indonesia." [speaker] *International / Cross-Cultural Psychology Section Symposium.* Calgary, AB: Canadian Psychology Association Conference.

Hedva, B. 2006, rev. ed. 2009. "Spiritually Directed Therapy Protocol Training Manual." [Unpublished training materials]. Calgary AB: Finkleman Communications.

Helman, C.G. 2000. *Culture, Health and Illness.* 4th ed. Boston: Butterworth Heinemann.

Human Rights Watch. 2003. *Aceh Under Martial Law: Human Rights Under Fire.* [Briefing paper]. Available at: http://hrw.org/backgrounder/asia/aceh 060503bck.htm.

Human Rights Watch. 2001. "Indonesia: War In Aceh." Issue Report 13 (4). New York.

International Medical Corps. 2004. *Aceh: Closest to the Epicenter, Furthest from Help.* Available at: http://www.imc-la.com/loc_indonesia_aceh123104.shtml.

Korn, E. R. and Johnson, K. 1983. *Visualization: The Uses of Imagery in the Health Professions.* Homewood, IL: Irwin Professional Pub.

McKellar, P. 1968. *Guided Image: Experiences and Behavior.* Harmondsworth, UK: Penguin.

Neher, A. 1980. *The Psychology of Transcendence.* New Jersey: Prentice-Hall.

Noddings, N., and Shore, P. J. 1984. "Intuitive Modes." In *Awakening the Inner Eye: Intuition in Education,* 68–89. New York: Teachers College Press, Columbia University.

Ramacharaka, Yogi. 1905. *The Science of Breath.* Yogi Publication Society. 19–22.

Rogers, R., and Carl, P. D. 1942. *Counseling and Psychotherapy: Newer Concepts in Practice.* San Francisco: Houghton Mifflin Company.

Seleem, Ramses. 2001. *The Illustrated Egyptian Book of the Dead: A New Translation with Commentary.* New York: Sterling Publishing Company.

Trauma Pages. 2006. Available at: http://www.trauma-pages.com/.

Tsunami Facts. 2005. Indonesian Government. Available at: http://aceh.net/reconstructionupdate.html.

World Health Organization. 2005. "Mental Health Assistance to the Populations Affected by the Tsunami in Asia." In *Asia Introduction and Population Perspective.* Available at: http://www.who.int/mental_health/resources/tsunami/en/index.html.

World Health Organization. 2005. *Mental Health and Psychosocial Care for Children Affected by Natural Disasters.* Available at: http://www2.reliefweb.int/rw/rwt.nsf/db900SID/LHON-69UESC?OpenDocument.

Yatim, Danny L. 1999. "Aceh's Early Heroines Ignored by History Books." *The Jakarta Post* (April 21).

NOTES

1. Save Emergency For Aceh (SEFA) is a humanitarian organization established on September 11, 1999, in response to the worsening humanitarian condition in Nanggroe Aceh Darussallam (NAD). It was founded by several young university graduates and students of Aceh. SEFA's vision and mission is to deliver humanitarian assistance and to bring about social transformation in Aceh's more disadvantaged communities.

2. D' Souza R., F. Rodrigo. 2004. "A Spiritually Augmented Cognitive Behavioral Therapy." *Australian Psychiatry* 12: 148–52. Finding spiritual meaning through self-transcendent values has been shown to reduce relapses and improve well-being in an Australian randomized control trial of patients with depression, schizophrenia and terminal diseases, in which 79 percent of the patients surveyed rated their spirituality or religious beliefs as either important or very important.

More than half (60%) said that rituals and practices helped them cope with psychological pain.

3. Ramacharaka, Yogi. 1905. "The Science of Breath." *The Yogi Publication Society,* 19–22. "Prana" is the name by which we designate a universal principle, which principle is the essence of all motion, force or energy, whether manifested in gravitation, electricity, the revolution of the planets, and all forms of life, from the highest to the lowest."

Chapter 10

ECOLOGICAL WORLDVIEW

From Ego to Eco

Scott Carlin,
Ani Kalayjian,
Michelle Kim, and
Elissa Jacobs

Nature is a community and not a machine.

—Ian Barbour

CLIMATE CHANGE: FROM EGO TO ECO

Climate change is a watershed in human history. It requires fundamental shifts in our ideas, relationships, and practices. However, what we need and still lack is a clear understanding of why it is happening. It is possible that climate change, habitat destruction, toxic plumes, and many other ecological ills all stem from a single source, which is that we misperceive our world and our role in it. The tremendous damage that is currently occurring to the natural world cannot be stopped simply with new technologies, new laws, or shifts in market pricing signals, because none of these solutions address the root problem. Only by embracing an accurate understanding of who we are and our relationship with Mother Earth can we begin to heal the devastation that we have caused.

This chapter describes the source of the Western world's misperception that we own the earth and introduces an alternative ecological worldview, while recommending models that help us to understand and adopt this idea of our right place in nature.

LITERATURE REVIEW

In misperceiving our world, we have also damaged ourselves. In our modern disposable society, we have become obsessed with quantity and have lost sight of the importance of quality, moral accountability, and personal integrity. The meaning of our work is measured increasingly by the magnitude of our paychecks. However, this materialism has only heightened our own personal vulnerability. The pace of work is continually accelerating as the workday grows longer. In addition, corporations have relocated jobs to other countries. Since our world is now premised on self-interest and manipulation, it has become harder to trust and build relationships. Instead, we rely on experts rather than friends and neighbors. Also, media propaganda has replaced truthful information. The commercialization of culture—seeking happiness through consumerism, professionalism, and social status—has weakened personal connections to family, community, and the natural world. Happiness and satisfaction have become more ephemeral, individuals have become more isolated, and relationships have become more confusing and less enduring.

Such ecological and social problems stem from an inaccurate mental model of the world that has evolved over several centuries of western thought. The Enlightenment Era was preoccupied with the question of human freedom. Could humans create conditions conducive to their own liberation through reason? Philosophy and the search for truth took a scientific turn. During the early 1600s, Francis Bacon (1620) began advocating a new empirically based, inductive model of reasoning, an early forerunner of the scientific method. However, it was Descartes (1641) who radically reshaped our view of the world. He asserted that the world was entirely knowable through deductive reasoning and mathematics. According to Descartes, the biology and chemistry of living organisms could be fully explained using these principles. Sir Isaac Newton's (1687) scientific breakthroughs seemed to confirm Descartes' vision. Capra (1982) writes that Newton, "accomplished a grand synthesis of the works of Copernicus and Kepler, Bacon, Galileo, and Descartes . . . which remained the solid foundation of scientific thought well into the twentieth century" (63).

Nature became viewed as mechanistic, reductionistic, deterministic, and dualistic, similar to a machine. Its parts could be disassembled and reassembled at will. This mechanistic view replaced the prevailing Christian model of nature, which was derived from Aristotle's Great Chain of Being—all life forms were hierarchically linked into a larger whole (Lovejoy 1974). Science assumed that once we understood all of nature's components, we could explain, and thereby determine, everything that happened in nature.

Beginning with Descartes, philosophers and scientists viewed the world around them as a series of objects to be manipulated and controlled. This dualistic world of knowing subject and passive mechanical objects remains a fundamental part of our contemporary worldview, even though several decades of scientific research have deemed this perceptual framework false.

The study of economics was also greatly influenced by these revolutionary ideas. If biology could be fully defined by mathematics, so could economics. Economics focused on creating a calculus to maximize human wealth and material prosperity. Early mechanized objects, like clocks, inspired Descartes' theory. Scientific metaphors then transferred back to society, giving rise to far grander visions of industrial mechanization.

During the Romantic period, many English writers penned scathing critiques of the new mechanistic worldview. For example, William Blake (1804) wrote of England's "dark Satanic Mills." These writers anchored their philosophies in older medieval organic traditions which rejected scientific reductionism. According to these writers, the world was creative, wild, and the whole was much more than the sum of its parts. In America, transcendentalists such as Thoreau (1854) developed critiques of industrial abuses of nature along similar lines. From different philosophic traditions, communists and anarchists also developed philosophical frameworks in opposition to capitalism's exploitive practices (see for example, Marx 1867 and Kropotkin 1888).

In the 20th century, the devastation of two world wars, which culminated in the detonation of atomic bombs in Hiroshima and Nagasaki, plunged the world into a moral and intellectual crisis. Groping for words to describe the first successful test detonation in New Mexico in 1945, J. Robert Oppenheimer (1965) quoted the Bhagavad Gita, "Now I am become Death, the destroyer of worlds." If the Enlightenment period was premised upon emancipation, modern technologies are its antithesis.

By the 1940s, Frankfurt School theorists Adorno and Horkheimer had developed a new philosophic critique aimed at rescuing human freedom from instrumental rationalism—the Newtonian worldview. The Frankfurt school analysis revealed that efforts to dominate nature as a means towards material prosperity had, through the trappings of civilization, resulted in repression, not freedom.

During the 20th century, new advances in physics led to major revisions in Newtonian science. The world was not deterministic. At the subatomic level, scientists were able to show that particles were probabilistic. Furthermore, Werner Heisenberg demonstrated that a researcher's intent influenced the outcome of experiments, and thus undermined the dualistic view of nature (Capra 1982).

The traditional Newtonian worldview is no longer an accurate representation of reality, yet it continues to play a powerful role in our culture. We continue to assume we are separate from nature and that we have a right to exploit its resources. We believe that nature has no intrinsic value and that nature's machinery is comprised of interchangeable parts.

Feminists see many parallels between the subjugation of nature and women. Mother Nature has been repressed and almost deleted from our anthropocentric and patriarchal world. However, the much older organic traditions of nature constrain human behavior. As Carolyn Merchant noted, "One does not readily slay a mother, dig into her entrails for gold, or mutilate her body" (1980, 3). For feminists, moving beyond the domination of nature will also require that we transcend existing patriarchal social relations.

Despite these rich theoretical insights into the nature of the current ecological crisis, policy debates about climate change remain wedded to an outdated worldview rooted in Newtonian physics. Therefore in order to manage this crisis effectively, we need to adopt a new and improved ecological worldview.

AN ECOLOGICAL WORLDVIEW

A worldview includes all the domains of our life and guides and determines our way of being in the world. Traditionally, people's models of the world and/or nature are derived from religion and science.

Scientific discoveries of the 20th century, often described as revolutionary, gave rise to a radically new view of the world, in which nature is understood as being evolving, historical, emergent, relational, and uncertain:

- evolving—everything around us is in a state of flux, and the universe itself is evolving
- historical—the universe has a history and a beginning
- emergent—when a complex system is developed, there arise "new modes of existence, new activities, and new kinds of behavior" that are beyond the sum of these components (Peacocke 2004, 40)
- relational—nature is viewed as a community of all forms of life and non-life, of which we are a part
- uncertain—nature is governed by a complex combination of law and chance

This new vision of reality can also be called an ecological worldview. Reality is seen as exhibiting chance, creativity, and emergence. The world is understood as a network of interaction—a web of mutual dependencies.

Also, it is organic—every event occurs in a context, which affects it and which in turn affects the whole. Furthermore, an event is also an entity in its own right and with its own individuality. This ecological vision shares its essential elements with some recent philosophical models, such as process philosophy and deep ecology.

PROCESS PHILOSOPHY

Process philosophy was developed by Whitehead (1929) and others as a systematic metaphysics that is consistent with the evolutionary view of nature. It identifies reality with change and dynamism—dynamic inter-relatedness. This extends to the natural world; humanity lives in interdependence with nature. The basic components of reality are depicted as processes of becoming, which can also be viewed as active moments of experience, rather than passive objects. The influence of contemporary discoveries in biology and physics is evident in the process view of reality as a dynamic web of interconnected events. Nature is characterized by change, chance, and novelty, as well as order. Process thought and ecology share the same themes of relationality and mutual interdependence. According to both, "nature is a community and not a machine" (Barbour 1990). Note that feminists usually agree with process thinkers' emphasis on a holistic relationality and an inclusive mutuality.

DEEP ECOLOGY

Deep ecology is a new branch of ecological philosophy that considers humans as an integral part of the environment—a component of the Earth and not separate from it. A process of self-realization—or re-earthing—is used for an individual to intuitively gain an ecocentric perspective. This notion is based on the idea that the more we expand the self and identify with others (people, animals, ecosystems), the more we realize ourselves. Deep ecology is called deep because it is concerned with fundamental philosophical questions about the role of human life as one component of the ecosphere; deep ecology avoids a narrow focus on either the biological sciences or utilitarianism and instead cultivates an ecological consciousness grounded in nonexploitation, according to Devall and Sessions (1985, 8).

RECOMMENDATIONS

1. Earth Democracy

   Earth Democracy offers a powerful new framework for integrating ecology, democracy, economics, and human rights. Shiva (2005) defines Earth

Democracy using 10 key principles. The first principle is "all species, peoples, and cultures have intrinsic worth." Many projects around the world illustrate this power of Earth Democracy in action. Below, we highlight three examples relating to forests, food, and water.

a. Wangari Maathai's *Green Belt Movement* (2009) in Kenya has planted over 40 million trees which has produced numerous ecological and human benefits. Wangari, "The Tree Mother of Africa," provides "a perfect example of aligning personal, social, and Earth practices" (Carlin et al. 2008).

b. Food Democracy—People have a universal right to food. Therefore, food production systems need to be restructured to better meet the basic needs of all people. Currently, the United States is struggling to combat an obesity epidemic, and the consumption of resource-intensive beef is growing fastest in China. However, in many African nations there is an epidemic of malnutrition. We are certainly capable of restructuring food production to provide greater levels of health to both developed and developing nations. Individuals also have a right to know what they are eating. Food companies/manufacturers should be required to disclose all ingredients and the use of genetically modified organisms (GMOs).

c. Water Democracy—Water is part of the global commons and thus it should not be privatized. The world needs to take responsibility for equitably sharing this critical resource and using its scarce supplies in ecologically sound ways. In 2004, Uruguay became the first nation to add water as a human right to its national constitution. Several other nations are examining similar changes, including Colombia, El Salvador, and Bolivia.

2. The Declaration of Interdependence

The Declaration of Interdependence offers a promising new framework for thinking and acting from the perspective of global citizenship. The Declaration was developed by CivWorld (2003) and states:

We the people of the world do herewith declare our interdependence as individuals and members of distinct communities and nations. We do pledge ourselves citizens of one CivWorld, civic, civil, and civilized. Without prejudice to the goods and interests of our national and regional identities, we recognize our responsibilities to the common goods and liberties of humankind as a whole. We do therefore pledge to work both directly and through the nations and communities of which we are also citizens:

• To guarantee justice and equality for all by establishing on a firm basis the human rights of every person on the planet, ensuring that the least among us may enjoy the same liberties as the prominent and the powerful;

- To forge a safe and sustainable global environment for all—which is the condition of human survival—at a cost to peoples based on their current share in the world's wealth;
- To offer children, our common human future, special attention and protection in distributing our common goods, above all those upon which health and education depend;
- To establish democratic forms of global civil and legal governance through which our common rights can be secured and our common ends realized;
- To foster democratic policies and institutions expressing and protecting our human commonality; and at the same time;
- To nurture free spaces in which our distinctive religious, ethnic, and cultural identities may flourish and our equally worthy lives may be lived in dignity, protected from political, economic, and cultural hegemony of every kind.

3. Spiritual Practices from Joanna Macy

    For several decades, Joanna Macy has been developing spiritual practices that help individuals and communities to strengthen their sense of ecological consciousness. Below we highlight three of her more valuable exercises: Gaia Meditation, Despair Ritual, and Mirror Walk.

    a. Gaia Meditation

        The Gaia Meditation was developed by John Seed and Joanna Macy to help citizens to identify with the earth. The Gaia meditation can be performed alone, in pairs, or larger groups. The meditation begins:

What are you? What am I? Intersecting cycles of water, earth, air, and fire, that's what I am, that's what you are. WATER—Blood, lymph, mucus, sweat, tears; inner oceans tugged by the moon, tides within and tides without. Streaming fluids floating our cells, washing and nourishing through endless river ways of gut and vein and capillary. Moisture pouring in and through and out of you, of me, in the vast poem of the hydrological cycle. You are that. I am that (Macy and Brown 1998, 185–86).

> The meditation continues on for two pages deepening the listener's connection to the earth's primal elements. Toward the conclusion, the listener is reminded that in our many life journeys:

we died to old forms, let go of old ways, allowing new ones to emerge. But nothing is ever lost. Though forms pass, all return. Each worn-out cell consumed, recycled . . . through mosses, leeches, birds of prey . . . Think to your next death. Will your flesh and bones back into the cycle. Surrender. Love the plump worms you will become. Launder your weary being through the fountain of life" (186–87).

The Gaia Meditation is an excellent tool for helping individuals to reconnect to the grand cycles of life and remember their own material and spiritual connections to that web. Its rich, earthy language vividly portrays the cyclic, material nature that each of us participates in every day, but all too often ignore. The more we reconnect to this fecund material reality, the more we honor the truth of our ecological existence.

b. Despair Ritual

The Despair Ritual derives from Chellis Glendinning's efforts to cope with the nuclear energy accident at Three Mile Island. Glendinning drew inspiration from the Chinese practice of "speaking bitterness." After the communist revolution:

People confessed not their sins but their sorrows. This had the effect of creating emotional solidarity. For when people poured out their sorrows to each other, they realized they were all together on the same sad voyage through life, and from recognition of this they drew closer to one another, achieved common sentiments, and took sustenance and hope (Belden 1949, 487–88).

According to Macy and Brown (1998, 105), despair work offers individuals the chance to "'touch bottom,' in experiencing and expressing their pain for the world." In so doing, "people lose their fear of it." This can give people a common ground, "a place of deep connection and commitment." For some, this can be a process of deep emotional release; like grieving, it can alter their sense of being. Macy and Brown argue that this process allows us to:

shift the weight of our despair, turn it and raise it into new understandings. The Chinese character for crisis is a combination of two forms: one means danger, the other opportunity. On this fulcrum, danger turns into opportunity. Or it is like a hinge. This hinge can swing us from pain to power because it is anchored in their common source: our interexistence within the web of life (114).

The Despair Ritual can be completed in 90 minutes, but will generally require a larger block of time so that people can gather, engage in preliminary exercises and also have plenty of time to process their emotions and experiences with the Despair Ritual.

c. The Mirror Walk

The Mirror Walk provides a deepening of awareness and gratitude for life. It emphasizes deep ecology and allows us to imagine ourselves as being a part of the larger world or earth community. The Mirror Walk is an excellent introductory exercise because it is an effective, gentle strategy for fostering trust between participants. This is a simple exercise, best done outdoors in a natural setting. In pairs, individuals take turns being guided as they keep their eyes closed. Since some individuals are deprived of sight, they will naturally use their other senses more intensely. Their partner is encouraged to guide them either by arm or hand towards sensory stimulating things in the environment e.g., fragrant flowers, the trunks of trees, birds singing, etc. Periodically, the guide points his/her partner's face in a certain direction and says "open your eyes and look in the mirror" (Macy and Brown 1998, 88). The partner, who is being guided, opens his/her eyes for only a few moments to take in the sight. When explaining this exercise to participants, remind them all to remain completely silent except for when the guider tells the guided to "take a look."

Gaining new perspectives from an ecological vision, suggested by contemporary sciences, process philosophy and deep ecology, we claim that this new ecological world view can help us move from our human-centered to an earth-centered norm of reality and value.

4. Biopsychosocial and Eco-Spiritual Model

The Mental Health Outreach Program developed by Ani Kalayjian (Meaningfulworld.com) utilizes a series of seven consecutive steps through which various aspects of traumatic exposure are assessed, identified, explored, processed, worked through, and reintegrated. The following are the seven steps of the Biopsychosocial and Eco-Spiritual Model:

1. *Assess Levels of Post-traumatic Stress:* Participants will be given a written questionnaire, the reaction index scale, revised and used by Dr. Kalayjian in previous disasters to determine the level of post-traumatic stress symptomatology. Also added are questions pertaining to meaning and purpose in life, based on Viktor Frankl's Logotherapeutic Approach.

2. *Encourage Expression of Feelings:* One at a time, each member in the group is encouraged to express his or her feelings in the here and now, in relationship to the disaster each has experienced. In post natural as well as human-made disasters the predominant feelings expressed were that of shock, fear, uncertainty of the future, flashbacks and avoidance behaviors, anger at the perpetrators or leaders, sleep disturbances, and nightmares.

3. *Provide Empathy and Validation:* Survivors' feelings will be validated by the group leaders using statements such as "I can understand . . ." or that "it makes sense to me . . ." and sharing information about how other survivors from around the world

have coped. Also used is intentional therapeutic touch, such as holding a survivor's hand. Here it is reinforced that the survivor's feelings of grief, fear, anger as well as joy of surviving are all natural responses to the disaster, and need to be expressed. When trauma ruptures the individual's links with the group, an intolerable sense of isolation and helplessness may occur. Providing validation and empathy in such a group will correct these effects by reestablishing the mutual exchange between the individual and the group.

4. *Encourage Discovery and Expression of Meaning:* Survivors will be asked "What lessons, meaning or positive associations did you discover as a result of this disaster?" This question is based on Victor Frankl's logotherapeutic principle that there could be a positive meaning discovered in the worst catastrophe, as well as the Buddhist assertion that it takes darkness to appreciate and reconnect with the light. Again, each member of the group will be invited to focus on the strengths and meanings that naturally arise out of any disaster situation. Some of the positive lessons learned were: interpersonal relationships are more important than material goods; importance of releasing resentments; importance of working through anger and achieve forgiveness; importance of taking charge of one's own life; and the coming together of nations for the purpose of peace and solidarity.

5. *Provide Didactic Information:* Practical tools and information are given on how to gradually move back to one's home or workplace utilizing the systematic desensitization process. The importance of preparation will be reinforced and how to prepare will be elaborated. Handouts will be given to teachers and prospective group leaders on how to conduct disaster evacuation drills and create safe and accessible exits. Booklets will be given to parents and teachers on how to relate to their children's nightmares, fears and disruptive behaviors. Assessment tools will be given to psychologists and psychiatrists. Handouts will be provided on grief as well as on how to take care of oneself as a caregiver.

6. *Eco-centered processing:* Practical tools are shared to connect with Gaia, Mother Nature. Discussions and exercises around environmental connections are held. Ways to care for one's environment are shared. Start with one's environment and expanding to the larger globe being mindful of system's perspective and how we can impact our environment, as well as how the environment impacts on us. List of mindful acts are shared to help co-create an emerald green world.

7. *Provide breathing and movement exercises:* Breath is used as a
   natural medicine and a healing tool. Since no one can control
   nature, others, and what happens outside of one's self, survivors
   are assisted in controlling how they respond to disaster. This will
   be an experiential section of the model. Survivors are provided
   with instructions on how to move and release fear, uncertainty,
   and resentments. In addition, survivors are instructed on how
   to use breath towards self-empowerment as well as to engen-
   der gratitude, compassion, faith, strength, and forgiveness in
   response to disasters.

UN PERSPECTIVES

Although on the surface, it would seem that climate change is just an
environmental issue, it is also an economic and social issue that affects
countries globally. As a result, the United Nations has created an intergovernmental body to focus on such dilemmas.

In recent reports from the UN's Intergovernmental Panel on Climate
Change (IPCC 2007), the science of climate change is very clear: human
activities have caused the warming of the climate system. Specifically over
the period from 1995 to 2004, a total of 250 million people were affected
by disasters with losses of 89,000 lives and costs of around US\$ 570 bil-
lion. Seventy-five percent (75%) of these disasters are related to weather
extremes, according the United Nations International Strategy for Disaster
Reduction (2007). Climate change is also changing the face of disaster
risk, not only through increased weather risks but also through increases
in societal vulnerabilities from stresses on water availability, agriculture,
and ecosystems.

While all people around the world are affected by climate change, all
people are not affected equally. For example, indigenous peoples are
among the first to face the direct consequences of climate change, since
they are more closely connected with the environment and its resources.
In addition, climate change exacerbates other difficulties that indigenous
communities face, such as political marginalization, loss of land, and
human rights violations. However, what is even more distressing is that
indigenous people contribute very little to the underlying causes of climate
change and are actually helping to enhance the resilience of ecosystems.
The United Nations Permanent Forum on Indigenous Issues (2007) is an
important venue for addressing these concerns.

Small island countries are sensitive to climate change and some of
them have already had their very existence threatened as a result of these
changes. In particular, many small island developing states have testified
at the United Nations (2008a) that they have been "experiencing sea-level

rise, increasingly severe hurricanes and other extreme weather events, drought, coral bleaching and declining fish stocks."

Some African states are also experiencing climate-related hardships. "Ministers from the Sudan, Mozambique and other African States" have told UN (2008) officials that "their countries were already going through worsened droughts and flooding, accelerated deforestation and loss of arable land." Leaders of both developed and developing countries agree that swift, cooperative action is needed to aid vulnerable states so they can humanely adapt to climate changes and restore already degraded environments for future generations. Such efforts should be implemented in combination with other development and environmental efforts. Governments, international organizations, and the business sector should work together under a comprehensive approach led by the UN.

Recently, the United Nations (2008b) Secretary-General Ban Ki-Moon identified climate change as a major global challenge and personal priority. He has taken a leadership role in supporting efforts by the international community to address the problem by bringing world leaders together and ensuring that the United Nations contributes to the solution. The Secretary General argues that the UN is in a unique position to help combat climate change.

One potential way to combat climate change is to boost investments in renewable energy and effective technologies and to promote lifestyle changes that reduce the burning of fossil fuels. The United Nations (2008c) has reported on Iceland's pioneering efforts to battle global warming; they have developed innovative ways to use natural resources to produce electricity, heat, and hot water, while protecting the environment. Iceland's president, Olafur Ragnar Grimmson, hopes that his country will inspire other countries by demonstrating how, in a relatively short period, a country can shift from dependence on coal and oil for 80 percent of its energy to almost 100 percent clean energy. Specifically, Iceland was able to achieve such results by tapping into geothermal energy. Mr. Grimmson also believes that solar and wind energy technologies can be combined to create new sources of clean energy.

CONCLUSION

The described impacts of climate change demonstrate that it is crucial for the future generations of mankind but also for us, we who are living now, to change our materialistic society. We need a new understanding of our rightful place in this world, as part of it rather than as its owners. We need to appreciate other people from different nations as equals who have the right to live a healthy life, without lack of basic needs such as water and food. When destroying nature, we destroy the foundation of our lives and those of our children. The climate crises can be stopped if we manage to understand the consequences of capitalism and adopt this new view of the world. A few recommendations as how to gain this comprehension are listed within this chapter. Take a look and give them a try; after all, the barrier between our present situation and a safe future is only in our heads.

REFERENCES

Adorno, T. W., and Horkheimer, M. [1947] 1997. *Dialectic of Enlightenment.* London: Verso Books.

Bacon, F. [1620]. *Novo Organum.* [English Translation 1863] Available at: http://www.constitution.org/bacon/nov_org.htm.

Barbour, I. 1990. *Religion in an Age of Science.* Available at: http://www.religion-online.org/showchapter.asp?title=2237&C=2072.

Belden, J. 1949. *China Shakes the World.* New York: Harper and Brothers.

Blake, W. 1804. *Jerusalem.* Available at: http://www.progressiveliving.org/william_blake_poetry_jerusalem.htm.

Capra, F. 1982. *The Turning Point: Science, Society, and the Rising Culture.* New York: Bantam Books.

Carlin, S. et al. 2008. "From Ego to Eco: A New World View," in Roeder, Larry, et al. (eds.) *NGO Framework for Action Report.* Available at: http://www.climatecaucus.net.

CivWorld. 2003. *Declaration of Interdependence.* http://www.civworld.org/declaration.cfm.

Descartes, R. 1641. *Meditations on First Philosophy.* Available at: http://filepedia.org/meditations-on-first-philosophy.

Devall, B., and Sessions, G. 1985. *Deep Ecology.* Salt Lake City: Peregrine Books.

Green Belt Movement. 2009. *About Wangari Maathai.* Available at: http://www.greenbeltmovement.org/w.php?id=3.

Kalayjian, A. 2002. "Biopsychosocial and Spiritual Treatment of Trauma." In *Comprehensive Handbook of Psychotherapy,.* Vol. 3 eds., Robert Massey and Sharon Massey, New York: Wiley. 615–37.

Kroptkin, P. [1888] 1974. *Fields, Factories and Workshops Tomorrow.* London: Freedom Press.

Lovejoy, A. 1974. *The Great Chain of Being.* Cambridge, MA: Harvard University Press.

Macy, J., and Brown, M. Y. 1998. *Coming Back to Life.* Gabriola Island, BC: New Society Publishers. Available at: www.joannamacy.net/.

Marx, K. [1867] 1976. *Capital: A Critique of Political Economy.* Translated by Ben Fowkes. New York: Vintage Books.

Merchant, C. 1980. *The Death of Nature.* New York: Harper and Row.

Newton, Sir I. [1687] 1999. *The Principia: Mathematical Principles of Natural Philosophy.* Translated by Bernard Cohen, I., and Anne Whitman. Berkeley: University of California Press.

Oppenheimer, J. R. 1965. Interview in *The Decision to Drop the Bomb*. Produced by Fred Freed. NBC. Available at: http://www.atomicarchive.com/Movies/Movie8.shtml.

Peacocke, A. 2004. *Evolution: The Disguised Friend of Faith?* West Conshohocken, PA: Templeton Foundation Press.

Shiva, V. 2005. *Earth Democracy: Justice, Sustainability, and Peace.* Boston: South End Press.

Thoreau, H. D. 1854. *Walden.* Available at: http://thoreau.eserver.org/walden00.html.

United Nations. 2008a. *Small Island Countries Say Climate Change Already Threatens Very Existence.* Available at: http://www.un.org/News/Press/docs/2008/ga10689.doc.htm.

United Nations. 2008b. *UN Secretary-General Ban Ki-moon's Initiatives on Climate Change.* Available at: http://www.un.org/climatechange/background/sginitiatives.shtml.

United Nations. 2008c. Press Conference On "How To Prevent Climate Change." (February 21), Available at: http://www.un.org/News/briefings/docs/2008/080221_Climate_Change.doc.htm.

United Nations Intergovernmental Panel on Climate Change. 2007. *Climate Change 2007: Synthesis Report.* Geneva: IPCC. Available at: http://www.ipcc.ch/publications_and_data/publications_ipcc_fourth_assessment_report_synthesis_report.htm.

United Nations International Strategy for Disaster Reduction. 2007. *Disaster Risk and Climate Change.* Available at: http://www.unisdr.org/eng/risk-reduction/climate-change/docs/Disaster%20risk%20and%20cc%20flyer.pdf.

United Nations Permanent Forum on Indigenous Issues. 2007. *Climate Change and Indigenous Peoples.* Available at: http://www.un.org/esa/socdev/unpfii/en/climate_change.html.

Whitehead, A. N. [1929] 1978. *Process and Reality.* New York: Free Press.

Chapter 11

LONG-TERM IMPACTS ON PERSONAL AND SPIRITUAL VALUES FOR FRENCH CANADIAN ELDERLY VICTIMS OF A FLOOD IN QUÉBEC, CANADA

A Question of Resilience

Danielle Maltais and
Simon Gauthier

Pain can make a whole winter bright,
Like fever, force us to live deep and hard,
Betrayal focus in a peculiar light
All we have ever dreamed or known or heard,
And from great shocks we do recover.

—May Sarton

INTRODUCTION

When faced with natural disasters, certain individuals, senior citizens for instance, are more vulnerable than others because they do not have easy access to community resources (Kalayjian 1995; Zakour and Harrel 2003). Many senior citizens, especially those with limited means, do not own homeowners' insurance and often live in rundown buildings. Many times, they do not own a vehicle, which can lead to evacuation problems during floods, earthquakes, or hurricanes (tornadoes). Zakour and Harrel (2003) estimate that people who are affected in a negative way when exposed to a disaster have limited access to support services because of different types of social injustices. These social injustices include unequal distribution of resources in their communities (the poorer neighborhoods having fewer community members to develop prevention and disaster victim support programs), the presence of faulty collective infrastructures including roads, bridges, aqueducts, and geographic barriers hindering help distribution to poorer neighborhoods. Senior citizens, particularly those with physical or mental challenges, limited means, or without social support, are at risk of injury or death, or of developing post-disaster health problems. Chan et al. (2003) and Osaki and Minowa (2000) demonstrate that women and senior citizens are particularly at risk of dying during an earthquake and in the year following the event. In spite of the fact that senior citizens are very vulnerable when it comes to natural disasters, research dealing with the consequences of disasters on the biopsychosocial health of senior citizens is relatively sparse compared to those concerning young adults, children or teens.

Most studies concerning senior citizens in the field of disasters address the frequency of psychological problems like post-traumatic stress, anxiety or depression after exposure to a disaster (Goenjian et al. 1994; Maltais, Lachance, and Brassard 2002; Phifer 1990; Ticehurst et al. 1996). Other research looks at the relationship between perceived and received social support and the post-disaster health of senior citizens (Kaniasty and Norris 1993; Kaniasty, Norris, and Murell 1990; Maltais et al. 2003), while a limited number of researchers address the resiliency process (Cyrulnik 2004) as well as the positive and negative impacts on personal values and beliefs of senior citizens who are exposed to disasters (Chung et al. 2004). This chapter describes the different perceptions researchers have of the coping abilities of elders, displays the traumatic reactions of the latter after a disastrous flood, and presents the means by which some of these elder people managed to find resilience.

VIEWPOINTS OF THE AUTHORS CONCERNING THE CAPACITY FOR SENIOR CITIZENS TO ADAPT

Different points of view clash when we speak of the issue of how senior citizens adapt when faced with a natural disaster and a traumatic event. Thus, certain researchers estimate that senior citizens represent a segment of the population particularly at risk of developing health or psychological problems after being exposed to a traumatic event such as a flood, an earthquake, or a hurricane (tornado) because they are less likely to receive attention, they are more likely to resist evacuation and are more perturbed by life's violent events (Carr et al. 1997; Krause 1987; Lewin, Carr and Webster 1998; Miller, Turner and Kimbal 1981; Ollendick and Hoffman 1982; Phifer 1988, 1990; Phifer and Norris 1989; Phifer and Tanida 1996; Ticehurst et al. 1996). These authors emphasize that, following a traumatic event, senior citizens have greater risks of developing health problems.

Actually, older individuals are more susceptible of suffering many chronic health problems in general; disasters make them even more susceptible and more at risk. The social network of older aged people can be weaker due to greater loss surrounding them (spouse, friends, and neighbors). These factors, as a whole, increase the stress at a time in life where the coping capacity weakens progressively and increases senior citizens' vulnerability. According to the supporters of this perspective, older individuals would rather use rigid, regressive and inadequate defense mechanisms. Exposed to a similar trauma, older victims would have a tendency to react with greater desperation to the multiple demands and constraints inherent in disasters than younger people (Bolin and Klenow 1982–1983).

Having less energy and diminished physical capacity, senior citizens would have a greater need for outside help to accomplish everyday chores (transportation, shopping, etc.) and to answer financial and legal consequences brought on by the disaster. This perspective highlights the fact that senior citizens confronted by a traumatic event are more inclined to be depressed (McNaughton et al. 1990), perceive their lifestyle negatively and have a weaker immune system (McNaughton et al. 1990). Eldar (1992), Fields (1996), as well as Thompson et al. (1993) also consider that senior citizens are less inclined to take evacuation alerts seriously and are generally more resistant to leaving their homes. Fields (1996) also mentioned that senior citizens more often find themselves alone in their homes when a disaster occurs, which increases the risk for harmful consequences from disasters. Elderly people (65 years and older) would also have a tendency to complain less than younger individuals (Kaniasty et al. 1990), they would probably not use enough of the formal help resources, and generally request less support from their relatives and community organisms (Bolin and Klenow 1982–83; Kaniasty, Norris and Murrel 1990; Ticehurst et al. 1996). Bolin and Klenow (1982–83) also estimate that senior citizens suffer more than other adults from the loss resulting from the sentimental value of what was destroyed, and that they would have more difficulty in bouncing back economically. Finally, in an analysis of the writings on the consequences of traumatic events on the senior population, it is emphasized that senior citizens are more at risk than younger adults of developing physical health problems, of dying, of presenting a more precarious financial situation, of living through deaths of loved ones, and of seeing their environment and their neighborhood fairly modified following a disaster (Bohonis and Hogan 1999; Chan et al. 2003; Osaki and Minowa 2000; Sanderson 1989; Wade et al. 2004). These authors have found that in comparison with younger adults, senior citizens are more at risk of greater physical injuries, of experiencing substantial economic loss, and of accumulating more debts following a disaster.

On the other hand, others believe that the elderly, and particularly those 65 and older, cope better than younger adults. These researchers base their arguments on the accumulation of seniors' life experience and on their greater capacity to adapt to consequences generated by stressful events. This viewpoint is elaborated from two major theories: ripening and inoculation. Supporters of the ripening theory argue that senior citizens react less intensely to stressful events than younger adults, while the supporters of the inoculation theory consider that seniors, because of their previous exposure to traumatic situations, are protected from undesirable effects on their health. In this perspective, previous experiences would allow senior citizens to mobilize the necessary resources in order to face different stresses produced by their exposure to disaster more effectively. The resilient capacity of aged individuals would thus be greater than that of younger people (Bolin and Klenow 1982–1983; Finnsdottir and Elklit 2002; Green et al.1996; Hutchins and Norris 1989; Kato et al. 1996; Norris and Murrel 1988; Thompson, Norris and Hanacek 1993; Tyler and Hoyt 2000; Weintraub and Ruskin 1999). Thus Kato et al. (1996), Green et al. (1996) as well as Gibbs (1989) assess that people's capacity to adapt increases with age, while Ruskin and Talbot (1996) and Norris et al. (1994) consider that previous exposure to difficult situations increases aging adults' resistance to stress and makes them more resilient. In fact, aged victims have recuperated quicker after a powerful hurricane (Bolin and Klenow 1988) showing less fear and desperation than young survivors, especially during aftershocks. Moreover, family and emotional agitation would be less present with older victims (Bolin and Klenow 1982–1983) and alcohol consumption would be lower (Miller, Turner, and Kimball 1981).

After an earthquake, senior citizens also reported fewer intrusive thoughts (reminiscences, thoughts, and dreams) than younger victims (Goenjian et al. 1994). Other researchers also noted that previous exposure to disasters contributes to ease people's adjustment to a subsequent disaster and attenuates post-traumatic symptomatology (Kato et al. 1996; Norris and Murrel 1998; Phifer and Norris 1998). However, Gibbs (1989) points out that seniors' experience is useful only if the previous disaster is managed with success and if the senior citizens have the necessary skills to adapt to different kinds of stress. Green et al. (1996), consider that the greater capacity of senior citizens to adapt to the consequences of their exposure to a disaster can be explained by, among other things, their religious commitment and frequent visits to sacred places. Moreover, as senior citizens are more likely to perceive disasters as acts of God, they seem to develop less resentment and rage towards the powers that be and, consequently, deploy calmer and more serene attitudes.

A few other studies have demonstrated that senior citizens are not more affected than younger victims and that a victim's vulnerability and resilience are not elements related to age. So, when speaking of anxiety, depression, avoidance strategies, sleep disorders, nightmares, intrusive thoughts, forgetfulness, and lack of self-confidence, senior citizens' reactions would then be similar to other age groups (Burger, Van Staden, and Nieuwouldt 1989; Fields 1996; Goenjian et al. 1994; Hovington et al. 2002; Livingston et al. 1992; Ollendick and Hoffman 1982; Shore, Tatum and Volmer 1986).

Other researchers also estimate that, among senior citizens, only certain elderly groups are more at risk of showing health effects or postdisaster psychological problems; such as senior citizens receiving very little social support or receiving social security, those having chronic illnesses and functional limitations, those individuals who have reached middle age or very old people (Fields 1996; Gignac, Cott, and Badley 2003; Gleser, Green, and Winget 1981). According to Eldar (1992) senior citizens of 65 years or older who show locomotion problems or loss of autonomy have more difficulty evacuating their homes than younger individuals and thus expose themselves to a greater degree to injury and stress. According to Phifer (1990), low income senior citizens would also suffer greater psychological distress following a disaster, and the psychological welfare of male victims would be more threatened. However, other researchers (Guarnaccia et al. 1993; Krause 1987; Ticehurst et al. 1996) observe that elderly women are more at risk of suffering from psychological and physical health problems. According to Krause (1987), after exposure to a heavy storm, women remain more affected than men 16 months after having been exposed to this type of disaster. Ticehurst et al. (1996) also consider that people of 65 years of age and older, presenting high levels of post-traumatic symptoms (often they are females), use avoidance as a strategy to adapt. In many studies done with disaster survivors, researchers have shown that elderly people who consider that the help received was insufficient presented a higher level of anxiety, somatization, depressive manifestations, and post-traumatic stress (Cook and Bickman 1990; Green, Grace and Gleser 1985; Joseph et al. 1992; Kaniasty and Norris 1993; Maltais, Lachance and Brassard 2003; Solomon et al. 1993).

Research conducted in Quebec two years after the July 1996 flood (Maltais et al. 2003) with people aged 50 years or older, found that those who thought that they had received less help than for which they had wished were still afflicted with more difficult living conditions and had more health complications than those survivors who were satisfied with the help they received. In addition, those survivors who were unsatisfied with the help received, compared to the ones who thought they had received more than enough help, had a more negative perception of their physical health. The survivors who were unsatisfied with the help received also showed more depressive manifestations, anxiety, insomnia, social dysfunction, and somatic symptoms than those who were satisfied. For their part, Norris, Phifer and Kaniasty (1994), Logue, Hansen and Struening (1981), as well as Phifer (1990), reported that people aged 55 to 64 showed more depressive manifestations than younger adults and than the elderly, 65 years and more, following their exposure to a flood (Norris et al. 1994; Phifer 1990) or to a tornado (Logue et al. 1981). Green et al. (1996) note that two years after the Buffalo Creek tragedy (collapsing of a dam), it was the 40–54 age group who showed more anxiety symptoms, while those aged between 25 and 39 showed more quarrelsome symptoms.

SENIOR CITIZENS' RESILIENCE WHEN EXPOSED TO A DISASTER

In spite of conflicting viewpoints on senior citizens' capacity to adapt in order to overcome the different stresses linked to their exposure to a disaster, studies have shown that many senior citizens are able to overcome these stresses and show resilience.

Resilience manifests itself when an individual is confronted by an adverse condition susceptible of interfering with or threatening his development, such as disasters (Bolin and Klenow 1982–1983; Melick and Logue 1985; Wright and Masten 2005). With senior citizens, it is possible to note a great diversity in the adaptive responses to stressful events. This phenomenon is explained by the fact that resilience is a process and it depends on the interactions between different protective and risk factors emanating from the individual himself as well as from his environment (Cyrulnik 1999). The protective factors increase the probabilities that the survivors can undertake a normal development, while the risk factors increase the individual's vulnerability when faced with a traumatic event by reducing his chances of developing fully (Wright and Masten 2005). As noted by Rutter (1987), a given factor can constitute a shelter for one person and a risk for another, depending on the circumstances. Moreover, these factors must necessarily be interrelated with other variables (for example an adequate social support and being present during the disaster). Thus, resilience depends on individual and environmental resources that can help people overcome their hardships.

In reference to the elements that can transgress or favor the resiliency process with elderly victims, certain authors (Krause 1987; Perry and Liddell 1997; Chung et al. 2005; Seplaki et al. 2006) assert that it is crucial to study resiliency under different dimensions (individual factors, environmental factors, etc.) in order to avoid any stigmatization that could emanate from only one point of view. For example, reducing people's adaptation to strictly personal aspects such as age could result in reinforcing the misconception that older people do not possess the necessary resources to solve their problems. Three types of factors stand out in the research on resilience and must necessarily be taken into account in the analysis and interpretation of the facts: the personal factors, the factors inherent to the disaster, and the environmental factors. On a personal level, senior citizens' perceptions with regard to the traumatic event itself, to others, and towards life in general, seem to be important elements in the resiliency process (Chung et al. 2004; Melnick and Logue 1985; Wagnild and Young 1990). In fact, the way in which an elderly person perceives a disaster as a menace, a challenge, or an opportunity will influence the presence or the absence of anxiety, depression, loss of control, as well as the choice of adaptation strategies (isolation, drug and alcohol consumption, search for help) used to face different stresses (Chung et al. 2004; Melick and Logue 1985; Norris and Murrell 1988). For example, elderly individuals who perceive themselves as being more vulnerable tend to use more sedatives and tranquilizers as well as alcohol to overcome their emotional reactions when exposed to a disaster (Melick and Logue 1985). The way elderly people interpret a traumatic event would also be influenced by other individual elements such as prior experiences (repeated failures or overcome challenges) and actual experiences (retirement, physical incapacities, or health problems), the level of self-esteem and of self-confidence, disposition, defense mechanisms, certain demographic variables, religious beliefs, and so on. (Cyrulnik 2004; Kinsel 2005; Wagnild and Young 1990). These studies emphasize that on the one hand, the experience of difficult existential events can make individuals more vulnerable to a future traumatic event; on the other hand this can serve as an element of protection in the sense that the past experience could have allowed elderly people to get either more or less capacity for adaptation (Norris and Murrell 1988; Phifer 1990). For example, elderly persons who have overcome many difficult situations may have acquired a stronger confidence in self, a confidence that will allow them to believe in their capacity to master future difficulties. Inversely, stress generated by a disaster could be linked to previous difficult experiences (loss of a loved one, diminishing of physical capacity), thus increasing significantly the vulnerability of senior citizens confronted with a traumatic event like a natural or a technological disaster.

The level of self-esteem and self-confidence could also influence the choice of adaptation strategies used by senior citizens in order to face a traumatic event. Those with positive self-esteem are capable of appreciating internal resources they possess and thus put them to use more effectively (Wagnild and Young 1990; Werner 1995). A persevering and optimistic disposition may bring elderly individuals to believe in their personal abilities and deploy actions to continue to reconstruct their life after a disaster (Kinsel 2005; Wagnild and Young 1990). A pessimistic disposition, however, could lead senior citizens to distrust their capacity to confront adversity, and consequently they would be more susceptible to use ineffective adaptation strategies, such as social isolation, alcohol, and medication consumption. These strategies can lead to the development and the reinforcement of negative symptoms such as anxiety and depression (Deater-Deckard et al., as cited by Goldstein and Brooks 2005).

Senior citizens who constantly assign a negative sense to disasters are more inclined to use defense mechanisms (adaptation strategies directed toward emotion) such as dissociation, to present a post-traumatic state of shock (Chung et al. 2004), and depressive manifestations (Livingston et al. 1992). Religious beliefs allow elderly individuals to perceive the hope for better days differently. Moreover, participation in a religious association could offer an important support in difficult times (Kinsel 2005).

Being a multifactorial process, senior citizens' resilience when confronted with a trauma cannot be explained by personal characteristics alone (Cyrulnik and Greene 2002; Perry and Lindell 1997). Certain authors show that factors related to the traumatic event also alter senior citizens' capacity for resilience (Chung et al. 2005; Phifer, Kaniasty and Norris 1988; Phifer and Norris 1989). The area of impact seems to have some bearing on this process, as a survivor in the vicinity of the disaster could experience more negative effects than a survivor removed from the area (Chung et al. 2004). Also, the time of exposure to the trauma (short/long) could be either a risk or a protection because the victim who is exposed for a long period of time could be caught with more negative consequences. The type of disaster (natural/technological) and the moment of impact (night/day) make up other characteristics of the disaster that may or may not favor senior citizens' resilience (Chung et al. 2005). Environmental factors like the social support received or perceived and the cultural vernacular also represent elements that can modify senior citizens' resiliency when confronted to a disaster (Bolin and Klenow 1982–1983; Bolin and Klenow 1988). Indeed, beliefs generally conveyed by the environment (family, community, culture) have an effect on the viewpoint elderly people form of the traumatic incident, viewpoints affecting in turn the feelings they experience and the adaptation strategies they set up in order to resolve their problems (Chung et al. 2004; Cyrulnik 1999). These beliefs are linked to the way a society defines the concept of trauma to the elderly and tinges the services offered the elderly who are confronted with a disaster (Cyrulnik 2004). For example, in a society in which the beliefs are negative with regard to elderly people, they could thus be brought to believe that they could in fact be incapable of resolving their problems (Cyrulnik 1999; DeMuth 2004). These socially conveyed and individually internalized thoughts are susceptible of blocking all resiliency processes, leading to senior citizens staying confined in their state of distress and of perpetual victimhood as a way of facing life's obstacles (DeMuth 2004).

Poulshock and Cohen (1975) nicely demonstrate the power of social stigmata by noting the incongruity between interiorized beliefs, personally reported beliefs, and the adaptation strategies used by senior citizens. In fact, even if they perceive themselves to be sick or extremely sick, they rarely use help services when disaster strikes. The authors explain that senior citizens unconsciously hope to avoid being labeled mentally ill by not resorting to the services of social agencies. For their part, Kohn et al. (2005) put forward the idea that senior citizens experience more psychological distress (demoralization, despair) in a community that does not give supportive services (to those with loss of physical mobility) to the elderly population. This situation would hinder the elderly population from recovering psychologically and physically (Kohn et al. 2005). Narrowmindedness is not the only factor that explains why senior citizens in difficulty might not use external help. Availability of adequately appraised help (perfect adaptation between perceived needs and help received by senior citizens) from family, spouse, and friends would make up crucial protection factors favoring the resiliency process in elderly people confronted with a disaster (Bolin and Klenow 1988; Phifer 1990; Seplaki et al. 2006). There are also other dimensions than social support coming between the occurrence of a disaster and the resiliency of senior citizens. For example, an elderly person who has acquired a high self-esteem may experience less difficulty in managing problems in an autonomous manner.

Finally, social service philosophy claiming that those people who ask for help are those who in effect receive help cannot apply to senior citizens because they do not display the same help request behavior (Fletcher et al. 1996), behavior that can be influenced by a multitude of elements (risk and protection) mentioned earlier. Cyrulnik (2004) summarizes well the possibilities of resilience by emphasizing that elderly trauma victims who get better more quickly are those who, before the trauma, had acquired internal and external resources enabling them to stabilize their individual condition. Among these internal resources, we find securing attachment styles, the positioning of constructive defenses (altruism, sublimation, dreaming, project, humor, creativity, and metallization), a high self-esteem, and a feeling of competence and efficiency. Positive social support and friendly networks constitute strong external resources that can modulate the person's perceptions with respect to the event itself and its environment.

SHORT- AND LONG-TERM EFFECTS OF THE JULY 1996 FLOOD ON THE PERSONAL BELIEFS AND VALUES OF SENIOR CITIZENS

In order to identify the consequences of a flood on the physical and psychological health of senior citizens as well as the impact of such an event on their values and beliefs, different studies, one of which was a longitudinal study, a two-phase measure with a mixed research tender, were done in Quebec, Canada, two, three, and eight years after severe flooding in 1996. This flood provoked the evacuation of more than 16,000 people, the destruction of 426 main homes and damaged 2,015 other residences in the Saguenay-Lac-St-Jean region. About a dozen municipalities, rural and urban, also suffered important damage to collective property (roads, bridges, aqueducts, and electrical distribution, etc.). Faucher (2002) estimates that the losses linked to the July 1996 floods reached more than one billion Canadian dollars. This amount includes the cost of reconstructing the collective property for the private individuals (± $620 million), indemnities paid by insurers (± $165 million), losses suffered by community organisms (± $50 million), and the expenses linked to the management of the rising water in the region's hydraulic basin (± $170 million). Faucher (2002) specifies that this cost does not include certain losses or hard to measure expenses, like the time lost for transportation, noninsurable items, or the work of the volunteers.

Two years (in urban municipalities) and three years (in rural areas) after this disaster, a total of 124 elderly survivors aged 55 years and older, and 107 elderly non-victims of the same age group participated in two studies based on the mixed approach (integration of quantitative and qualitative methods). These elderly people answered different questions (open-ended and open) about their physical and psychological health and the impacts of the flood on their close family, their social life, and their spiritual values. Eight years after the July 1996 floods, 62 victims and 44 non-victims were met with again.

Two or three years after the July 1996 floods, the victims showed more uncertain physical or psychological health and a more difficult lifestyle than non-victims. The flood victims were, among other things, more likely than non-victims to think that their physical health was average or poor and to declare the appearance and exacerbation of health problems. More victims than non-victims also reported being afflicted with financial difficulties and considered they had cut back on their social activities. The victims also showed more manifestations of post-traumatic stress syndrome and of depression than elderly non-victims. According to the anxiety-insomnia scale, their social dysfunction and somatic symptom scores were also higher, while their psychological welfare was lower than that of non victims.

Eight years after the July 1996 floods, the data showed that psychological health had increased as much for the urban as for the rural victims (the scale scores tended to diminish) but that the differences still persisted between the victims and the non-victims with reference to their psychological health. For example, in the urban environment, elderly victims showed, even after eight years, significant differences from the elderly non-victims in relation to the presence of post-traumatic stress and social dysfunction. These victims also obtained a significantly higher global score to the scale of the *General Health Questionnaire* (28 items: Goldberg and Hillier 1979) showing that their global psychological health was not generally as good as that of the elderly non-victims. In the rural environment, again eight years after the floods, elderly victims showed significantly more post-traumatic stress and depression manifestations than non-victims. The elderly victims were also more likely (78.9%) than elderly non-victims (41.2%) to think that their physical health had deteriorated during the eight years that followed the July 1996 floods.

In spite of the presence of physical and psychological health problems in elderly victims, a good many of them have identified positive aspects from their experiences which helped them in the meaning-making process. The following six post-traumatic growth factors as well as meaning-making were identified in the elderly in this study:

SHORT-TERM POST-TRAUMATIC GROWTH AND MEANING-MAKING

1. Confidence or optimism toward the future: Many elderly victims mentioned feeling more optimistic about the future, because the floods allowed them to realize that local and extraterritorial solidarity can manifest themselves in these circumstances. They now believe they will get help when in difficulty. Even if they say they are confident about what the future holds, those who answered noted that they attach less importance to their financial situation than before and that they take things much more lightly, day by day, without too much planning or project elaboration.

2. Personal feelings of safety: A few of those who answered felt safer because they relocated farther from the water's edge or because they were living in a new home, in spite of feeling a greater vulnerability in relation to the elements of nature and of feeling less security, fearing more and stronger natural disasters.

3. Personal growth: A good number of senior citizens think that their level of self-esteem grew because they realized the pertinence of the choices and the options they favored during the flood and during the reconstruction phase. A few of those who answered noted they had a better self-esteem because, many times, they had to insist on their rights with different people and authorities and show tenacity. The ability to express oneself is also an aspect that some have admitted to getting out of the experience. Some elderly have also stated giving less importance to other people's opinions and displaying more determination in the elaboration of their projects. Many survivors consider themselves better equipped to react to a possible disaster and cite the fact that having lived through such a test has brought them a feeling of competence underestimated until now. The diminishing of prejudice, the sensitivity towards difficulties others have survived through, the increased open-mindedness and empathy are also aspects associated with personal growth. Certain participants also said that the flood made them discover personal resources (autonomy, resourcefulness, etc.) they did not know they had. Many of those who answered believe they will be able to use the resources at their disposal more efficiently if a similar event arises.

4. Spirituality: In general, the victims' religious beliefs or spiritual values stayed the same. However, many of the interviewed elderly mentioned that their belief in God helped them face the hardships. Their prayers and connection to their religion was a protective factor and helped them in the process of discovering a new meaning in their life.

5. Questioning personal values: A few victims stated that the losses or the damage they suffered led them to a deep consideration on the importance granted to material things, even if it demands a certain effort. Many of the interviewed elderly also stated that their priorities have changed and they now give more importance to their conjugal and family relationships and being more sensitive to the hardships others may have to deal with in their lives. Many have noted feelings of reconciliation, a better understanding and a strengthening of the ties between spouses and the other members of their entourage. The hardships lived through at the human relationship level in the first months following the flood, caused by the different stresses, made way for deeper feelings, a better comprehension and communication as well as an undeniable mutual support.

6. Acceptance of outside help: Among the interviewed elderly people, many mentioned having learned how to ask for help and to accept and to receive help from their immediate surroundings, but also from others, including the help offered by paid workers and volunteers. Moreover, these survivors also noted that they will be more willing to help those other survivors who still experience problems.

CONCLUSION

The studies carried out with the elderly have allowed us to note that natural or technological disaster victims may notice a deterioration of their health, but that they are susceptible of experiencing positive changes to their beliefs and personal values. In spite of the differences of opinion among researchers concerning elderly people's capacity to overcome the different stresses linked to the exposure to a disaster, we find that in many of these inventoried studies the authors note that in severe disaster contexts, the elderly have shown resilience in spite of the negative repercussions these events have had on their psychological and physical health. The July 1996 flood is a good example of how senior citizens, in spite of their material losses, the varied stresses they experienced, and the temporary modification to their lifestyles, showed unsuspected qualities and strengths that will enable them to resolve their problems and defend their interests with the authorities who are sometimes refractory to the survivors' needs.

REFERENCES

Bohonis, J. J., and Hogan, D. E. 1999. "The Medical Impact of Tornadoes in North America." *The Journal of Emergency Medicine* 17 (1): 67–73.

Bolin, R., and Klenow, D. 1982–1983. "Response of the Elderly to Disaster: An Age-Stratified Analysis." *International Journal of Aging and Human Development* 16: 283–96.

Bolin, R., and Klenow, D. J. 1988. "Older People in Disaster: A Comparison of Black and White Victims." *International Journal of Aging and Human Development* 26 (1): 29–43.

Burger, L., Van Staden, F., and Nieuwouldt, J. 1989. "The Free State Floods: A Case Study." *South African Journal of Psychology* 19 (4): 205–9.

Carr, V. J., Lewin, T. J., Webster, R. A., and Kenardy, J. 1997. "A Synthesis of the Findings from the Quake Impact Study: A Two-Year Investigation of the Psychosocial Sequelae of the 1989 Newcastle Earthquake." *International Journal of Social Psychiatry and Psychiatric Epidemiology* 32: 123–36.

Chan, C. C., Lin, Y. P., H. H. Chen, H. H., Chang, T. A., Chen, T. S., and Chen, L. S. 2003. "A Population-Based Study on the Immediate and Prolonged Effects of the 1999 Taiwan Earthquake on Mortality." *Annals of Epidemiology* 13: 502–8.

Chung, M.C., Werrett, J., Easthope, Y., and Farmer, S. 2004. "Coping with Post-Traumatic Stress: Young, Middle-Aged and Elderly Comparisons." *International Journal of Geriatric Psychiatry* 19: 333–43.

Chung, M.C., Werrett, J., Easthope, Y., and Farmer, S. 2005. "Differencing Post-traumatic Stress Between Elderly and Younger Residents." *Psychiatry* 68 (2): 164–73.

Cook, J.D., and Bickman, L. 1990. "Social Soutien and Psychological Symptomatology following a Natural Disaster." *Journal of Traumatic Stress* 3: 541–77.

Cyrulnik, B. 1999. Un Merveilleux Malheur. Paris: Odile Jacob.

Cyrulnik, B. 2004. "Peut-On Parler de «Résilience» chez les Âgés?" In *Vieillissement et Résilience,* ed. A. Lejeune, 7–12.

Deater-Deckard, K., Ivy, L., and Smith, J. 2005. "Resilience in Gene-Environment Transactions." In *Handbook of Resilience in Children,* eds. S. Goldstein, and R.B. Brooks, 49–63. New York: John Riley.

Demuth, D.H. 2004. "Another Look at Resilience: Challenging the Stereotypes of Aging." *Journal of Feminist Family Therapy* 16 (4): 61–74.

Eldar, R. 1992. "The Needs of Elderly Persons in Natural Disaster: Observations and Recommendations." *Disasters* 16 (4): 355–58.

Faucher, G. 2002. "Les Coûts Économiques des Catastrophes Récentes Subies par le Québec." Revue trimestrielle de l'Institut de la statistique du Québec: 8–16.

Ferraro, F.R. 2003. "Psychological Resilience in Older Adults following the 1997 Flood." *Clinical Gerontologist* 26 (3–4): 139–43.

Fields, R.B. 1996. "Severe Stress and the Elderly: Are Older Adults at Increased Risk for Post-traumatic Stress Disorder?" In *Aging and Post-traumatic Stress Disorder,* ed. P.E. Ruskin and J.A. Talbot, 79–100. Washington, DC: American Psychiatric Press.

Finnsdottir, T., and Elklit, A. 2002. "Post-traumatic Sequelae in a Community Hit by an Avalanche." *Journal of Traumatic Stress* 15 (6): 479–85.

Fletcher, J., Webster, R.A., Carr, V.J., and T.J. Lewin. 1996. "The Psychosocial Impact of an Earthquake on the Elderly." *International Journal of Geriatric Psychiatry* 11: 943–51.

Gignac, M.A., Cott, C.A., and Badley, E.M. 2003. "Living with a Chronic Disabling Illness and then Some: Data from the 1998 Ice Storm." *Canadian Journal on Aging* 22 (3): 249–59.

Gibbs, M.S. 1989. "Factors in the Victim that Mediate between Disaster and Psychopathology: A Review." *Journal of Traumatic Stress* 2 (4): 489–514.

Gleser, G.C., Green, B.L., and Winget, C. 1981. *Prolonged Psychosocial Effects of Disaster. A Study of Buffalo Creek.* London: Academic Press.

Goenjian, A.K., Najarian, L.M., Pynoos, R.S., Steinberg, A.M., Manoukian, G., Tavosian, A., and Fairbank, L.A. 1994. "Post-traumatic Stress Disorder in Elderly and Younger Adults after the 1988 Earthquake in Armenia." *American Journal of Psychiatry* 151: 895–901.

Goldberg, D., Hillier, P.V., Hillier, V.F. 1979. "A Scaled Version of the General Health Questionnaire." *Psychological Medicine* 9: 139–45.

Green, B.L., Gleser, J.C., Lindy, J.D., Grace, M.C., and Leonard, A.C. 1996. "Age Related Reactions to the Buffalo Creek Dam Collapse." In *Aging and Post-traumatic Stress Disorder,* eds. P.E. Ruskin and J.A. Talbot, 101–25. Washington, DC: American Psychiatric Press.

Green, B.L., Grace, M., and Gleser, G. 1985. "Identifying Survivors at Risk: Long-Term Impairment following the Beverly Hills Supper Club Fire." *Journal of Consulting and Clinical Psychology* 53: 672–78.

Greene, R.R. 2002. "Holocaust Survivors: A Study in Resilience." *Journal of Gerontological Social Work* 37 (1): 3–18.

Guarnaccia, P.J., Canino, G., Rubio-Stipec, M., and Bravo, M. 1993. "The Prevalence of Ataques de Nervios in the Puerto Rico Disaster Study: The Role of Culture in Psychiatric Epidemiology." *The Journal of Nervous and Mental Disease* 181 (3): 157–65.

Hovington, C., Maltais, D., and Lalande, G. 2002. "Les Conséquences des Catastrophes sur la Santé Biopsychosociale des Aînés: Résultats de la Recension des Écrits." In *Catastrophes et État de Santé des Individus, des Intervenants et des Communautés,* ed. D. Maltais, 289–320. Chicoutimi: GRIR-UQAC.

Hutchins, G.L., and Norris, F.H. 1989. "Life Change in the Disaster Recovery Period." *Environment and Behavior* 21 (1): 33–56.

Joseph, S., Andrews, B., Williams, R., and Yule, W. 1992. "Crisis Soutien and Psychiatric Symptomatology in Adult Survivors of the Jupiter Cruise Ship Disaster." *British Journal of Clinical Psychology* 31: 63–73.

Kalayjian, A.S. 1995. *Disaster and Mass Trauma: Global Perspectives on Post Disaster Mental Health Management.* Long Branch, NJ: Vista Publishers.

Kaniasty, K., and Norris, F.H. 1993. "A Test of the Social Soutien Deterioration Model in the Context of Natural Disaster." *Journal of Personality and Social Psychology* 64 (3): 395–408.

Kaniasty, K., Norris, F.H., and Murrel, S.A. 1990. "Received and Perceived Social Soutien following Natural Disaster." *Journal of Applied Social Psychology* 20 (2): 85–114.

Kato, H., Asukai, N., Miyake, Y., Minakawa, K., and Nishiyama, A. 1996. "Post-Traumatic Symptoms among Younger and Elderly Evacuees in the Early Stages following the 1995 Hanshin-Awaji Earthquake in Japan." *Acta Psychiatrica Scandinavica* 93 (6): 477–81.

Kinsel, B. 2005. "Resilience as Adaptation in Older Women." *Journal of Women and Aging* 17 (3): 23–39.

Kohn, R., Levav, I., Garcia, I.D., Machuca, M.E., and Tamashiro, R. 2005. "Prevalence, Risk Factors and Aging Vulnerability for Psychopathology following a Natural Disaster in a Developing Country." *International Journal of Geriatric Psychiatry* 20: 835–41.

Krause, N. 1987. "Exploring the Impact of a Natural Disaster on the Health and Psychological Well-Being of Older Adults." *Journal of Human Stress* 13: 61–69.

Lewin, T. J., Carr, V. J., and Webster, R. A. 1998. "Recovery from Post-Earthquake Psychological Morbidity: Who Suffers and Who Recovers?" *Australian New Zealand Journal of Psychiatry* 32: 15–20.

Livingston, H. M., Livingston, M. G., Brooks, D. N., and McKinlay, W. W. 1992. "Elderly Survivors of the Lockerbie Air Disaster." *International Journal of Geriatric Psychiatry* 7 (10): 725–29.

Logue, J. N., Hansen, H., and Struening, E. L. 1981. "Some Indications of the Long-Term Health Effects of a Natural Disaster." *Public Health* 96: 67–79.

Maltais, D., Lachance, L., and Brassard, A. 2002. "Les Conséquences d'un Sinistre sur la Santé des Personnes Âgées de 50 Ans et Plus: Étude Comparative entre Sinistrés et Non-Sinistrés." *Revue Francophone du Stress et du Trauma* 2 (3): 147–56.

Maltais, D., Lachance, L., Brassard, A., and Simard, A. 2003. "Satisfaction Face à L'aide Reçue et État de Santé Biopsychosociale Post-Désastre." *Canadian Social Work Review* 29 (1): 39–59.

McNaughton, M. E., Smith, L. W., Patterson, T. L., and Grant, I. 1990. "Stress, Social Support, Coping Resources, and Immune Status in Elderly Women." *Journal of Nervous and Mental Disease* 178 (7): 460–61.

Melick, M. E., and Logue, J. N. 1985. "The Effect of Disaster on the Health and Well-Being of Older Women." *International Journal of Aging and Human Development 21* (1): 27–38.

Miller, J. A., Turner, J. G., and Kimball, E. 1981. "Big Thompson Flood Victims: One Year Later." *Family Relations* 30: 111–16.

Norris, F. H., and Murrel S. A. 1988. "Prior Experience as a Moderator of Disaster Impact on Anxiety Symptoms in Older Adults." *American Journal of Community Psychology* 16 (5): 665–83.

Norris, F. H., Phifer, J. F., and Kaniasty, K. 1994. "Individual and Community Reactions to the Kentucky Floods: Findings from a Longitudinal Study of Older Adults." In *Individual and Community Responses to Trauma and Disaster: The Structure of Human Chaos,* ed. Ursano, R. J., McCaughey B. G., and Fullerton, C. S. Cambridge, MA: Cambridge University Press.

Ollendick, D. G., and Hoffman S. M. 1982. "Assessment of Psychological Reactions in Disaster Victims." *Journal of Community Psychology* 10: 157–67.

Osaki, Y., and Minowa, M. 2000. "Factors Associated with Earthquake Deaths in the Great Hanshin-Awaji Earthquake, 1995." *American Journal of Epidemiology* 153 (2): 153–56.

Perry, R. W., and Lindell M. K. 1997. "Aged Citizens in the Warning Phase of Disasters: Re-Examining the Evidence." *International Journal of Aging and Human Development* 44 (4): 257–67.

Phifer, J. F. 1988. "The Impact of Natural Disaster on the Health of Older Adults: A Multiwave Prospective Study." *Journal of Health and Social Behavior* 29: 65–78.

Phifer, J. F. 1990. "Psychological Distress and Somatic Symptoms after Natural Disaster: Differential Vulnerability among Older Adults." *Psychology and Aging* 5 (3): 412–20.

Phifer, J. F., Kaniasty, K. Z., and Norris, F. H. 1988. "The Impact of Natural Disaster on the Health of Older Adults: A Multiwave Prospective Study." *Journal of Health and Social Behavior* 29: 65–78.

Phifer, J. F., and Norris, F. H. 1989. "Psychological Symptoms in Older Adults following Natural Disaster: Nature, Timing, Duration and Course." *Journal of Gerontology* 44: 207–17.

Poulshock, S. W., Cohen, E. S. 1975. "The Elderly in the Aftermath of a Disaster." *The Gerontologist* 15 (4): 357–61.

Ruskin, P. E., and Talbot, J. A., 1996. *Aging and Post-traumatic Stress Disorder.* Washington, DC: American Psychiatric Association.

Rutter, M. 1987. "Psychosocial Resilience and Protective Mechanisms." *American Journal of Orthopsychiatry* 57 (3): 316–31.

Sanderson, L. M. 1989. "Tornadoes." In *The Public Health Consequences of Disasters,* ed. M. Gregg, 39–49. Atlanta, GA: Centers for Disease Control.

Seplaki, C. L., Goldman, N., Weinstein, M., and Lin, Y-H. 2006. "Before and After the 1999 Chi-Chi Earthquake: Traumatic Events and Depressive Symptoms in an Older Population." *Social Science and Medicine* 62: 3121–3132.

Shore, J. H., E. Tatum, and W. Vullmer. 1986. "Psychiatric Reactions to Disaster: The Mt. St. Helens Experience." *American Journal of Psychiatry* 143: 590–95.

Solomon, S. D., Bravo, M., Rubio-Stipec, M., and Canino, G. 1993. "Effects of Family Role on Response to Disaster." *Journal of Traumatic Stress* 6 (2): 255–69.

Tanida, N. 1996. "What Happened to Elderly People in the Great Hanshin Earthquake." *BMJ* 113: 1133–1135.

Thompson, M. P., Norris, F. N., and Hanacek, B. 1993. "Age Differences in the Psychological Consequences of Hurricane Hugo." *Psychology and Aging* 8: 606–16.

Ticehurst, S., Webster, R. A., Carr V. J., and Lewin, T. J. 1996. "The Psychosocial Impact of an Earthquake on the Elderly." *International Journal of Geriatric Psychiatry* 11: 943–51.

Tyler, K. A., and Hoyt D. R. 2000. "The Effects of an Acute Stressor on Depressive Symptoms among Older Adults." *Research on Aging* 22 (2): 143–64.

Wade, T. H., Sandhu S. K., Levy D., Lee, S., LeChevalier, M. W., Katz, L., and Colford, J. M. 2004. "Did a Severe Flood in the Midwest Cause an Increase in the Incidence of Gastrointestinal Symptoms?" *American Journal of Epidemiology* 159 (4): 398–405.

Wagnild, G., and Young, H. M. 1990. "Resilience among Older Women." *Journal of Nursing Scholarship* 22 (4): 252–55.

Weintraub, D., and Ruskin, P. E. 1999. "Post-traumatic Stress Disorder in the Elderly: A Review." *Harvard Review of Psychiatry* 7 (3): 125–83.

Werner, E. E. 1995. "Resilience in Development." *Current Directions in Psychological Science* 4: 81–95.

Wright, O. M., and Masten, A. S. 2005. "Resilience Processes in Development: Fostering Positive Adaptation in the Context of Adversity." In *Handbook of Resilience in Children,* ed. S. Goldstein and R. B. Brooks, 17–37. New York: Springer.

Zakour, M. J., and Harrel, E. B. 2003. "Access to Disaster Services: Social Work Interventions for Vulnerable Populations." *Journal of Social Service Research* 30 (2): 27–54.